COMMON SENSE FORESTRY

Books for Living Wisely from Mother Earth News

Mother Earth News came into being when astronauts were flying to the moon and young people were questioning the status quo. People began to seek answers in Mother Nature. They turned back to the land, seeking a simpler, more grounded, and more fulfilling way of life.

Times change, and so do fashions and phrases. The world is still full of questions, but the answers are more likely to involve concepts of ecology, interconnectedness, and sustainability. No one talks of going "back to the land" much, but we still find answers in Nature, and in our own natures.

The partnership between Mother Earth News and Chelsea Green has a common taproot in the Earth. The Books for Living Wisely series will reflect the common mission of the two companies: to introduce new people to ideas that are at once exciting, important, and basic.

Bryan Welch
PUBLISHER, MOTHER EARTH NEWS

Stephen Morris
PUBLISHER, CHELSEA GREEN

COMMON SENSE FORESTRY

Hans W. Morsbach

Illustrations by Robert W. Hutchison

CHELSEA GREEN PUBLISHING COMPANY

White River Junction, Vermont

Designed by Suzanne Church.

Printed in Canada.
First printing, December 2002.

05 04 03 02   1 2 3 4 5

Printed on acid-free, recycled paper.

Due to the variability of local conditions, materials, skills, site, and so forth, Chelsea Green
Publishing Company and the author assume no responsibility for personal injury, property
damage, or loss from actions inspired by information in this book. Recommendations in this
book are no substitute for site-specific advice available from forestry professionals. Always
follow manufacturers' guidelines and use common sense when operating tools and machinery.

Library of Congress Cataloging-in-Publication Data

Morsbach, Hans W., 1932-
Common sense forestry / Hans W. Morsbach.
p.   cm.
Includes bibliographical references and index.
ISBN 1-931498-21-0 (alk. paper)
1. Woodlots. 2. Forest management. 3. Forests and forestry. I. Title. I. Series.

SD387.W6 M67 2002   2002031483
634.9'2—dc31

Chelsea Green Publishing Company
Post Office Box 428
White River Junction, VT 05001
(800) 639-4099
www.chelseagreen.com

To my mother,
Hanni Morsbach-Weigert,
who showed me how to grow things.

CONTENTS

ACKNOWLEDGMENTS

I am indebted to the many Wisconsin foresters who taught me to appreciate and manage my woodland. Among them are: Todd Kenefick, Mark Mittelstadt, John Nielson, Paul Pingry, Rich LaValley, and Aaron Young. Furthermore, I would like to thank Jerry VanSambeek and Melvin Baughman for their suggestions. Ecologist Gigi LaBudde enlightened me on the problems of invasive species. Gordy Christians of the Hayward (Wisconsin) State Nursery was kind enough to relate some of his seeding experiences, which was particularly helpful because there is little useful information published on the subject. Much wisdom herein is thanks to these folks. The mistakes are mine alone.

I learned a great deal from German foresters Wilhelm Bode, Gus Hopp, Joachim Kohl, Wolfgang Lipphardt, Klaus Meyer, and Hans Volker. Mr. Bode's book, *Waldwende*, introduced me to the concept of Dauerwald and influenced me profoundly.

I am also indebted to my accountant, Rich Schaefer, for reviewing the chapter on income tax; to Wendy Edelberg, for her help with the economic analysis; and to Bob Drea for his help with the photographs. A project I began years ago, the Hedgerow Foundation, has had great influence on my woodland and this book. I would like to thank the Richard H. Driehaus Foundation of Chicago for funding the Hedgerow Foundation.

My friend, fellow forest enthusiast, and editor, "Diamonds" Dave Mulcahey, contributed significantly to this book. He made writing this book an enjoyable experience. My buddy Jake Spicer was an enthusiastic supporter from the very beginning. He made many valuable suggestions, including the nonbotanical term "pernicious grass." I would also like to thank Steve Morris and Alan Berolzheimer at Chelsea Green Publishing for seeing the book through, and Fern Bradley for her immensely useful editorial contributions.

I also would like to thank my fellow woodland owners, Bob Holst, Larry Krotz, Dave Johnson, James Njus, and Larry Severeid, for their interest and support.

Lastly, I would like to thank my family for tolerating my literary obsession. My wife, Kathy, has been a model of forbearance. My faithful dog, Pooch, a puli, has been good company.

PREFACE

When I first became interested in cultivating trees, I looked for a "how-to" book. Because humans have been cultivating trees forever, I was sure that someone would have written a concise, readable little book to guide me in my tree-planting efforts. To my surprise, I could not find one, so I turned to the voluminous academic literature on forestry. This, I soon discovered, is difficult to understand and obviously not intended for small-woodland owners. So, twenty-five years later, after planting tens of thousands of trees, I took up the challenge of writing this simple, common-sense guide for woodland owners.

A friend gave me a booklet entitled "Woodlands in Wisconsin," which contains this maxim: "The only general rule in silviculture is that there are no rules."* The more I became involved with trees, the more I learned to appreciate this wisdom. In silviculture, principles I had assumed to be self-evident turned out not to be clear at all and even controversial. For example, I had assumed that clear-cutting was always bad—just look at the denuded mountains in our Northwest. But I have since accepted that clear-cutting is defensible in certain situations. I also had thought that the use of chemicals was always bad, but now I accept that herbicides can be very useful in preparing a site for seeding and planting. I had assumed that, given fertile ground, almost any local species of tree would flourish—which is not at all true. I found that there are many questions in forestry without clear answers: Should I plant trees or seed them? How close should they be to each other? Should I have a monocultural plantation or a mixed forest? Would my forest benefit from my leaving it alone? On these and other questions of procedure, most foresters are bound to hold strong yet differing opinions. So it became apparent that a competent woodland owner had to pick up know-how on his own. If I could not find an authoritative book to guide me, I would have to learn from experience. There is only one slight problem with this approach: In forestry, it may take a generation or more to find out whether any procedure is truly workable. I will never know whether some of my tree-growing schemes will stand the test of time. I can only that hope my children will notice and perhaps appreciate some of my silvicultural feats.

I am a small-woodland owner, not a forester. Much of what I know I have learned from other woodland owners, from the literature available, and from

* This quote is attributed to a W. Pfeil, 1860, as quoted in S. A. Wilde, "Woodlands of Wisconsin" (Cooperative Extension Programs, The University of Wisconsin, 1977).

professional foresters. I have spent years observing, experimenting, and discussing methods and practices with small-woodland owners from all over the Midwest. This book relates my experiences and observations. I recognize that many scholars have written learnedly on the subject. I do not mean to contest them, and I bow to their superior knowledge. And yet, I feel that I can offer would-be tree farmers practical, accessible advice. I should note that my experience is only of my own Wisconsin woodland. Although certain forestry principles may apply universally, woodland owners in other geographic settings may encounter situations far different from mine. So I pass on my hard-learned lessons to other woodland owners in the hope that they will be useful. I have tried to present the material—much of it in the mainstream, some on the cutting edge—in a direct, reader-friendly manner. Although humans have been engaged in growing trees for millennia, the science of nurturing a forest is changing continually. So do not look at this book, or any other, as the final authority on silviculture.

It will please me enormously if this book helps readers grow straighter trees with less difficulty than I encountered on my plantation. I will be equally pleased if it motivates readers to grow a mixed forest. Better yet, it would be wonderful if my book inspires readers to purchase some woodland. Small, private woodlots account for 86 percent of U.S. hardwood acreage. Owners of such woodlands play a key role, much greater than most of them realize, as stewards of this valuable resource. This book is dedicated to them.

Though I would encourage you to read the book from cover to cover, this is not at all necessary. Because most chapters are designed to be comprehensible individually and as part of the whole, the occasional repetition of material covered elsewhere in the book is necessary.

If you, the reader, should have any suggestions or comments about my book, I would be grateful to hear them. I urge you to visit my web site, www.woodlandmanagement.com, which will feature periodic updates and dialogue between forest enthusiasts.

Hans W. Morsbach
5745 S. Harper Ave.
hmorsbach@mindspring.com
Chicago, Illinois 60637

one

COMING INTO A
SMALL WOODLAND

When I bought a farm in Richland County, Wisconsin, in 1972, I knew nothing about farming. In a way I surprised myself when I decided to buy the farm. It was a very impulsive decision, and most certainly I did not know, nor did I think, about the commitment I was about to make. I was a small businessman in Chicago and really had no spare time. I bought the farm from a friend, who was renting it to a neighbor who grew corn and hay and raised cattle. The land is hilly country, and the tenant farmer failed to employ conservation practices, such as contour strips, which resulted in severe erosion. Equally damaging to the land were his grazing bovines, which devoured most of the seedlings and saplings in and around the woods. It didn't take long to realize that the arrangement with the tenant farmer was bad for me and bad for the land.

So I decided that I would raise my own herd of cattle, but I abandoned this endeavor as soon as my steers got pinkeye. Few things are more difficult than segregating a steer from a herd for medical treatment. It takes a cowboy with a lasso to do that, and, as I mentioned earlier, I'm really just a city dude from Chicago. Eventually I sold all my cattle at a loss. Next I tried to raise bees, but I never acquired the promised immunity to stings. Mercifully for me, all the bees died one cold winter.

When the county forester from the Department of Natural Resources (DNR) proposed that I start a tree farm, I was ecstatic.* He suggested that I plant fifty thousand walnut trees. It would be cheap, easy, and convenient for me. He would arrange for everything—seedlings, equipment, labor—and the government would pay most of the expense. My involvement would be minimal. I knew that walnut trees, once they matured, would be quite valuable. If only one in ten of my fifty thousand trees made it, my grandchildren would become multimillionaires! My forester assured me that the presence of a walnut stand would greatly enhance the value of my farm and that he personally knew of groups of well-to-do doctors eager to pay a thousand dollars per acre (triple the value of my land at the time) for land planted with walnut trees. Here was a great opportunity to make money. Growing walnut trees promised to be profitable and easy; trees don't jump fences, get pinkeye, or sting. Why, I wondered, did neighboring dairy farmers still put up with chores twice a day instead of growing walnut trees?

That spring the trees were planted and the DNR even gave me an "outstanding forestry" award for my farsightedness. I did not realize until years later how absurd it was that such a prestigious award had been given to a city slicker who was unable to tell an elm from a hickory. The award neither made me a forester nor made my trees grow. Gradually it began to dawn on me that growing walnut trees involved more trouble and expense than I had been led to believe. For starters, most of my trees grew very, very slowly. Many grew crooked and some not at all. Eventually I learned that grasses and weeds around the trees had to be controlled. Because the weeds were bigger than the trees, I bought a bush hog, a heavy-duty mowing attachment for my tractor, and mowed between the rows. Unfortunately, from the tractor's seat it's hard to tell grass from a walnut. I ended up mowing down many of my precious seedlings.

I also learned that walnut trees in an open-field plantation do not want to grow straight. Like most trees, walnuts grow toward the light. If the light comes from all sides, the resulting tree will be shaped more like a bush than a tall, stately tree that harbors a seventy-foot veneer log. If I had known then how a tall veneer log should look, I would have realized immediately how difficult my undertaking was to become. But very slowly, bit by bit, I have learned the ins and outs of walnuts and other hardwoods. The process continues.

Along with my friends Bob Holst, a musician, and James Njus, a lawyer from St. Paul, I have worked many weekends over the last twenty years, pruning and herbiciding around my walnut trees. As amateur tree farmers, we each have different theories about how to prune and care for walnut trees, and these theories have changed over time. Pruning is tree therapy, an attempt to cajole a tree to do something it normally does not want to do on its own. The therapy is sometimes gentle, sometimes extreme; all too often it is ineffectual and even lethal. Bob, James, and I tested a wide variety of techniques and subjected our poor walnut trees to

* County foresters are typically employed by the DNR to advise individual woodland owners on management and subsidies. Throughout this book I will use the terms "county forester" and "DNR forester" interchangeably. In addition, there are consulting foresters whom you can hire for a fee (these will be discussed in greater detail in chapter 18).

Outstanding hero . . . or sucker? S.W.C.D. stands for Soil and Water Conservation District.

various experiments. For a brief time, one member of our team totally sheared all the side branches from the trees as far as he could reach, producing thin "flag poles." We went through a period when "tree balance" was our motto (this was achieved by trimming branches so that the result would be a symmetrically balanced tree with a straight leader, the twig in the center destined to become the main stem of the tree). There was another period when James would protest, "*You* may not know who the leader is, but the tree does." In fact, we found this to be generally true, but not always. After years spent trying to force our trees to grow straight by sheer will, nagging questions persisted: Why should we prune hundreds of trees per acre when only about fifty will be harvested? Why do walnuts in dense, mixed woods grow tall and straight without pruning?

We learned by trial, error, and observation. We consulted experts who often had divergent views; we read professional and academic literature and discovered that an astonishing amount of thought and research has been devoted to walnut cultivation. We found only some of the literature useful and concluded that caring for a plantation of walnut trees is intrinsically problem-ridden. Twenty years after the initial planting, many of our trees are doing quite well. Especially where the conditions are favorable, trees are fifty feet tall and of veneer quality. On eroded ridge land and other poorly chosen sites, however, the results have been dismal. Our success has been a mixed bag, and we'd certainly do it differently if we had it to do over again. But that, as you'll learn, is one of the joys of stewardship.

My bush hog attaches to the back of my tractor and mows everything thinner than my wrist.

WHY YOU SHOULD WANT A FOREST

Every other week or so I go through the same ritual: cajoling my wife or my brother-in-law James or some of my friends to accompany me in the rustic seclusion of my farm outside Cazenovia, Wisconsin. It's a long drive for anybody I try to solicit, so I suppose I shouldn't be surprised that some weekends I get no takers. The first half of the trip, especially—over the grid-locked expressways of the city, out through sprawl of the suburbs, across the monotonous agroindustrial abstraction of northern Illinois—is more than enough penance for a week's worth of sins.

Still, the farm is paradise, even if I sometimes have a sore ass by the time I get there. I've spent some of my happiest times there. Kathy and I were married nearby, in a little Quaker town. We celebrated at the farm, and everybody remembers it as the best wedding they've ever been to. The farm has been a gathering place for the family ever since—a place for holidays and parties, a retreat for friends, a haven for rest and relaxation. Over the years, Kathy and I have filled the house with wonderful old gadgets and furniture you used to be able to pick up for nothing at auctions in the neighborhood. I use a lot of them, or lend them to my Amish neighbors.

I am always onto some scheme or other, schemes that strike me as interesting ways to make my woodland productive. I have harvested oak from my forest to make booths for my restaurant, furniture for an other business venture, and stairs for my house. I built a deck with black locust posts and a black walnut balustrade. Currently I am engaged in a little venture with my neighbor Harvey Miller. We're making slab tables out of wood cut on the farm. We are setting up a wood shop, a sawmill, and a kiln. I would like to call them "Amish" tables, since Harvey is the carpenter and he is Amish, but Harvey protests that the Amish cannot use their religion to commercialize anything. He suggests the tables be called "country style" or "rustic." I guess that's what we'll have to do.

Admittedly, the work I put in isn't always productive or efficient. I have spent countless hours in field and forest and barn, toiling or playing or walking or dodging falling trees and turtled tractors. I've spent hours observing wildlife, or shooting it, fiddling with equipment, or hatching some silvicultural scheme, or conducting some crazy experiment. I

should say "we," because I have been blessed with willing and sometimes even useful companions. My guests spread tree seeds, build scarecrows, hunt, drive the tractor, cut wood, and work in the garden. There is no end to the projects we think up (and some we actually accomplish). We flooded the valley and made a beautiful four-acre lake full of bass. We have created a varied and beautiful network of paths, all well maintained. We always work hard, even the city slickers, and to properly evaluate the fruits of our labors we make many inspection trips in the Gator, an incredibly useful and fun vehicle, something that resembles a cross between a golf cart and a tank. The Gator is manufactured by John Deere, and comes in four- and six-wheel models. It has a low center of gravity and can negotiate incredibly steep terrain. I have never tipped it, though I've come close many times. The Gator is always loaded with the proper equipment when we tool around, so we can stop at any spot and impulsively cut down an unwelcome tree, liberate a little oak tree from competing trees, or do a little pruning or thinning.

At night there is play time. We drink wine and play hearts and liar's poker and backgammon for a dollar a point. My brother-in-law James and I have had a running feud on the backgammon table. We keep score on the dining room wall. After more than twenty years, the point differential is nearing a thousand. To avoid embarrassment I will not say who is winning.

Over the years, I've built a deep bond with my land. It's full of special places. There is the lake. And the steep wooded hill that overlooks the lake and the farm-

The Gator, by John Deere, is part tank, part golf cart, immensely useful, and a toy non-pareil. It improved my pleasure in life.

house. I recently cut some trees down near its ledges for vistas. On the other side of the hill you can see for miles in every direction. Then there is the Hidden Passage, a path that runs down the middle of several rows of white pines. It is high on a hill, and in the summer it's a cool place to walk or Gator in the breezy shade. (Or at least it was, until I got a little too zealous at pruning.) Nearby are the graves of my previous pooches. All around the farm are hunting stands, each with its particular lore. And hawks' perches, wood piles, experimental plots, scarecrows, and fallen trees I've fashioned into "bridges" over my Gator paths. There are different patches I know by their vegetation. There are stands full of oaks and others dominated by sugar maples (which my Amish neighbors tap to make maple syrup). There are extremely fertile spots, like the one near a creek bed where my acorn planting grew into a dense thicket of oaklings. Everywhere I rove on my farm I find hidden trees, those wonderful specimens planted by serendipity, favored by fate, and destined to be fine veneer trees. And, of course, there are the groves of walnuts, all planted in lines where farm fields used to be. After all these years of sweat and tears, some of those groves are starting to look leafy and inviting in the summer.

The farm is such a major part of my life. I am blessed by fortune to have it. I think about it all week long, and I'm loathe to leave it when I'm there. I believe anybody, given a few acres, will understand the pleasures I've known. All you need to do is take the first step.

WHAT YOU NEED TO START YOUR WOODLAND

To reduce forest stewardship to its barest essentials, all you need is a piece of land. Let's say you have a half-acre of land that you do nothing with at all. In a matter of a few decades it will revert to forest. If you don't believe me, I can show you a neighborhood on the South Side of Chicago that residents abandoned wholesale twenty-five years ago when the steel mills started closing down. Today many lots where houses once stood are covered with forty-foot-tall pioneer trees.

But if you have an acre of land, or more, chances are you will want to speed the process of forestation along. Perhaps you will want to choose the kinds of trees that will grow there. Here again, not much is required. Gather seeds, disturb the earth (i.e., dig it, scratch it, rototill it, plow it) and sow away. When I began my forest schemes so many years ago, I was too impatient for such basic measures. I wanted to plant seedlings by the thousand. Well, I've come around to the wisdom of simplicity. My most recent projects have been spreading seeds.

Still, woodland management accomodates big ideas, large-scale effort, and costly equipment. If you've got the ways and means, you can do some pretty awesome stuff. The point is, you needn't feel you don't have the time or the money or the know-how to create a woodland for your own enjoyment. It's an avocation that suits any schedule, fortune, or inclination.

Taking care of your woodland can be a lot of work. If you have more than ten acres, get used to the idea that you will never get everything done. It's more important, in my opinion, to leave time to just walk around and enjoy your land. As I write this, I am aware that I have to mark several dozen crop trees to be cut, and I have to arrange for a team of Amish horses to drag out the timber. I need to mow between rows of young trees to disturb mouse habitat. I also have to arrange to have eroded roads bulldozed. In addition, I have to attend to a problem with my tractor's hydraulics. Besides all this, my wife complains about an increase in the mouse population in the house. Do all these problems diminish my pleasure of ownership? I guess not, because I can't wait to be back at the farm next weekend. Remember: Your own enjoyment is the most important thing of all.

IS THERE FAME, HONOR, OR RICHES IN WOODLAND MANAGEMENT?

Don't make the mistake I did and let rows of planted hardwoods put dollar signs in your eyes. True, real estate appreciation has made buying country acreage a no-brainer. But as a general rule, you will do better with your money in other investments. Forestry has many rewards, but making a lot of money is not one of them.

Nor should you count on the respect, or for that matter the understanding, of your farming neighbors. If you want to do a little socializing in the country, it's hit or miss whether you'll find neighbors with compatible interests. This varies region by region, of course. New England is populated by hundreds of thousands of small-woodland owners, and you can probably find a neighbor with whom you can discuss the latest editorial in the *New York Times* over a cup of tea. But my farm is located in Wisconsin's dairyland, where farmers

A DIFFERENCE IN PERSPECTIVE

In a moment of candor, one of my neighbors opined that my tree plantation was downright immoral. He stopped his pickup truck on the back road that runs past my land to give me a piece of his mind about my project. "Growing trees where grain used to be just ain't right," he told me. A little more ominously, he added: "I heard them talk in the tavern about burning down the trees. I told them not to do it because they might get caught." It became clear to me how differently my neighbors and I understand the world and our places in it. To them, I am undoing the work of their forebears, who painstakingly cleared the land of trees to make it arable in the first place. I am also, perhaps, denying sustenance to the hungry of North Korea and Sudan. Happily, in the past twenty years tree farming has become more acceptable and even some of my neighbors now appreciate my forest.

---

struggle to make a meager living. My sport-utility vehicle is a symbol that indicates I've come to play. I am very aware that I am a local oddity. My lifestyle is just very different from many locals, and some resent my relative wealth—it does not help that my real estate taxes are reduced by my participation in a state forestry program. Doing business with neighbors is difficult: When I pay too much, I'm a sucker; when I bargain, I'm cheap. It's hard to find a middle ground. Further complicating neighborly relations in Richland County is the presence of Amish farmers, who have their own conflicts with the local "English" population. I try not to get involved; I like them all. We chat about the weather and local news, and we may have an occasional beer together (even my Amish neighbors will accept one), but my family and I do little real socializing with our neighbors. It's perhaps for this reason that few urban tree farmers can hack country living for long periods of time. I have been around longer than any other weekend woodland owner in the township, and I've seen plenty come and go.

We've all come a long way since I bought my farm. My intention in this book is to pass on to you what I have learned the hard way. But for the wisdom that mistakes impart, much of our time and effort would be wasted. I am convinced, however, that with a few timely suggestions, the amateur tree lover can turn any parcel of land, wooded or not, into a preserve of natural beauty and gain the satisfaction that comes from husbanding nature to productive ends.

The experiences and recommendations I outline in this book will differ at times from the methods encouraged by the government, industry, and academia. For example, I argue that direct seeding—as opposed to the conventional method of planting seedlings—will yield a more pleasing and profitable forest in the long run, and that a mixed forest is environmentally more sound than a monocultural plantation. At the same time, recognizing that each person will approach his or her woodlot with different amounts of time, energy, and money, I present and discuss a number of alternatives for realizing your aspirations, including the conventional techniques I have found disappointing on my own farm. In all cases, I try to discuss these alternatives in the context of my own experience and those of foresters and other woodland owners I know. I relate my im-pressions and recommendations on equipment, herbicides, and other tools of the trade, and offer advice on how to get the most benefits from government pro-grams. I caution you to be realistic about your expectations of success and profit. The riches to be gained from your forest are—and perhaps rightly so—most likely to be of the spiritual kind.

SATURDAYS WITH AUGIE

My friend "Diamonds" Mulcahey writes:

In my years of going to Cazenovia with Hans, he's introduced me to some pretty interesting people. One of my favorites is Augie Laechelt. Hans met him years ago when he stopped at Augie's place near LaValle, in Sauk County, to buy some honey. He's made a habit of visiting Augie from time to time ever since. I've dropped in a few times, too. We go to collect acorns from the stately red oaks that shade the pretty house Augie built a while back.

When we visit, Augie's always game to give a tour. He'll show us his garden, his hives, his equipment for extracting honey, the two-story workshop he built a few years back when his honey operation was in full swing. I was impressed by the wasp trap he made with a five-gallon bucket, some wire mesh, bait, and a piece of plexiglass. You sucker the wasps in and then they suffocate. It's an ingenious contraption, and adaptation of an old barn trick for catching flies.

Augie's been keeping bees since 1955, full time since 1967. He's semiretired now, down to two hives. Once I naively asked Augie if he ever got stung. "Have I ever got stung?" he repeated in mock amazement, as he took off his shoe and started peeling away his sock. "I'll show you some fresh ones!" I asked how on earth he got stung on the tips of his toes. "I did it myself," he said. "I grab a couple of bees, and hold them by my toes until they sting me."

No, Augie's not a masochist. He's got arthritis, bad enough so he can't get to sleep some-times. A doctor had prescribed medicine, but Augie didn't like dropping a few bucks a day on pills. So he applied a secret beekeepers have known for ages: Bee venom soothes arthritis. Every time the pain gets bad, Augie gets himself stung. The venom must work wonders, be-cause Augie doesn't appear to have slowed down much. Recently when we drove up, he was up on his roof putting the finishing touches on a handsome new chimney stack. I should mention, Augie's going on 88.

two

THE TEN COMMANDMENTS FOR SMALL-WOODLAND OWNERS

I. ENJOY YOUR WOODLAND.

Your woodland should be a source of pleasure and joy. Sounds, animal activity, and interesting vegetation are everywhere. Let nothing interfere with the enjoyment of your forest.

II. BUY NEAR.

One key to enjoying your woodland is buying land that's quick and easy to get to. Buying woodland nearer to "civilization" also makes good investment sense, because it is more likely to appreciate in value than more remote land.

   On the other hand, if you live in a sprawling metropolitan area or a part of the country where the landscape is boring, as I do, you may decide a longer drive is worth it. And regardless of location, chances for real estate appreciation are very good, roughly on par with alternative investments.

III. DO NOT EXPECT TO MAKE MONEY.

It is very unlikely that you'll see any profit from cultivating trees. Sure, a timber sale can bring in a windfall, but it takes about a century for a hardwood tree to reach maturity. Considered over the long run, your rate of return is much less than you would get by buying a certificate of deposit. There may be a little money in practicing short-rotation forestry, such as growing pines for pulp, but this sort of tree farming is not friendly to nature, not nice to look at, and no fun.

If return on your investment is what you're after, place your hopes in appreciating land values rather then timber sales.

IV. DON'T BUY MORE LAND THAN YOU CAN MANAGE.

Your pleasure is more likely to come from observing and working your land than from its size.

V. DO NOT EXPEND TOO MUCH TIME, EFFORT, AND MONEY ON YOUR TREES.

Small-scale forestry is a poor investment but personally very enriching. Only do it to the extent that it gives you pleasure.

VI. BE KIND TO THE ENVIRONMENT.

Doing nothing is one way to be kind to your woodland. This means do not clear-cut, do not use chemicals, and minimize the use of your lawn mower. (You will soon observe that in the country, a tract of land in its natural state is a lot more interesting and less work than a manicured lawn.) If you desire to actively benefit the environment, there are steps you can take, such as eliminating nonnative species, encouraging trees that provide food and shelter for wildlife, and allowing old trees to recycle themselves.

VII. CONSULT EXPERTS IN YOUR FORESTRY PRACTICES—BUT REMEMBER WHO'S BOSS.

No matter the size of your land, you can improve it with forestry. As a starting point, I suggest that you contact a forester. Foresters can get you useful literature, possibly prepare a management plan for your woodland, and suggest certain forestry practices. They also will inform you if your state has any programs benefiting small woodland owners. If you participate in any government subsidies or other programs, you are bound to honor your commitments. Follow foresters' advice, but if it conflicts with what you want to do, follow your instincts.

VIII. FAVOR MERCHANDISABLE TREES.

While you will not get rich growing trees for the market, there is no reason why you should not favor the trees that are most likely to have timber value sometime in the future. You may plant tree seeds directly or plant seedlings and follow accepted forestry practices to make them marketable. Follow the German *Dauerwald* philosophy, which calls for growing timber in mixed forests of native tree species, unevenly aged, in a biodiverse environment with abundant wildlife.

IX. REPRESS YOUR ANAL COMPULSIONS.

Often woodland owners apply their city values to their dealings with woodlands. They think they have to mow, to grind trimmed branches into tiny wood chips, and to eliminate natural ground vegetation. Remember that nature recycles more efficiently than you do and that the waste created by natural vegetation is essential to environmental health.

Another anal compulsion is the tendency to grow trees like row crops. Trees grow best in a natural environment together with all kinds of other vegetation. A plantation is boring and prone to infestation and disease. If you do plant seedlings, mix the species up as much as you can. They will grow better, foster more wildlife, and provide more enjoyment.

X. BE A GOOD CITIZEN AND AN ACTIVIST.

Attend conferences of woodland owners' associations. You'll find these organizations just about everywhere. They offer useful lectures (even though you should not believe everything you hear) and opportunities for vendors to sell their wares. You will learn a great deal, and you will enjoy meeting others who share your interests. Make your land available as a demonstration site to help educate other, less-experienced woodland owners.

Become politically active. Prevail on the government to recognize the importance of private woodland owners in preserving our natural environment. The United States government offers very generous support to farmers, yet it gives nothing to small-woodland owners. This is an outrage!

While farmers overproduce and pollute the waterways and aquifers, woodland owners play an important part in preserving pure water, preventing floods, and maintaining the equilibrium of our climate. Write your congressional representative to see that this injustice is rectified.

three

BUYING LAND

The most important advice I can give to the aspiring forester is this: Choose your land well—you might be living with it the rest of your life. I have owned my Wisconsin farm for thirty years. I love it more than my home in Chicago, although the four hours it takes me to get there are wearisome. On my way to my land I pass equally beautiful woodland and farms half the distance from home, and I often wonder if I would make a different choice if I had it to do all over again. Of course I would. I bought my land impulsively and did not bother to consider alternatives. On the whole, I've done well, but I suspect I could have done better. Following is some advice that could save you from repeating my mistakes when buying your own woodland.

Buy near. Many woodland owners spend countless hours traveling from their city residence to their woodland. Good land tends to be more expensive the closer it is to urban centers, so buyers will travel hundreds of miles to find a sweetheart deal. Fair enough. But in my experience it is better to pay more and own less than to spend a lot of time traveling. You will derive the most pleasure from being in the country, not getting there. Moreover, the farther your woodland is from your home, the more difficult it will be to find time for the many duties of tending your trees. A nearby location may be best for you, and it may be a better investment as well.

Consider why you want to tend a woodland. If you just want to enjoy a pretty setting, you should have a general idea where the countryside is the most appealing. Often the prettiest land, with pleasant hills and pretty rock formations, may not be very fertile, but that may not matter to you. Fertility is important for farming and timbering, but much less for wildlife. What is important for wildlife is habitat and food sources. Some species of trees, such as oak and aspen, are especially beneficial for wildlife. For hunting, forested land interspersed with meadows seems to work best.

Think about the setting that appeals to you most. Aspects of a setting you enjoy could include the contours of the land, the vegetation, and such factors as fertility or remoteness from civilization. After identifying your ideal setting, narrow your search to regions nearby that offer those qualities. For example, consider the country around my home in Chicago. Pretty much anything south is fertile, flat, very expensive, and, to me, boring. The fields of central Illinois are the most fertile in the world, but the country only starts to get lively in the northwest corner of the state, near the Wisconsin border. It's a trade-off: If I were only interested in fertile land, no matter how aesthetically uninteresting, I could have bought property much nearer my home. Instead, I bought in southwestern Wisconsin, and I have a varied, lovely woodland with a little lake, hills, pretty rock formations, fertility in the valleys, and interesting vegetation. But it is 226 miles away. In retrospect, I should have bought land in northwestern Illinois, in the beautiful bluff country near the Mississippi. The land is not fertile, but the wildlife is great and it is hundred miles closer to Chicago. Hindsight is twenty-twenty. Still I love my land and wouldn't trade it for any other.

Figure out where you want to buy your land and then generate leads. A few years ago, after reading a book published by the Worldwatch Institute entitled *Who Will Feed China?*, I surmised that grain land would be a good investment. I hit upon a fun scheme to generate leads for real estate. I identified areas in Minnesota and North Dakota where land values seemed reasonable, and I marked the larger towns in the area on a road map. I asked my daughter, Sarah, to contact the local papers and insert an ad saying that a Chicago businessman seeks to acquire land. I do not claim that my scheme was particularly clever, but it did yield an incredible volume of mail. I received many good leads, and in the end I bought well. I especially enjoyed corresponding with a lot of country folks. Interestingly, most mail came not from landowners but from prospective tenant farmers who wanted to work the land if it should become available. I have since sold the land. It turned out that my premise was flawed: Soybeans can be produced more cheaply on cleared Brazilian rain forest land than in the United States.

Get an idea of how big an acre is, then figure out how many you can handle. When land is surveyed, it is divided into square-mile parcels known as a section. Each square mile has 640 acres. Often land is sold in multiples of 40 acres. A 160-acre square is known as a quarter section. Forty acres make a quarter-quarter section, the equivalent of a square parcel with quarter-mile sides. Forty acres is a good-sized parcel of land and will keep you busy. When buying rural land smaller than forty acres, beware that many counties require a minimum-size parcel of land for a building permit. In Richland County, Wisconsin, for instance, you are not allowed to build on less than thirty-five acres, except in subdivisions of land incorporated in a town.

I own four farms in Richland County, totaling about five hundred acres. Although I am intimately familiar with my home farm, I do not have the time and energy to take care of some of the more remote acreage. My forester recently informed me that a stand of oaks needs be harvested soon and that I could realize a gain of about $40,000. The oaks are on the very bottom of a ravine that I had not visited in a decade! When the county forester has to tell me to harvest a stand of oak I have overlooked, it is a clear sign that I have more land than I can handle.

Acquiring buildings with your land may be a bargain. When I bought my first farm of 140 acres in Wisconsin, the purchase price included several sheds, a great barn, and a beautiful farmhouse. The replacement value of the house alone was worth the $33,500 I paid for the property in 1972. Essentially I bought tillable land, and there was little mention of the timber value and buildings. These days, real estate prices tend to factor in the value of buildings and timber. Even so, chances are that the standing houses, barns, and sheds will be less costly—not to mention more charming—than ones you would build.

Water is great for recreation and beauty—and enhances your land's value. After I bought my farm, I dammed the valley, and there was enough spring water to make a four-acre lake. The project was financed by the Department of Natural Resources (DNR) because of its value for flood control. Since then new regulations for constructing dams have become restrictive, and the DNR may not allow you to convert wetland into a lake. (This may vary from state to state.) Generally, you can use water originating on your land, but you cannot dam a creek that flows through your property. Sometimes the presence of water makes real estate agents drool, and it may unreasonably inflate the price of the property.

Wooded land is preferable to tillable land. It is relatively easy to convert wooded land into fields; the reverse is not true. It takes generations and much effort to establish a forest. Wooded land is becoming more valuable as well. When I bought my farm in 1972, tillable land was considered more desirable than wooded acres; the woodlands were sort of thrown into the bargain. Now the reverse is true because many buyers are city folks more interested in woodsy ambience and wildlife than farming. Land values have appreciated considerably since I bought my farm. A wooded two-hundred-acre farm I purchased in 1972 for $45,000 will soon be on the market for $400,000—after I harvest about $75,000 of timber.

Assess the timber potential of your woodland. To many city slickers, "woods is woods." As Ronald Reagan said, "You see one tree, you've seen them all." Don't believe it. There can be huge differences in the value of forests. Before buying, you should consider the value of standing timber as well as the growing potential of the land. Frequently timber is cut before the land is sold. If there is standing timber, the longer, straighter, and fatter the trees, the greater their value (see chapter 4 for details). If you hear stories about somebody financing a woodland purchase by felling the trees on it, do not believe that you can duplicate the feat. Such deals constitute a rare imperfection in the market, and it takes an expert to sniff them out.

Subsidies may make land more affordable. There is one advantage to acquiring working farm acreage: It may be covered by a government subsidy that will pay you a fair amount of money for doing nothing except being a good steward of soil and water. The Conservation Reserve Program (CRP) pays something like $60 an acre (the amount is a function of fertility) per year for ten or fifteen years if you agree not to plant crops (trees are not considered a crop). Technically, this subsidy is only available on soils highly susceptible to water or wind erosion. Since the government is also interested in subsidizing farming and decreasing agricultural production, much land is considered erodible and qualifies for CRP payments. The present value of the CRP payments may constitute a sizable portion of the purchase price of the property.

Make sure you understand where the borders of your land are. It is not a given that your land ends at a fence line. You need to know where your borders are, especially when it's time to cut timber. You want to avoid cutting your neighbor's trees by mistake, or letting him cut yours. It makes for poor neighborly relations. Farm borders are often more complicated in New England, where land was changing hands before it was conventionally surveyed.

Consider seeking advice from a consulting forester. If you have never owned woodland, it pays to seek advice from a consulting forester. Foresters may provide you with a great deal of useful information, such as the availability and prices of similar land on the market, the value of standing timber, the fertility of the land, and alternative schemes for woodland management. Best of all, they can walk the land with you and help make you aware of many special features a novice would undoubtedly miss. Spending a few hundred dollars to understand, evaluate, and appreciate your land is an excellent investment. The county forester can give you a listing of consulting foresters. Note that the county forester cannot provide services for you until you own the land, and even then he might be too busy.

Be patient. In buying anything, patience is a virtue. Don't let a salesperson convince you that you are about to pass up a deal of a lifetime. Your dream place is out there waiting to be found.

four

IS YOUR LAND SUITABLE
FOR A BEAUTIFUL FOREST?

Unless you happen to own a desert ranch, chances are that your land can grow a respectable forest. Almost any site can foster attractive trees. It's hard to say whether your forest will produce the sort of trees you can sell for a lot of money; that depends on a number of variables. But regardless of the goals you set for your forest, you will be more likely to succeed if you match the site with the most suitable vegetation. It may be difficult for you to assess a site's quality on your own, so don't hesitate to consult experts. A soil expert from the Natural Resource Conservation Service (NRSC, an agency of the United States Department of Agriculture) can help you, as can your county forester or a consulting forester. County foresters may be willing to help, free of charge, and sometimes they are even delighted to share their knowledge with you.

Suggesting that you consult experts may appear to be an easy way out of explaining difficult forest phenomena—a bit like a medicine bottle suggesting that you see your doctor. I have as much faith in foresters as I do in doctors—which is to say, a great deal—but I also assume that their competence varies. In any case, even though you will often need to seek a forester's guidance, there is much you should learn on your own. This chapter will acquaint you with some basic concepts of site suitability, enough to help you ask the right questions.

ASSESSING YOUR SOIL

You will learn much about the soil on your land by learning its natural and agricultural history, subjects an NRSC expert can surely tell you all about. In the prairie states, flat land is generally very fertile, thanks to the thick and nutrient-rich layer of humus laid down by prairie grass over thousands of years. In Illinois, for example, it is not uncommon for topsoil to be more than six feet deep. In forests, by contrast, the soil tends to be much less fertile because there is less decaying organic matter. In hilly agricultural land, years of plowing has often caused much of the topsoil to be eroded into valleys. Some ridge land has been enriched by alluvial soil deposited by the wind. This is the case on my farm in Wisconsin, where Mississippi River dirt was blown for millennia onto neighboring hills. In other regions, glaciers swept away fertile soils and deposited gravel or sand. (This can be a problem, as sand does not hold moisture.) You should attempt to learn the history and makeup of your soil. It's fun and interesting.

To figure out what trees to cultivate, it helps to know the composition of your soil. You (or your vigorous offspring) can dig a hole about four feet deep and invite a soil expert to give you a lecture on the ins and outs of your soil situation. If you're lucky, he'll bring along a coring device. You can take him on a hike around your property to take cylinder samples of the soil. Unless your land has been severely eroded you will have a layer of dark topsoil consisting of some organic matter (up to 5 percent). This layer may be quite thin (less than an inch) or thick, as is common in the prairie plains. Below the topsoil are other layers that can impede root growth, such as clay, a high water table, or rocks. Clay in particular is a problem, although when it is mixed with dirt (such as loam) it may be more or less fertile. Your local NRCS office can provide you with a colorful soil map showing various soil classifications. There are scores of soil types, principally used to gauge agricultural fertility. It is easy to learn some of the basic types such as alluvial (organic matter windblown from river beds), loam (a fertile mixture of sand, clay, and organic matter), and muck (composted soil of high acidity). It is nice to know the terms, but for our purpose the knowledge is not all that important.

A more reliable way to judge fertility is to look at prevailing vegetation. Experts look at different weeds, flowers, and ferns as indicators of what tree species will thrive on a specific plot of land. For instance, the presence of maiden-hair fern or jack-in-the-pulpit is a sign that the land may be fertile, while the presence of blueberry plants typically indicates a dry, nutrient-poor soil and acidic (low pH) soil. To help evaluate your land and plan future projects, I recommend that you walk your property with your forester and ask him to point out indicator plants. Keep in mind, however, that it is not individual plants that signify the fertility of a site, it is the *community*, or mix, of plants that gives clues to its profile. Understand, too, that floristic composition will be of less help in evaluating fields and meadows. Reading patterns of vegetation is a complicated matter, well beyond the scope of this book. For further guidance, there are useful handbooks to consult.* Unless you are a trained forester, however, you will very likely waste hours of vexation trying to glean the smallest nuggets of practical guidance out of such resources. You will do much better to confer with a forester. At any rate, all foresters, ecologists, and soil experts agree that looking at plants gives you better information than analyzing the soil. And it's easier and more fun than digging holes.

THE SITE INDEX

Foresters have a measure to gauge the suitability of a site for different kinds of trees. It's called the "site index." This simply expresses the expected height of a tree species at age fifty. Your forester should be able to tell you what the site index is for a given species on your land. For example, on land with a site index of forty for walnuts, an average walnut tree will grow to forty feet in fifty years. Given that the typical index range for walnut trees is between fifty and ninety feet, it may not be a good idea to cultivate veneer hardwood on that site. Keep in mind, though, that while the site index is a helpful guide, it is not infallible. I have had excellent results growing walnuts next to white pines on apparently infertile ground where no forester should have ever suggested planting walnuts. The walnut trees growing next to pines are healthier and stronger than other stunted walnut trees planted a few yards away. The lesson seems to be that trees are affected by conditions not considered in the site index. Does this invalidate the index? Not necessarily, but the interpretation it presents should be taken with a grain of salt. The walnut trees next to the pines are only twenty-two years old, but some already are fifty feet tall. Will they grow to veneer dimension? I sure hope so, but as so frequently happens in forestry, I will never find out, because my lifespan is much shorter than that of a walnut tree.

* The Department of Forestry, Ecology, and Management at the University of Wisconsin has published a book on floristic plant communities useful for drawing inferences on soil and climatic conditions: *A Guide to Forest Communities and Habitat Types of Central and Southern Wisconsin* (Madison: The University of Wisconsin Press, 1996). My forester was using this handbook and suggested it to me. Your forester will likely be able to recommend a similar guide appropriate to your region. Also look into the publications of your local state university extension service.

ASSESSING THE EXISTING TREES

The best way to gauge a site's quality is to look at the trees already standing on it. The taller the trees, the better and more fertile the site. In a forest, trees will attain a given height whether they are fat or skinny, whether the spacing is dense or loose. A tree's height is a better indicator than its diameter. If prevailing trees are puny, it is unlikely that your land will generate stately veneer-quality trees. Vigorous trees with large crowns and smooth bark are generally good signs. (Walnuts are an exception—deep grooves in walnut bark are a sign of fast growth.) On the other hand, smaller-diameter trees with mossy bark and dead branches in crowns are often signs of poor soil fertility. Lush vegetation, such as brambles and shrubs also indicate fertility. If your land has been recently logged, you may want to take a close look at the tree stumps to get an idea of what size trees your land can support. Crown shape of softwoods (conifers) is a good indicator of health: the crowns of vigorous trees are pointed, while those of weaker ones are flattopped.*

OTHER FACTORS

Another factor to consider in choosing where to plant your new forest is the "aspect" of the site—that is, the land's position relative to the sun. It's easy to get confused about what aspect means. Think of it this way: When you stand on a slope looking down, if you're facing north, the site has a northern aspect. The most productive sites tend to be on northern and eastern aspects, since they receive less sun and retain more moisture, which benefits your forest.

In addition to soil, moisture is an essential ingredient to tree growth. It is generally accepted that on normal soil, annual precipitation should be at least twenty inches. Some soil, however, such as the sandy region to the east of my farm in Wisconsin, will not absorb moisture. As a result, only certain species of trees will thrive in those conditions. In the aforementioned sandy region conifers and scrub oak should do well. In Wisconsin, the presence of an irrigation set-up is an indication that the soil is sandy.

It stands to reason that the more fertile a site, the better the quality of its trees, right? Actually, too much fertility can be a mixed blessing. I have encountered Edens of fertility, typically in low-lying depressions, where ambient vegetation becomes so rampant that tree seedlings are drowned in a sea

* Mollie Beattie, "Woodlot Management," *Blair and Ketchum's Country Journal* (July 1981).

of weeds. Invading vegetation such as thistles, giant ragweed (which can grow twelve feet tall in sixty days), and pigweed can be difficult to eradicate. Not until your seedlings are liberated will they do extremely well, but your trouble getting them started will be richly rewarded.

MATCHING TREES TO YOUR SITE

It is essential that you carefully select the most sensible trees for your site. Planting trees on unsuitable sites is a horrible mistake. It is more gratifying to own a mixed stand of random (or even garbage) trees than an underperforming stand of walnuts or oaks. Since 1978, when I planted acres of walnuts on unsuitable land, forestry has learned from its mistakes. A friend in a nearby county also had an unfortunate experience. He planted oaks, ash, walnuts, white pine, and spruce on his county forester's suggestion. It was nice that the species were mixed together, but the forester should have anticipated that the deer and/or pernicious grasses would kill the oaks, white pines, and walnuts. He also might have anticipated that the owner was not the kind of person to do a lot of work on his stand (the owner believed that once planted, the seedlings would take care of themselves). Only the spruces and ashes survived, in part because the deer left them alone. The point I am trying to make is that it is very important to select the most suitable kind of vegetation for your site. A situation where you are the proud owner of a plantation of trees favored by the local deer population should be avoided. A good forester will help you find a reliable range of possibilities for any particular site. Even the best forester is not infallible, but an incompetent one will waste a lot of your time and money. In any case, whenever a forester suggests a given procedure, it's instructive and prudent to see another site where it has been done.

If your land does not have an ideal soil profile, do not despair. Remember, the trick is to find a match between plants and the site. Even if your land appears to be totally infertile (if, for instance, you have purchased an abandoned gravel pit), it will be suited for some pleasant vegetation, albeit not veneer oak trees. Brambles are a good beginning for a gravel pit. Aspens may take root, and although they won't become fat they will begin forming a forest climate. In time a gravel pit may become a great source for blackberries and attract all sorts of wildlife. It may become a nesting ground for swallows, bats, or even a few snakes. Rabbits will like it, and they in turn will attract predators. You and nature can mold even the most barren and forbidding piece of land into an exciting and lively habitat. It's a fun challenge.

MANAGEMENT PLANS

If you have had any dealings with your county forester, chances are that he has a management plan for your woodland. In Wisconsin, the management plan is a prerequisite for obtaining cost-share money or a reduced state real estate tax levy (more about this below). Generally, a management plan is a record of what forestry procedures have been done on your land and what procedures are suggested in the future. If you take cost-share money or other subsidies, you are obligated to follow the management plan. This is hardly onerous: The plan is a nonthreatening document and consists of things you would most likely want to do anyway. And it allows a lot of leeway to meet your forestry objectives.

Having a plan drawn up is a straightforward process. Your county forester will walk your land, describe it in writing, and suggest a likely approach to managing the land. Typically the plan will read something like this: "This stand with a northern aspect consists of a mixed forest that had been logged about twenty years ago. . . . Recommended action is TSI." Or something like this: "This 10.5 acres of mature white oak should be logged before the year 2005. To assure regeneration, we suggest logging in the winter following ample acorn production." In my experience, the foresters' recommendations have been sound and consistent with my understanding of the principles of good forestry.

Most woodland owners will have their management plan written up by their county forester. The DNR, however, does accept management plans written by licensed consulting foresters. Management plans written by consulting foresters can be more specifically geared to the interests of the woodland owner than those written by the DNR—and, in distinction to the latter, they cost you money. (In chapter 18, I will discuss at greater length the wonderful things a consulting forester can do for you.) In some states (e.g., Vermont), management plans are customarily prepared by a consulting forester at the woodland owner's expense.

THE MANAGED FOREST LAW

Wisconsin's Managed Forest Law gives about sixteen million dollars to small woodland owners to subsidize real estate levies. The purpose of this law is to:

encourage the growth of future commercial crops through sound forestry practices while recognizing individual owners' property objectives and society's needs for compatible recreational activities, forest aesthetics, wildlife habitat, erosion control, and protection of endangered resources.

It's a wonderfully conceived law with noble, achievable objectives. (Some other states have similar laws.) Under the law the state pays all real estate taxes above $0.74 per year per acre (or $1.74 if public hunting is excluded). In return, the landowner obligates himself to (1) follow the management plan, (2) desist from building on the land, and (3) pay 5 percent of any timber harvest to the state. If he decides to build on the land, he will have to repay the state the money he has received plus 12 percent interest. In all, this is a very sensible plan, and I recommend you take advantage of it.

ARE MANAGEMENT PLANS RELEVANT?

While the management plan is the bread and butter of the forestry profession, surprisingly few woodland owners know about it. Once it's drawn up, it tends to do little more than occupy file space both in the DNR office and in your desk drawer. Most woodland owners do not have a clue what it is all about. I once overheard some county foresters discussing how many woodland owners actually knew what was in their management plan—they figured it was 2 or 3 percent. I was among the 97 percent for years. A management plan to me was a bureaucratic document enabling me to obtain cost-share funds. I could not have cared less about the plan itself. Now, in retrospect (and having educated myself in the process of writing this book), do I feel I missed out on anything? I think so. I have always enjoyed spending time with my forester walking through the woods, not looking at paperwork. But I must admit, had I read my management plan carefully when I got it—and had I reviewed it periodically—I would have had better insight into my land and even a better understanding of silviculture. It would have formed a better basis for discussions with my forester, and, on the whole, I would have done a little better with my woods.

five

STARTING YOUR FOREST

My Aunt Nancy's great-grandfather came from Germany and homesteaded in southern Kentucky in 1830. At that time he planted a single walnut tree on his front lawn. This tree enjoyed ideal growing conditions: The soil was well-drained and loamy, and there was lots of sun all around. Grandpa knew all about pruning and took very good care of this tree. The tree grew to be one hundred feet tall with no lateral branching for sixty feet. Some years later, his granddaughter, Aunt Nancy's mother, cut the tree and sold it, using the money to finance Aunt Nancy's education at Carleton College, where she later went on to become a professor. It is unfortunate that her great-grandfather did not live long enough to know about the wonderful use of his walnut tree.

Nice story, isn't it? Of course, it is pure fantasy. First of all, it takes a lot longer than one hundred years for a walnut tree to become fat enough to pay for anybody's tuition. Secondly, it is impossible for an open field walnut to grow this tall without developing huge lateral branches. Now look at the drawing of the tree on page 26. It shows an open field walnut tree of low lumber value. I intended the tree to become a hundred-foot grandpa tree with no lateral branching, but while I was napping, the lateral branches got so big that I could no longer prune them. So I decided to leave it as a demonstration tree. It's beautiful in its own way, and every year it produces bountiful nuts, but it will never

This walnut tree grew too many lateral branches to even be valuable for lumber. I call it my "demonstration tree," since it shows convincingly the value of pruning and management.

pay tuition anywhere classier than the school of hard knocks.

HIDDEN TREES

When I was a greenhorn forest owner, I delighted in discovering trees growing in the weeds or trying to break through a stand of sumac or prickly ash to find a place in the sun. How wonderful to find such a tree! It may become a beautiful specimen and make me rich. Such a lovely little tree will have to be helped along, I thought—I must *liberate* it. Out comes the chain saw to eliminate all competitive vegetation within ten feet. What a happy tree this would be! Of course, through experience I learned that this approach was all wrong. As long as a little tree has access to the sun without being shaded by a larger neighbor, there is no need to interfere. When a tree is doing well already, do not mess with it—at least not yet. Liberating an individual tree may cause it to develop large lateral branches and the result will be another demonstration tree like the one described above, devoid of lumber value.

Most trees are planted in open fields. This is not necessarily the best way of starting your forest, just the way it is routinely done. But often the best trees grow where you do not expect them, where you may have forgotten them, or where not you, but squirrels, have planted them. You may find such a tree at the edge of your forest growing skinny and straight with a small crown. The tree is striving for sunlight, always fearful of being crowded out by neighboring trees. (See color photo #3.) If it fails to contact sunlight by maintaining a place in the canopy, it knows it

will die. By stretching upward, it will grow long and skinny, and thereby assume the desired shape of a beautiful lumber tree.

Such trees are wonderful to find and nurture. I call them hidden trees. Squirrels are very adept at planting seeds in fortuitous spots to generate such miracle trees. Of course, you can do many things better than most squirrels, and there is no reason why you can't successfully hand-plant individual trees or seeds in out-of-the-way places. The results are often extraordinary. While you can plant shade-tolerant trees such as maples in the shade, shade-intolerant trees such as oak, aspen, or walnut need direct sunlight.

Many of my best trees are "hidden" trees, planted at the edge of woods or in weedy and bushy spots where neighboring vegetation provides side shading. They grow straight with relatively little care. It surprises me that forestry literature universally advises against planting in small clearings or on the edge of forests. Experts warn against planting any area less than a couple of open acres. I don't know how such misinformation became orthodoxy. In my experience, planting individual trees anywhere is a good idea as long as the tree can get direct sunlight. Hidden trees are great candidates to develop into future crop trees in your perpetual mixed forest. I have many hidden trees on my farm, and they give me profound pleasure.

WORK WITH NATURE

The most important virtue to have in forest management is an unshakable trust in nature. Always try to understand nature; work with nature, not against it. You should observe nature, learn from nature, and use nature's ways to your own ends. Always try to position plants where they like to grow naturally. For example, if you want to grow a stand of oaks, expose the dirt on a small area with direct sunlight, plant seedlings or some acorns, and then let nature do its thing. If you try to plant aspens in the shade or in a field of certain species of grass, they will not flourish. In this chapter I will outline some basic forestry principles that will enable you to predict what methods are more likely to lead to desired results.

If you were to leave your woodlands totally to nature, you would be a naturalist. A very prestigious organization, The Nature Conservancy, purchases land all over the world and typically leaves it to nature with little interference. Following the same principles, you might just as easily foster a paradise of biodiversity.* Over time, your land would revert to something similar to its original state. The problem, however, is that you may not live long enough to see much of the transformation. Nor should you assume that leaving your land alone is necessarily the surest way toward a biodiverse paradise. Nonmanagement is better than poor management, but your management aims are best met by working with nature to transform your woodland to your tastes. This chapter will give you some understanding of how you can predict the growth of your trees and speed nature's processes along.

You are the steward of your land and should determine the objectives of ownership. Nature offers you incredible latitude to transform your land to your designs. You can choose a park setting, a natural forest, a monocultural tree farm, or a combination of all of the above. I recommend aiming for a mixed species and uneven-aged forest, since it will offer many of the desired objectives of woodland ownership: beauty, rich wildlife, and timber production. Besides being fun and beautiful, a mixed-species forest resists natural disturbances, fosters incredible wildlife, and generates wonderful trees.

In guiding your trees to grow according to your design, it helps to understand that much plant behavior is predictable. A trained forester can project how a tree is likely to grow based on its position relative to other plants and the peculiarities of the species. To help make this clear, I will introduce three key phenomena of plant behavior: shade tolerance, disturbance, and succession.

SHADE TOLERANCE

You may be surprised to learn that plants, like people, can be tolerant or intolerant. In fact, shade tolerance is an important ecological principle. It is a measure of how much or how little sun a plant needs to survive. It's not that any plant is "tolerant" or kind enough to relinquish sunlight to a

* I will explain biodiversity in more detail in chapters 13 and 15. It is the interactions of the wide variety of plants, beetles, bugs, fungi, lichens, trees, shrubs, mammals, birds, amphibians, insects, and microscopic organisms that inhabit an ecosystem. It would be erroneous to maintain that non-management will always lead to biodiversity. The Nature Conservancy, a well-respected environmental organization, often employs burning and at times herbicides to restore sites to their original vegetation.

neighbor; most plants will grab as much sunlight as possible. Tolerant trees, like maples, can survive with relatively little sun, while intolerant trees, such as aspens or oaks, need direct sunlight to live. A shaded oakling may survive a short time with little sun but will die within one or two growing seasons. A tolerant maple, on the other hand, can hang around for years in a shady spot, growing very little. If an opportunity develops—for instance when a canopy tree dies—it will lap up the available sunlight and grow large.

Shade Tolerance of Common Woodland Trees

*The table below grades trees by degree of tolerance to shading.**

VERY INTOLERANT:

aspen	cottonwood
tamarack	willow
balsam poplar	jack pine

INTOLERANT:

butternut	red pine
black walnut	paper birch
hickory	black cherry

INTERMEDIATE:

ash	white spruce
elm	sycamore
oak	white pine
hackberry	shagbark hickory
yellow birch	

TOLERANT:

basswood	red maple
silver maple	box elder
black spruce	ironwood
cedar	

VERY TOLERANT:

beech	hemlock
balsam fir	sugar maple

* Source: *Forestry Facts #79*, School of Natural Resources, Department of Forestry, University of Wisconsin.

DISTURBANCE

Disturbance is an event that drastically alters the composition of a forest. Examples of disturbance are climatic changes, floods, fires, severe insect infestation, droughts, severe cold spells, strong winds, ice storms, clear-cutting, pasturing, pollution, volcanic eruptions, landslides, and earthquakes. Depending on the severity of the disturbance, the forest may be destroyed or only slightly damaged. Ecologists have documented numerous disturbances and cycles of disturbances. Many are caused by humans, such as the burning of Brazilian rain forests, clear-cuts in British Columbia, and the prairie burnings by Native Americans. While disturbances are irregular, some occur often enough to have a significant impact on ecosystems. Forest fires, for example, are a great boon to shade-intolerant trees, primarily by wiping out slow-growing competitors for sunlight. Many of the jack pine's seeds remain in its cones until they are released by the heat of a fire; thus, forest fires play a key role in the regeneration of this species.

SUCCESSION

In nature, soil moisture, soil fertility, and patterns of light and shade are always in flux. As these conditions change, the land may attract a new set of vegetation. The process by which a forest is populated by a new community of plants is known as "succession." For example, here is how succession often works after a prairie fire: The fire destroys surface vegetation, exposing the soil surface. Within a short time an abundance of grasses, brambles, and weeds emerge, and seeds from birches or aspen may blow onto the site and germinate. They are all fast-growing, shade-intolerant species, referred to as "pioneer" plants. In a short time the pioneer seedlings will form a new overstory (i.e., canopy of foliage), making the shaded area below inhospitable to their own seeds and other pioneer plants. Where some light penetrates the canopy, trees with an ability to thrive with moderate sunlight, such as oak, ash, and hickory, may establish themselves. These species gradually take over the canopy and succeed the original pioneer trees as they die (birches and aspens mature at the age of about eighty). These hickory, oak, and ash trees cast so much shade that their own offspring cannot grow below them.* Over time, new understory is formed by the arrival of shade-tolerant trees, such as maples, ironwood, and basswood. They hang around patiently until a canopy gap develops, which they will fill. Once the shade-tolerant trees dominate the canopy, the forest reaches a state of a mature equilibrium that will persist until a new disturbance of one kind or another occurs. (In fact, without disturbance our woodlands would be overwhelmingly dominated by shade-tolerant trees.) It is interesting that in the last sixty years aspen forests have decreased by half

---

* Some tree species employ other methods to discourage unwanted competition of offspring. The cherry tree produces a pathogen that kills small cherry seedlings nearby.

in Wisconsin, while maples have increased by a third.* The mix of tree species has been affected by changes in the frequency of disturbance: Native Americans stopped burning prairies (which they formerly did to provide forage and to make game more visible to hunters), the voracious timbering by settlers subsided, and for a while forest agencies vigorously sought to reduce naturally occurring forest fires. More recently, foresters have changed their philosophy, allowing fires to occur naturally on a limited scale.

Your own management procedures should be based on the dynamics of succession. As a forester, you should anticipate that intolerant trees, such as aspens, will gradually give way to more tolerant species growing in their shade. The dynamics of succession are full of variables, and the artistry of a forester consists in part of knowing these dynamics and using them as tools in shaping a forest.

WHAT TREES SHOULD YOU CULTIVATE?

A word is in order here about what trees you should choose for your woodland. Nature may have made that choice for you already, and I would certainly encourage you to work with whatever trees are already growing on your land, even if they are not ideal. They will likely form a basis upon which to build by influencing the natural process of forest succession. However, you will have many opportunities to plant new trees and to choose between species of already existing trees, so let me mention the qualities of certain trees just as a way of orienting your thinking.

I confine myself to northern trees and will not attempt to be exhaustive in my coverage, simply because I can't be. Given where my farm is in Wisconsin, I can tell you about oaks but not about beeches. I can speak with a little authority about walnuts but not about chestnuts. Furthermore, I have tended to think about the trees I plant in terms of their timber value, especially when I started out. You may have other interests—historical, ecological, aesthetic, or the like—that don't place high value on timber sales. That's great. But if you don't know exactly what you want, you might start with the thumbnail descriptions below.

Conifers

Conifers tend to grow best in sandy soil, though the ones I planted as seedlings seem to do fine on my loamy farm. However, a state nursery supervisor told me conifer seeds have a hard time germinating unless there is a sand component in the soil. Conifers vary in their properties, just as hardwoods do, but on the whole they have been impervious to the pernicious grasses on my farm. (You'll read more

* A DNR publication entitled "A Look at Wisconsin's Forests" gives the following statistics: In 1936, 42 percent of all forested areas was occupied by aspens and birch and 21 percent by maple and basswood. In 1996 the respective proportions were 22 percent and 34 percent. One may reasonably assume that this is largely the result of the suppression of forest fires.

about this later on.) As a result, I have found them useful as trainer trees when interplanted among my hardwoods.

White pine, sometimes called northern pine, furnishes a light, soft, straight-grained wood with a yellowish tint. It's only moderately strong, so it is used in construction generally for finishing material. It's great for cabinet making and joinery. White pines tower over other pines, reaching as high as two hundred feet. White pine grows all over the northern United States and Canada and used to dominate in the upper Midwest as well. The species is susceptible to blister rust and the tip weevil and has intermediate shade tolerance. While I have never found authoritative information on this, I believe deer prefer to browse on white pine over red pine.

Red pine, also called Norway pine (although they are native to northern Wisconsin), can also be sold for timber. It is considered to be better for pulp than white pine, though both are fine pulp trees. Red pines are easier to take care of than white pines and are not susceptible to blister rust or weevils. They are shade intolerant, though, and don't grow quite as tall as white pines.

Spruce is best known to most Americans as the species of their Christmas tree. There are several varieties, including black, white, and Norway spruce. Black spruce is common in the northern United States and Canada, and these days is primarily used for pulp. Its wood is light and easy to work, but it is also very tough in fiber, a quality that made it a choice building material in the days of timber framing. It also used to be prized for piles and other submerged timbers, because it preserved well under water. But it seldom grows bigger than seventy feet high and nine inches in diameter, making it too small for modern lumber. In practical terms, other types of spruce are little distinguished from black spruce, except Norway spruce, which was formerly used in shipbuilding. Spruce is a food of last resort for deer but important feeding grounds and habitat for a great variety of birds and little critters.*

Cedar grows in two basic varieties in the United States. White cedar is soft, light, fine-grained and durable, but it lacks strength and toughness. Red cedar grows more slowly than white, but has the same texture to its wood. It has a pretty red color, though, and a distinctive pungent odor that has made it popular for protection against moths. Red cedar and white cedar are durable in water—red cedar more so—and consequently they are often used as outdoor construction finishes. White cedar is often made into shingles, while red cedar makes good sills, siding, and posts. Cedar trees tend to grow multiple stems, so to maximize timber production you have to cut off all but one stem.

Hardwoods

Hardwoods run the gamut from prize trees, such as oak and walnut, to the

---

* Much of the information on black spruce is from Virginia Barlow, "Black Spruce," *Northern Woodlands* 8 (Winter 2001): 35.

garbage trees such as prickly ash and box elder. Each should have its purpose in your woodland, even if that purpose is to hone your machete-slashing technique.

Oak is the gold standard of hardwoods. Historically in northern climes, it is the wood that civilizations were built on. A dozen or so species thrive in the United States, of which white oak is the hardest. Its wood is heavy, hard, cross-grained, and strong. In the past, oak was used for timber framing in construction, shipbuilding, and building casks and barrels. These days it is widely used for flooring, trim, veneer, and furniture. Its silver grain and high, durable polish make white oak one of the most beautiful woods for cabinet making, especially if lumber is quarter-sawn. Red oak is similar in appearance to white oak, but the grain is tighter and redder, and the wood is slightly softer. Today, red oak is put to the same uses as white oak, but formerly it was also split to make shingles. Unfortunately, red oak is particularly susceptible to oak wilt. You should check with foresters about incidence in your region before you plant red oaks.

Oaks are stately and wonderful trees, especially when their leaves turn. If your oaks are of mixed variety, your treeline will yield a riot of color in autumn, ranging from flame red to golden brown. The bur oak may be the most beautiful northern hardwood in existence. This gnarly-branched oak, which somewhat resembles the shape of coral when denuded, is one of the few trees that could survive the prairie fires set by Native Americans in centuries past. Awesome groves of bur oaks are some of the few aesthetic thrills peculiar to the Great Lakes region. Even oaks that produce little decent timber are nice to have around. If your soil is poor, you'll still be able to grow scrub oak. Oak of all varieties makes good firewood, which can even be burned green. Oaks tend to have intermediate shade tolerance, so it can take some effort to liberate them from competing trees in the forest, but the effort is well worth it.

Aspen, called "popple" or "poplar" in my part of Wisconsin, is a light and fast-growing tree. It's a pioneer tree, meaning that on a barren piece of land it's among the first species of tree that establishes itself, which is one of the reasons I like it. If you look at a grove of aspen, it's likely you're looking at one organism. Aspen trees we see aboveground are joined to each other by root systems that can stretch great distances. The wood from the aspen is typically made into pulp, although a fair amount of furniture is made out of it these days because it's cheap and easy to work. Because it is rather light, it is often used for gates and for pallets. In the pioneer days, settlers used "popple" for cabin logs, joists, rafters, and weatherboard. It's not a good firewood.

Ash is a large tree that produces heavy, hard, and very elastic wood. The best known uses for ash lumber are tool handles and baseball bats (although now they are starting to make bats out of maple as well). Ash is hard to work, so it's rarely used for carpentry. Whenever I have to cut an ash, I am always surprised how much more resistance it offers my chainsaw. I love ash trees because they grow straight and slender with very little lateral branching. Many times I wished that it could be so easy to grow walnut trees. The value of ash trees used to be higher when there was a greater demand for tool handles, wooden tennis rackets, and so forth.

Hickory is the heaviest, hardest, toughest, and strongest of all American woods. In the past it was widely used for implements requiring bent-wood details, such as oxbows, but even then it was not considered a good construction material. It's the densest wood in my forest, a top-shelf firewood, packed with carbon, which explains why it burns so well. Even when green it burns long and hot. Hickory is the best wood with which to smoke meat, and is popular at barbecue joints in my hometown. The shagbark hickory, with its bark seeming to peel in long strips, is a distinctive and attractive tree. Hickory bark can be useful as well. A folk chair craftsman I know cuts it into narrow strips to weave seats for his chairs. He claims it lasts forever.

Locust is a hard wood and difficult to work, but useful nonetheless. Very durable, it gets harder with age. It also resists termites, and thus was used for sills and foundation blocks in early construction. Locust was also fashioned into pegs for timber construction—so keep locust in mind if you ever want to build a log cabin on your land or, more realistically, if you want to harvest your own timber for fenceposts, dock posts, or other structural items that will be exposed to the elements. I used black locust from my farm as posts for a deck and to build run-off drains for my roads.

Black walnut is a species dear to my heart, in that I blew a small fortune planting thousands of the suckers all over the farm I bought several decades ago. Although the tree does not leaf out prodi-

giously, it is elegant. Its nuts are easy to collect, tasty, and quite fragrant when encased in their green hulls. The wood is lovely, with a dark, purplish, wavy grain. It has come in and out of vogue as a fine cabinet and veneer wood, but it is always among the most prized and valuable American hardwoods, traditionally used for gun stocks. Its irregular and knotted roots produce beautiful burled wood. Walnut is relatively durable wood, as well, so it also can be used unseasoned for fence rails.

Cherry wood, highly prized for its beauty, is light red to brownish red in color with a close fine grain that takes an exceedingly high polish. So it is one of the most desirable woods for cabinetry and veneer. Although its bark is interesting, the wild cherry is not particularly pretty, and the cherries the tree produces are small and generally up in the crown, out of sight. Its appearance notwithstanding, this is a tree you want to encourage wherever possible for its valuable and beautiful wood.

Birch wood resembles cherry in texture and, in some of its species, in color as well. The most common birches in American forests, white (or paper) birches, are distinctive for their peeling white bark, and are generally a pulp wood. Paper birch was widely used by Native Americans for thatching and canoes, and early homesteaders used birch bark as a water barrier underneath their sod roofs. It's a pretty tree to have in your woods, but there is no reason to cultivate it. The birch commonly used for cabinetry is yellow birch.

Maple is a large and beautiful tree and, along with oak, is a true-blue lumber hardwood. A heavy, hard, and strong wood, maple is wonderful for heavy-duty flooring. Its wood is light with a beautiful silver grain, especially when quarter-sawn. Some distinctive features are grain irregularities, known as curly maple and bird's-eye maple, which make the wood weaker but are highly prized by cabinetmakers for their beauty. Sugar maple is tapped for sap in early spring, which is then boiled to make maple syrup. Like the oak, maple has many varieties and is distinguished by beautiful foliage, especially in autumn.

Apple and pear trees are a wonderful compliment to your forests and fields. I have several apple trees on my farm, some in out-of-the-way places. It's nice to come across one in the fall and pick its fruit. I haven't cultivated orchards on my farm, but for those who are so inclined, orchard-keeping is an engrossing and highly rewarding avocation in its own right. The wood of these trees is handy as well. Their crooked and twisting grain make great ornament. A note of caution: Pear trees have the reputation of harboring pests, and they do not grow nearly as well as apple trees.

As I admitted above, my discussion of the trees from which you have to choose is by no means complete. I have not touched on a number of tree species I encounter in my own forests. Instead, I hope this discussion inspires you to think about the qualities that most excite you in the woods you will cultivate. As I will argue throughout this book, you should strive for a mixed

---

Firewood

Below is a table of the heat output of different species of wood. The first column shows the relative weight of different kinds of wood. The second shows how much heat, measured in British thermal units (BTU), a cord of that wood produces at 100 percent efficiency. *

	POUNDS PER CU. FT.	MILLIONS OF BTUs PER CORD
Cottonwood	24.8	13.5
Aspen	27.0	14.7
Pine	26.3	14.3
Paper Birch	37.4	20.3
Sugar Maple	42.1	24.0
Oak	48.7	25.7
Hickory	50.1	27.7

---

* Minnesota Extension Service, *Heating the Home with Wood* (University of Minnesota Natural Resources, 1983).

forest where many of these species exist in harmony. Depending on how engaged your state's Department of Natural Resources is, county officials may offer valuable guidance or, on the other hand, may try to influence you to favor some species over others. I encourage you to seek all information they can provide to you. But as the steward of your land, you must make the choices. Follow your own lights.

GENERATING A FOREST ON A FIELD

Many landowners want to convert open land into a forest. This awesome undertaking may be accomplished in three different ways, which I will discuss in the following three chapters. These methods: succession, planting, and seeding. There is no unanimity on which of these works best, and you should be suspicious of anyone who tells you that there is only one obvious way. As a practical matter, you may decide to choose your own hybrid scheme of establishing a forest. There is but one thing that I would categorically advise you to avoid: a monocultural plantation. I have learned that a mixed forest works best and that deciduous trees, especially on grassy lands, are more difficult to cultivate than conifers.*

In deciding on how to go about establishing a forest you should consider the following variables:

Proximity of your land to a forest. Depending on the nature of prevailing vegetation, your open land may benefit from a nearby forest. For example, some trees, such as aspens and locusts, have extensive underground root runners just under the surface, known as rhizomes, that send up vigorous sprouts, also referred to as suckers. Aspen suckers, supported by a huge root system sometimes several acres in size, can grow to ten feet in a few months. Oddly, aspen suckers have much bigger leaves than older aspen trees. Often aspens and locusts, using their root-structure as a base, can colonize an adjacent field and, significantly, are not bothered by pernicious grasses. But if you plant an individual aspen into pernicious grasses, it has a hard time getting established. (See color photo #4.) In addition to helping expansion via rhizomes, a nearby forest serves as an important and welcome source of seeds.

The equipment resources at your disposal. Hand tools and rototillers are useful for certain jobs, but a tractor with a chisel plow, or a Gator, will allow you to succeed more easily.

The amount of money and effort you are willing to devote to your forest. Your success at starting a forest is somewhat proportional to the resources you employ. If you have a lot of money, the easiest method might be to plant a mixture of seedlings about three feet apart that will yield rather fast and gratifying results. But

---

* Charles Darwin observed in *The Origin of Species* (1850) that wheat fields planted with diverse varieties of the grain were more productive than those planted with a single variety. This is because mixtures check the spread of pathogens and therefore disease. There is no reason to believe that the same does not hold true for trees—that is, monocultures are problematic.

even with minimal resources, you may get good results. If you go for a walk with a hand tool and a few nuts and acorns in your pocket, you should be able to get a few seedlings started. Little beginnings, such as a few seedlings next spring, can give you a wonderful high.

The presence of undesirable vegetation. If you own a pasture or hayfield where pernicious grasses grow, it will be difficult to establish a forest. Other kinds of vegetation, such as sumac or prickly ash, may also be a nuisance to your efforts.

Many traditional foresters will tell you that planting seedlings is the best way to start a forest. This, I believe, is not the most sensible method; it is, however, the prevailing method and likely the only one with which you're going to get expert assistance. At first, in fact, planting appears to produce satisfying results, since most trees survive. Yet over the long term serious problems may crop up, particularly the ill effects of pernicious grasses, along with the arduous maintenance tasks such as pruning. (Note, however, that planting conifer seedlings is less problematic—and cheaper—than deciduous trees because they are relatively unperturbed by pernicious grasses and have the wonderful propensity to grow straight.)

Some woodland owners on the cutting edge of forestry prefer seeding. But this method, too, can be disappointing: Results are difficult to predict with any degree of certainty. And succession? This is a seductively attractive alternative, because nature does all the work and (if you are lucky) it requires no chemicals. In some situations, such as a plot near an existing stand of trees, you will do well to let succession establish your forest. But without an adjacent stand of trees ready to invade the pernicious grass carpet, succession works very, very slowly. Of course, you may want to try a combination of all three methods and do a bit of experimentation of your own.

As a small-woodland owner you have an advantage not open to huge timber companies that frequently clear-cut and start new forests from scratch. You can nurture individual plants and give them a little help and encouragement every year. Most academic forestry literature, which is geared more to the Weyerhaeuser Corporation than to you and me, has little to say about babying individual oak seedlings or using canopy gaps to establish oak trees. So when a forester tells you the only way to establish a new stand of oaks is a clear-cut, you should voice a strong objection.

Suppose you plant or spot an oak seedling in an area overgrown by prickly ash or sumac. Possibly a squirrel may have planted the acorn and a small seedling appears. You should know (or learn) that an oak seedling overshadowed by larger established plants will assuredly die in one or two growing seasons. To help the seedling survive you should :

Identify the seedling so you can find it in subsequent years. You may do this with a flag or a plastic tube. Or you may just remember.

Give a seedling room to survive, if it is small. You should clear competing vegetation in a three-foot diameter circle. It is most important that the seedling has direct access to sunlight. You may have to repeat this liberation for a few years.

Know when to leave it alone. When the oak seedling has penetrated the canopy, your work is done. As a matter of fact, any further liberating becomes counterproductive, because the surrounding vegetation provides side shading that makes the tree grow into a straighter and more valuable lumber tree.

Fostering individual trees is fun, challenging, and labor intensive. You will learn to regard many a nurtured tree as a loving relative. In the next chapter I will introduce your bitterest enemy.

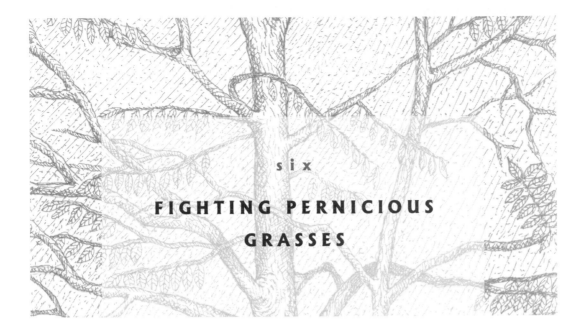

six

FIGHTING PERNICIOUS GRASSES

When I bought my farm, it was half woods and half agricultural land. Because I wanted eventually to cover most of the open land with walnut groves, I was faced with the necessity of confronting the number one foe of young hardwoods: pernicious grasses. ("Pernicious grasses," I should note, is not a botanical term but one suggested by a friend. It means simply those species of grass that stunt trees.) Fighting pernicious grasses proved to be much more difficult than I ever could have imagined. I understand that in some parts of the country, such as New England, the problem is the opposite. Much of the land there has not been used for agriculture for generations, and the problem land owners face is more how to keep the forest from reclaiming the pasture than vice versa. To keep an expanding forest in check is relatively easy; a semiannual mowing will solve much of the problem. However, if you want to plant trees in the midst of pernicious grasses, get ready for a fight.

THE PERILS OF PERNICIOUS GRASSES

When I started out as a tree farmer, I assumed that grass growing between my trees was innocuous ground cover and would not bother my seedlings. If it did, I would pick up my hoe and solve the problem. Little did I imagine how useless my hoe would be to fight grasses with resilient, five-foot-deep root systems—not to mention the damage hoeing would do to my seedlings. In fact, I continue to learn the hard way that controlling pernicious grasses is vital to the success of any deciduous tree plantation in a prairielike setting, and that it requires diligent and systematic measures. At one time my pasture land had been seeded with orchard grasses, a mixture of various species of grass, among them smooth brome, a nonnative variety imported from Germany. Smooth brome outcompetes all other kinds of vegetation, particularly deciduous trees. On my farm, smooth brome occupies large meadows, and its complete coverage has not changed in the thirty years I have owned the farm.

Counseled by the county forester, I planted my first seedlings into a field that had been a hay field. As part of the planting process, I applied a band of herbicide to kill competing vegetation, and for a while it appeared to have worked. All the seedlings survived and the grass appeared to be dead. But the following year the grass reappeared, and it became difficult to find my little trees. I tried to mow between the rows of trees, but I found it hard to spot the seedlings. As my mower lost its bearings, many seedlings were inadvertently chopped.

The smooth brome continues to stunt the greater part of my walnut plantings. (Other woodland owners I know have reported similar problems with tall fescue and quackgrass.) Why are these grasses so detrimental? When I first noticed that grass had declared war on my aspiring forest, I figured that it was a matter of grass sucking away moisture and strangling trees, but studies suggest that some grasses dominate by more effectively competing for nitrogen. Another problem is that some grasses (including smooth brome*) produce a phytotoxic (plant-poisoning) substance that inhibits growth of some tree species. The process is known as allelopathy, and its effectiveness may be observed in the large areas of grass on my farm that have remained unchanged for decades. When I planted, I left some areas untouched for aesthetic reasons. I fantasized that on some beautiful afternoon I would walk through my wonderful forest and see a deer family grazing between stands of trees. Since then, I have begun to regard this idyllic meadow as a green asphalt carpet. The brome grass cover tolerates no other vegetation. Not only is the grass toxic to tree seedlings, but it competes so effectively for nitrogen that other plants cannot establish themselves. Only a few trees have managed to pierce the grass carpet: some aspen, sumac, and prickly ash, which benefit from large common root structures connecting them to a nearby colony of trees. An occasional ash, cherry, or hickory may spring up, and pines seem relatively impervious to the grasses; but neither my beloved walnut trees nor the hundreds of oak trees I planted were any match for the grass.

---

* There are different subspecies of fescue and brome grasses. I only have experience with tall fescue and smooth brome. I will refer only to brome and fescue, as shorthand, in this book. It may be that different varieties of brome and fescue are more or less pernicious. Suffice it to say that they are exotic species in North America and, as such, may not have natural enemies. That generally means trouble.

CONTROLLING PERNICIOUS GRASSES

Among the numerous species of grasses, fescue and brome are especially vicious. Fescue typically has roots five feet deep, which makes it very difficult to eradicate. And no matter where you plan to establish your forest, you can count on battling pernicious grasses. One way to identify them in your region is to determine which species are native and which are not. The nonnative species are likely to give you trouble. You may educate yourself further by reading up on local ecology and by consulting your forester or other locally based professionals, such as botanists, ecologists, and the like. Over the last two decades, I have acquired a small body of knowledge on grass, which I'll share with you here.

Broadleaf weeds are generally more benign than grasses. Big weeds such as ragweed and Canada thistle may shade out tree seedlings and harbor bothersome rodents, but generally they are less likely than pernicious grasses to kill seedlings. Also unlike most grasses, broadleaf weeds are weak-rooted enough that after a rain they can be pulled out by hand. Trees often thrive among weeds. In late summer, trees growing among weeds display happy, dark green foliage and are photosynthesizing, while trees growing in the grass generally look stressed, with sparse and yellowing leaves. Though less bothersome than grass, some broadleaf weeds can cause problems. For instance, Canada thistles have completely covered a patch of newly emerging tree seedlings on my farm. A ragweed invasion can be equally annoying. Still, thistles and even giant ragweed can be more easily eradicated than fescue and brome grass.

Eradicate grass completely before planting or seeding. Without herbiciding, any deciduous trees (such as oaks or walnuts) you have planted into pernicious grasses may die or develop so poorly that they will never have commercial value. If by luck a few trees should survive, it will take them a very, very long time to establish themselves. A forester friend says one of the keys to successful reforestation is "to herbicide grass deader than a doornail." This sounds like good advice, especially when dealing with brome or fescue. The problem is that pernicious grasses will return! An application of herbicide will merely weaken the grasses. Zillions of grass seeds remain after you have killed all the grass plants. With five-foot-deep root systems it would require repeated applications of herbicides to kill grass deader than a doornail. Though experts maintain that repeated applications of Roundup will kill grasses, I have not figured out how to accomplish this feat. Besides, it would be quite costly and possibly injurious to the environment. Herbiciding will give you easier, quicker, and cheaper results than disturbing the grasses mechanically, but perhaps it's best to use both techniques in tandem. It's a tough battle.

As an alternative to herbiciding, plant something else to supplant or mitigate pernicious grasses. A friend recommends growing corn for two years before planting or seeding trees. Or you might consider planting some conifers with deciduous trees. Conifers resist pernicious grasses more so than deciduous trees.

Disturbing the soil may be useful. I came serendipitously upon the idea of disturbing the soil between rows of trees to stimulate weed seed germination. When I made my first attempts at seeding, I rototilled a stretch of ground to plant some acorns. The seeding was only marginally successful because a flock of turkeys dug up most of the acorns, but broadleaf weeds grew like crazy and overpowered the grasses. I have since concluded that disturbing the grasses between the rows of planted trees promotes weed growth. This disturbance can be effected by means of rototilling, discing, or chisel plowing. There is a downside, however: The weeds will attract mice, which will gnaw at your trees. Nevertheless, the mice will do much less damage to your trees than pernicious grass will. The procedure also may be more successful if you throw out some seeds before you chisel plow. For instance you could spread some tree seeds, or even clover or rye—all would help to subdue pernicious grasses. At my forester's suggestion, I recently planted ash seeds, but unfortunately they failed to germinate. (This is a pitfall of seeding: You can never be sure your seeds are viable.) However, my efforts were not in vain, as the chisel-plowing stimulated some weeds. But be forewarned that while chisel-plowing and spreading seeds may weaken pernicious grasses, it will not eradicate them.

Mowing does not control grasses. Mowing will not significantly affect pernicious grasses such as brome or fescue. Some tree planters mow, hoping to prevent grasses from producing seeds, but there are so many ambient seeds anyway that this effort is pointless. There are even ways mowing can be counterproductive: It may make the grass denser and thus more likely to choke your seedlings. If done with heavy equipment, especially on wet days, mowing will compact soil around seedlings, which can stunt tree growth.

That said, mowing has its uses, its main benefit being that it fairly reliably destroys mouse habitat. Mice love to gnaw on young bark in the winter, which effectively girdles the tree. A gnawed hardwood tree will almost always resprout (and there is little long-term damage), but nibbling will retard the tree's development. Mowing between rows of seedlings can keep mice at bay, but you should beware that it will make it easier for deer to nibble at your seedlings. On balance, I think that frequent mowing between seedlings is not a good idea. (One exception: If fast-growing shrubs such as prickly ash invade your plantation, periodic mowing is advisable.)

BY THEIR MOWING YOU SHALL KNOW THEM

Some naturalists come down hard on the mowing public. Bob Chenoweth, author of *Black Walnut* (Sycamore Press, 1995), writes: "After forty years of mowing, after several new mowing machines have been purchased and discarded, after countless hours of riding in circles, there will be nothing to show for this huge expenditure. . . . We are remembered by our acts, those we touch and those we leave behind. A mowed lawn or pasture will not be long remembered."

It has also been suggested to me that mowing reduces the chance of wildfire. Although I have never had fire damage, it is obvious that a fire could severely damage a young plantation. At any rate, while mowing can actually be more fun, time spent herbiciding is much more productive.

HERBICIDES

Many reasonable people are unalterably opposed to herbiciding. I believe the choice is not so simple. Admittedly, the enthusiasm for herbicide has often gone too far. For example, many forestry authorities recommend using herbicide to kill unwanted trees because it is a little less work than felling or girdling. On the other hand, even avatars of environmentalism, such as the Sierra Club and The Nature Conservancy, use herbicides.* Though I consider myself an environmentalist, I have been attacked by others for using herbicides. More sensitive naturalists feel that my use of herbicide puts me beyond the pale. Progressive German foresters maintain that herbicides are never justified, because safer procedures are available. But then, German foresters do not face a nonnative grass problem as we do. It is very difficult to fight pernicious vegetation in many parts of North America without herbicides. If herbicides are used with care and reason, their ill effects will be mitigated or counterbalanced by the resulting forest.

Yet the catch, as I will explain, is the difficulty of use. Be suspicious of any person who claims that herbiciding is an easy and foolproof procedure. I know from experience that using herbicides to control pernicious grasses and

---

* I learned this in personal conversations with representatives of each organization. Herbicides are often the only efficient way to eliminate nonnative species as part of the process of restoring the environmental health of a given piece of land. Burning is often a better alternative to herbiciding.

weeds in tree plantings is a complicated task. You may never master the art of herbiciding—few do. Consult your forester, who may be very helpful. But he, too, may experience unexpected results.

When to Use Herbicides

When planting into grassy areas, herbicides afford your seedlings some protection from pernicious grasses. Herbicides are equally useful in fertile areas where ambient weed seeds may overwhelm your little seedlings. I have in mind one particular patch on my land where in successive years giant ragweed killed trees I had planted both as seeds and as seedlings. Ragweed grows so fast (more than a foot a week) that it chokes the trees and makes it nearly impossible to spot seedlings. I killed the weeds by using a wick applicator to brush the herbicide directly on to the weeds at a level higher than the tree seedlings. (There is a non-chemical alternative: I have mowed weeds with my bush hog, raising the blade just above my tallest seedling.)

My first efforts at spraying herbicides weren't terribly effective. Given the size of my plantation and the limited amount of time and effort I was willing to devote to the task, only a small portion of my trees got sprayed. And even in the areas where I spread the herbicide, the results were disappointing. I am not sure whether the herbicide failed to kill the grass plants or whether seeds lingering in the soil simply germinated into a new grass crop. No matter: The grass always returned in a year or so.

In my woodland, I have never followed a regimen for herbicide. I have never applied it more than once every other year. In some spots where I applied no herbicide whatsoever, the grasses dominate to such an extent that the trees are puny and any survivors will take a long time to establish themselves. In time, the few surviving trees may shade out the grasses and survive, but this will take a very long time. Some surviving trees are about two feet tall after twenty-five years, barely holding on.

Herbicides for Woodland

Some of the herbicides available to tree farmers are frighteningly potent. One such poison, Oust, costs $736 for two pounds. The label says you should not get it into your eyes—useful advice, considering that a tablespoon of the stuff could wipe out a sizable vegetable garden. Three-quarters of an ounce in aqueous solution is the recommended dose per acre. Recently, I sprayed it around newly planted seedlings. (Do not copy this procedure; I did it as an experiment.) I needed enough Oust for two hundred small planting areas of four square feet each. I calculated the amount quite carefully and it came to one-eighth of a teaspoon, less than the salt you might put on a bite of hamburger. The experiment did not work well, in spite of (or because of) my precise calculation. Needless to say, I had to be very careful, as the smallest imprecision would have serious consequences to the plants.

Very generally, many factors determine the proper dosage of herbicide to apply, such as the kind of trees you are spraying near, what weeds and grasses you fight, what kind of soil you have, and which way the wind is blowing. I cannot claim to be an expert on these matters, and even the experts often fail to obtain the desired results. Forestry literature, both professional and academic, is full of praise for the effectiveness of herbicides, but it is suspiciously silent on the difficulties of applying them. Professional forestry writers shy away from giving explicit practical instructions—indeed, every professional who read the manuscript for this book warned me against doing so. Professionals instead command woodland owners to read the labels, which is a frustrating exercise. The directions are typically a small book, obviously written with the help of a corporate legal department, whose job it is to prevent lawsuits. These booklets contains a large volume of technical data that is essentially incomprehensible (and mostly irrelevant) to the average woodland owner. But somewhere in the instructions will be the recommendation for a maximum dose per acre, along with an admonition that any greater application violates Environmental Protection Agency (EPA) guidelines. Meanwhile, and strangely, television commercials promote these powerful poisons as user-friendly tools for controlling mundane domestic weeds. One ad shows a good-looking lady spraying Roundup on a harmless dandelion growing in a crack in her driveway. One wonders why she doesn't just kick the little plant or bend down and pull it out.

A further complication is that regulations are always changing with regard to permissible uses of herbicides for forestry applications. For example, twenty-five years ago, I used Atrazine as a pre-emergence herbicide. Today Atrazine is no longer permitted for woodlands. It was replaced by Simazine, but now this, too, is about to be phased out. As a consequence of this shifting situation, it is difficult for small woodland owners to get reasonable instructions on how to apply herbicide—even though their use is urged on them by most experts and the chemical industry.

If you want to use herbicide but are unsure of your judgment, I recommend erring on the side of caution while you experiment. A very knowledgeable friend dilutes five ounces of herbicide (generally Roundup) in three gallons of water in a backpack sprayer tank. If the weeds he seeks to kill eventually do not die, he increases the doses. Through experience you will arrive at the proper concentration in your spraying system.

Below I will discuss four common herbicides—Simazine, glyphosate, Oust, and Pendulum—because I have used them with relative success. Note, however, that this is in no way an exhaustive treatment of the range of herbicides available. New products constantly appear on the market. Whatever I describe here may be obsolete within a year.

Simazine is a pre-emergence herbicide that should be applied in early spring. It remains in the soil and kills germinating seeds when reacting with moisture. It kills sprouts before they emerge from the soil. The suggested dosage is two to three quarts per acre. This is a ballpark amount, and I encourage you to obtain specific advice on how much poison to use. The amount will depend on the soil type, the species of weed, and the size of the weeds. If you spray Simazine in early spring over both conifers and deciduous trees, be aware that the conifers may suffer, because the needles will absorb the poison more than deciduous seedlings do before they leaf out.

BLESSING OR CURSE?

Herbicides are considered necessary to modern agriculture, but only a small proportion of the chemicals applied ever reach their intended target. The remainder must be absorbed by the environment, where they do great damage. One of many serious consequences is the contamination of aquifers, a threat that has only recently come to public attention.* The scale of agrichemical warfare is overwhelming. Consider Michael Pollan's stunning account in the *New York Times Magazine*** of a typical potato grower's herbiciding regimen: Early in the season, the field is fumigated to kill all microbes. As soon as any weeds appear a herbicide is sprayed that is so toxic it kills any insect that eats the sprayed plants. (Unfortunately, Pollan does not discuss the effect on the birds eating the insects.) The weeds are sprayed twice more with herbicides. Fertilizers are then applied ten different times through an irrigation system, followed by eight applications of fungicides and two sprayings from airplanes. Some of the chemicals—such as Monitor, a herbicide known to cause neurological damage in humans—are so toxic that the farmer does not dare to walk on the field for at least one week after application (nor does he ever eat his own potatoes). Further adding to the chemical treatment is an insecticide Monsanto bioengineered into the potato plant. The Colorado potato beetle drops dead when it eats potato foliage. Much of the chemical treatment is designed to eliminate black spots on the potato, which are tasteless and whose only offense is aesthetic. Organically grown potatoes have the black spots but taste the same. The effect of all of these chemicals on the consumer is unknown and practically unregulated. Organic farmers grow just as many potatoes per acre but because of the black spots sell them for less. The organic farmer has to work harder, but is probably healthier and happier. I find such agricultural practices revolting, and I mention them here only as a caveat that, while I do endorse the intelligent use of herbicides in tree farming, it is necessary to maintain perspective about the blessings and the curses of agricultural chemicals.

* *State of the World 2001: A Worldwatch Institute Report* (New York: W.W. Norton, 2001). The cost of removing chemicals to make aquifer water potable is so high that some German municipalities (e.g., Munich) pay farmers large sums to convert to organic agriculture.

** Michael Pollan, "Playing God in the Garden," *New York Times Magazine*, October 25, 1998.

Glyphosate (best known by its most common trade name, Roundup) is the most widely used herbicide. It essentially kills everything green (except genetically altered soybean plants). In an overgrown area you should mow, and when the vegetation recovers zap it with Roundup. The sprayed plants will wilt and die, though they may resprout. The more luscious and juicy and green the foliage, the better it works. If your spray hits the leaves of a seedling by mistake, break them off. If you don't, the poison will severely stress the tree. It does not matter much if you get glyphosate on the bark. Suggested application is two to three quarts per acre.

Oust, according to its manufacturer's description, offers "broad-spectrum control of grasses and herbaceous weeds with residual activity." This is both a pre- and post-emergent herbicide, acting both on the plant to be eradicated and lingering on in the soil killing germinating seeds. It is used in concentration of about one-half to three-quarters ounces per acre. Oust is extremely potent, so you have to be very careful not to spray too much. An acquaintance once oversprayed a couple of acres and nothing grew on it for almost two seasons. My forester has recently suggested spraying one-half ounce an acre on a planting of small seedlings in the fall. This would kill many weeds and grasses, but it would also retard the growth of my seedlings. Nonetheless, it may be the best compromise solution. It will do more damage to the grass than to the seedlings. However, if your seedlings are tiny, such as spruces in their first spring, an application of Oust may not be a good idea.

Pendulum is a new product with the wonderful attribute of killing grasses but not deciduous trees. It can be applied to your plantation in spring at a rate of four to six quarts per acre.

Often herbicides are combined in a "cocktail." My forester now recommends the use of Oust (one-half ounce) and Simazine (three quarts) in the fall, and a combination of Simazine and Roundup in the spring before the seedlings leaf out. Remember that these recommendations and the currently suggested herbicides will change over time. Moreover, that exact recommendation may be ill suited to your conditions even if it works for mine. I urge you to take advice from your forester and to read the labels. Advice will vary; for example, some foresters (not to mention the product's label) recommend Simazine only for site preparation—not for your use on tree seedlings.

Applying Herbicides

Aside from being environmentally unsympathetic, the proper application of herbicides is difficult, unpleasant, and time-consuming. It helps to have the right equipment, but even that is no guarantee of the desired result. I rigged my first spraying setup to my tractor, resting the herbicide tank on a platform supported by the hydraulics, with a pump driven by the power takeoff. Assistants walking behind the tractor manned the spray nozzles at the ends of hoses, applying a circle of herbicide spray around each tree. Although I thought I had the right equipment and made all the necessary preparations, herbiciding with the tractor never seemed to go as smoothly as planned. The hoses had a tendency to get tangled, and inevitably a hose would get snagged and shower us with its milky poison. As the trees got bigger, the branches hit the tractor driver in the face, and the helpers holding the spray nozzles had to dodge the branches continuously. Not surprisingly, as time went on even my loyal friends expressed little enthusiasm for helping me with the task.

I have since bought a Fimco sprayer and mounted it on my Gator. This setup is much less unwieldy than the one on my tractor, and as a result I am able to spray more of my plantation than before. Yet even with the improved procedure, my pernicious grasses always resurface.

From my experience, here are my best suggestions for achieving reasonable control of grasses and weeds by applying herbicides.

Be careful to use the proper concentration of the herbicide. It is no easy matter to calculate the proper dosage of herbicide in your application. Suppose you're using Roundup, and the directions suggest using no more than two quarts per acre. Further suppose that rather than applying the herbicide evenly all over your acreage, you only want to spray it around three hundred oak trees. Now, given that you are only supposed to spray Roundup at the rate of two quarts (64 ounces) per acre, how many quarts should you use? You would have to consider the size of the circle you spray around each tree. Let's say the circle is four feet in diameter (which equals 12.56 square feet per tree). This means that for 300 trees you will spray 3,768 square feet (300 trees times 12.56 square feet/tree). We know that one acre, equaling 43,560 square feet, will require 64 ounces of herbicide. So, if 64 ounces is enough for 43,560 square feet, how many ounces are required for 3,768 square feet? The answer is:

Ounces for 300 trees (3,768 square feet) = 3,768/43,560 x 64 = 5.53 ounces

If you put 5.5 ounces of Roundup into a three-gallon canister, the mixture should be stretched to spray around 300 trees, which means each circular area around a tree should be sprayed with 1.28 ounces of the mixture.

128 ounces per gallon x 3 gallons/300 trees = 1.28 ounces

Your next task is to determine how long it will take you to spray 1.28 ounces. What you should do is to count aloud while you spray that volume into a measuring cup. Suppose it takes three seconds. This means that you should spray the area around each tree for three seconds. This assumes that the pressure in the tank is constant (naturally, the higher the pressure the more spray is ejected).

It is my estimation that if you come within 50 percent of the suggested dosage, you are doing well. You will also learn that if you apply too little, your

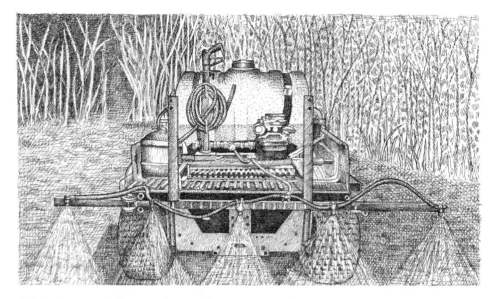

The Fimco sprayer, mounted on my Gator, makes applying herbicide relatively easy.

targeted weeds will not die, but only get a slight headache. Over time you will also learn that some weeds, such as burdock, resist being killed and require a slightly higher dosage.

Read the labels of the herbicides you use. I do not have the qualifications to comment on the potential harm these poisons can do—but they can be dangerous. It has been suggested, for instance, that herbicides may affect the reproduction mechanisms of humans.* So it is wise to be cautious. I have been showered several times with herbicides when a hose broke, without apparent ill effects. At the same time, some cautious tree farmers use masks to avoid inhaling herbicide spray. This is highly recommended, especially when mixing the chemicals, because you are exposed to a higher concentration of the chemical at that time. The use of special clothing and rubber gloves also is recommended. My wife insists on throwing all clothes into the washer after I spray.

Do not spray when it is raining too hard or when it is too windy. A moderate rain will accelerate your poison's rate of absorption, but a pouring rain may wash it away. However, there are exceptions to this rule: It is okay to spray Roundup even in the rain, but if you spray on a windy day, your poison may drift or even dry up and blow away.

---

* It is appalling that the U.S. government, in attempting to eradicate Colombian coca fields, uses fifteen times the dosage recommended for U.S. woodland owners.

Use wick application for tall weeds. Soybean farmers at times kill weeds taller than their crop with a wick applicator. The wick is a cloth saturated by a pipe filled with herbicide and attached horizontally to the front bumper of a vehicle. Some foresters use a manual wick applicator. Just brush the stuff on the leaves of the weeds. Colleagues of mine have used these to good effect, but I prefer to use a hand sprayer.

Do not herbicide promiscuously. I recommend using herbicides only to kill grass and not to eliminate understory or to kill trees to be culled. As I mentioned earlier, some foresters use herbicides to kill undesirable trees rather than felling or girdling them, or for "wildlife enhancement" after clear-cutting. These uses are often encouraged by the chemical companies. Generally such uses are unfriendly to the environment and not cost-effective—all in all, a lousy idea.

Consider the stovepipe procedure. If you have a small plantation and do not have extensive spraying equipment, you may want to apply herbicide using a stovepipe to shield the seedling. Simply put the stove pipe over your plant to protect it from the herbicide and spray Roundup around it with a hand sprayer. It works well. Some folks tell me that holding a sheet of plywood with a handle to protect your seedlings from the poison is easier to use. Be sure that only one side of the plywood shield is exposed to the spray.

Keep your nozzles and equipment clean. When using a large tank with a pump, it pays to leave the agitator running to prevent clogging. Keeping the agitator running will assure that the herbicide is uniformly distributed in the solution. Uneven concentrations of poison may kill your seedlings. When it's not agitated, powdered herbicide may settle and clog the system. This situation is to be avoided at almost any cost. Also, be careful not to get particulate matter in the nozzles, as it will block the spray.

Use of a blueing compound may be helpful. When herbiciding a large area, you may lose track of which sections of a field have been sprayed and which have not. Adding an agent to tint your herbicide mixture blue (see page 200) makes it easier to identify the area sprayed.

The Limited Effectiveness of Herbicides

Using more herbicide may get you better trees, perhaps, but it's not really worth it after a certain point. Recently, I attended a Walnut Council field day in Illinois, where we were shown a marvelous plantation of forty-foot walnut trees as straight as candles. The plantation was tended with the help of academicians who are the leaders among walnut aficionados. The well-tended, weedless grass under the trees was herbicided twice a year and mowed frequently. I was struck by the fact that the semiannual herbiciding was deemed

HERBICIDE DISPENSING EQUIPMENT

Canister. Most readers will be familiar with canister sprayers, which look a lot like fire extinguishers. Using them is simple and straight forward: You merely need to add the poison, pump, and you are ready.

Backpack sprayer. A backpack sprayer is similar to a canister sprayer except that carrying the equipment on your back is much easier. The hand pump enables you to pump with your left hand while you walk or use the sprayer with your right hand. It is very versatile, and I have seen woodland owners, even with a large acreage, use nothing but such a small backpack sprayer.

Sprayers with an engine-driven pump. I use a Fimco Sprayer, which fits on the back of my Gator, operates without hitches, and sprays an eight-foot-wide band with four nozzles from a fifty-gallon tank. It enables me to spray about three acres an hour. If you plan to reforest more than a couple hundred acres of land, a Fimco (or one of several comparable makes) should give you good results.

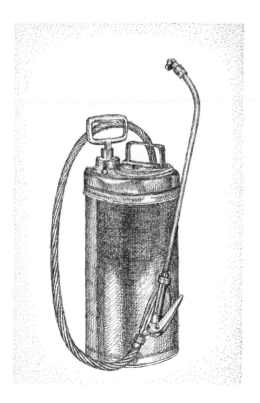

Canister sprayer.

Backpack sprayer.

necessary to control the grass even under a closed canopy. The cost of the frequency of herbicide applications most likely exceeded the timber value of the trees. The beauty of the trees may satisfy the vanity of the plantation owner, but it will do nothing for his pocketbook nor the environment.

ALTERNATIVES TO HERBICIDE

I have reluctantly concluded that herbiciding is a justifiable tool in forestry when used as sparingly as possible. Typically, though, the benefits of chemicals are quite visible while the damage done to the environment is hidden. Which is to say, the advantages of herbicide are very seductive. And their powers of seduction are reinforced by huge promotional efforts by the chemical industry. You should always look for alternatives to achieve your ends without the use of chemicals.

Below I will discuss the best alternatives to herbicides.

Natural Succession. Many invasive plants are shade intolerant, and they will be shaded out when the trees grow up. I am happy to state with near certainty that my pernicious brome grass will be shaded out as trees form a forest. It is still unfortunate that I am using herbicide in the interim to give my trees a start. If I had been better informed when I planted my trees (or if I was unalterably opposed to herbicides), I would not have planted oaks and walnuts, since other trees, such as most conifers, box elders, willows, and aspen, are less affected by brome grass.

Mowing. As I state throughout the book, I am no fan of mowing, especially in your front yard, where natively occurring vegetation is often much more interesting than a lawn. A case can be made for mowing off the blossoms of offensive plants, but that is not always effective. I have mowed the heads of giant ragweed in spring, but somehow there are always plenty of seeds left for the following growing season. As a matter of fact, the giant ragweeds appeared one season after I had disturbed the soil for seeding trees. Before this, I had never seen a giant ragweed in the area. Somehow, the seeds had been there all along and just waiting for me to disturb the soil and then cover the area like a ten-foot new snowfall. It is incredible—but you have to learn that there always seem to be a lot of seeds in the soil waiting for a season in the sun.

Girdling. A girdle is a one-inch-deep ring cut around the circumference of a tree, severing the life-sustaining cambium (see chapter 12). Some tree species respond quite well to girdling. For instance, black locust will generally die. By contrast, coppicing a black locust (i.e., cutting through its trunk) generates vigorous resprouting (see below). When I tried to convert a black locust patch to walnuts, a neighbor suggested I cut down the locusts and put

USING POISON TO BRING BACK THE PRAIRIE

I don't like spreading poison on my land. But the simple fact is that sometimes it's worth the benefit. It might be useful to relate to you my attempt to start a prairie grass patch. It turns out to be a lot more complicated than you might expect. When I decided to convert part of my pasture into a prairie landscape, I herbicided a few acres with Roundup in the fall and then disced it. The soil looked moist, fertile, happy, and ready for prairie grass seed. I was mistaken. A prairie grass expert advised me that I should herbicide the emerging grass in spring, and till it again and then repeat the procedure before planting the prairie grass. (And this was a man who did not strike me as someone who likes to spread a lot of poison without good reason.) He explained that even after herbiciding and tilling, millions of seeds of all kinds remain per square foot—seeds that would vigorously compete with the prairie grass seeds. Prairie grass seed costs hundreds of dollars per acre, so the land must be properly prepared.

Mechanical means are also needed to fight the orchard grass. I was instructed to mow my prairie garden in June of the first growing season, setting the mower about six inches off the ground. This will kill the existing grasses and give the newly seeded grasses a chance to establish themselves. (You will have a hard time finding the prairie grass plants. They are tiny the first year and it takes an expert to spot them.) Yet mechanical means alone are not sufficient to eradicate competing vegetation and reestablish native grasses. Herbicide must be used. The power of nonnative species is such that the storied tall grass that once filled the prairies and savannahs over thousands of square miles is on life support.

---

cooking salt on the stumps. That was nonsense—the locusts resprouted all over the place. Girdling works much better, since the injured trees seem to put their energies into surviving, but end up suffering a slow death. (See discussion of girdling in chapter 12).

Coppicing. Chopping off plants above the surface will leave the root structure intact with the result of vigorous sprouting. Some folks put some sort of herbicide on the cutoff surface. People claim it works, although I have never done it. A better option is to plant new seedlings into the coppiced stand and use the resprouts for sideshading of your trees. To make this scheme work, you will have to control the resprouts for a few seasons, since they will be much more vigorous than your planted seedlings.

Burning. Burning is a much in vogue with ecologists. I cover burnings elsewhere in chapters 7 and 20. Conceptually, burning plants with relatively small root systems is effective, and many invasive grasses and weeds fall into this category.

Scarification. As explained in chapter 9, roughing up the surface to make the soil receptive to seeds is a good strategy. A similar scheme could be used to disturb the grasses around trees. I have run a chisel plow between my trees with mixed success.

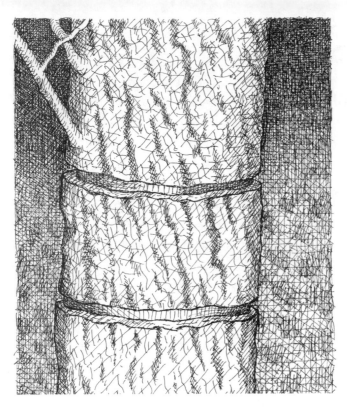

A girdle cut through the cambium will slowly kill a tree.

The result can be an influx of another species, such as Queen Anne's lace, which is at least less pernicious than brome grass.

Controlling pernicious vegetation is a tough proposition and may well be your greatest challenge as a woodland owner. Whenever possible, I urge you to favor natural ways to fight grasses, such as succession, which will be discussed in the next chapter.

seven

ESTABLISHING A FOREST
BY SUCCESSION

The significant advantages of the succession method are that it is cheap and natural—that is, it can be done without the use of herbicide. If you simply leave an open field undisturbed, brambles, weeds, and eventually pioneer trees may establish themselves. Once mature, the pioneer trees, typically aspens and birches, attract other hardwood trees, like nut trees, which in turn attract the more shade-tolerant trees, typically basswood and maples. If you are lucky, the transition to a forest may go relatively fast, by which I mean a half-century. However, if pernicious grasses are present this process may take much longer. As I related in chapter 4, brome and fescue grasses are poisonous to many deciduous trees and can cover land like a sheet of green asphalt, making it very difficult to establish a forest. With or without pernicious grasses present, certain techniques will help speed succession along. They include:

Burning. Burning is a strong successional technique if used wisely. A good way to get rid of tall grass and weeds temporarily, it is often especially useful in clearing the way for other management procedures, such as discing or chisel plowing. Burning can also promote the growth of species of trees resistant to fire. Some oak trees, such as the bur oak, have adapted to prairie burning by developing a thick fire-resistant bark. When the Native Americans were replaced by white settlers, the prairie burnings stopped, and the oaks became the most abundant tree in the emerging forests.

Don't be fooled into thinking that once you've burned your grass and weeds to the ground they're gone for good; they will reappear. Burning will have no lasting affect on grasses. How could it if the roots can be several feet deep? Furthermore, zillions of ambient seeds remain in the soil, resistant to being burned. If you decide to burn a field, you will need a burning permit from your state's DNR, a matter that can be dealt with by your county forester. If you have never done it before, you should engage experienced help to keep the fire under control. Since the DNR office will not issue a permit unless chances of spreading a fire are small, there is little danger of starting a major fire—except if you get too close to conifers, which can burn ferociously. Be careful: Take note of the wind's direction, and have plenty of friends, as well as shovels and rakes, on hand to control the fire. Burning is a fun experience. Generally there is a bit of excitement, just enough to make it interesting.

Scarification. If you hope that seeds from adjacent trees will germinate, or if you wish to spread seeds you have collected, it is important to expose the mineral soil of—or "scarify"—your field. Certain seeds, such as those of the aspen and the cottonwood, are very tiny and spread readily in late spring. I once visited a tree nursery where cottonwoods are "seeded" simply by exposing the soil. The nursery foreman said that surrounding cottonwood trees will always provide enough ambient seeds (visibly more like dust than seeds) to get enough seedlings started.

One traditional way to expose the dirt, as some forestry textbooks suggest, is to drag anchor chains behind a bulldozer. Since few woodland owners happen to have an anchor chain lying around (and since the equipment needed to drag it would undoubtedly cause severe compaction of the soil), you ought to find other ways to expose the dirt. For small operators, a rototiller or a disc will serve the same purpose. I have achieved the best results with a chisel plow mounted on the three-point hitch of a tractor. In certain plowed patches of my farm I've noticed aspens sprouting prolifically after chisel plowing, even though there were no other aspens for a quarter-mile. Of course, you can never rely on that sort of success. In any given year you may not stimulate any germination at all, which means starting from scratch the following year. Even if a few pioneer trees managed to establish themselves, don't hesitate to scarify again the next year. Many small trees will withstand a disc or a chisel plow thanks to their strong taproots, especially in the spring when there is more moisture in the soil.

Herbiciding. A nursery supervisor suggested that, as an alternative to scarification, I try herbiciding grass and weed vegetation next to a row of white spruces heavily laden with cones in order to allow little spruces to establish themselves. One year, I tried to scarify next to the white spruces, but no seedlings appeared. I now believe that the pH was too high for conifers, which do best in acidic soils.

Using a chisel plow is my preferred way to prepare a site for seeding.

Enhancing natural succession with available seeds and plants. If you have extra seeds or plants you can plant them into the successional vegetation. When planting seeds, be sure that there is some exposed soil. I have used a hand-held rototiller to expose the soil. In the fall, whenever you go for a walk and see seeds of plants you like, pluck them off, put them into your pocket and spread them onto exposed soil on your successional plot. When you see the plants the following year, you'll feel proud.

Encouraging individual plants. As a small woodland owner you should have the time to give attention to individual trees. Your favorite plants are much more likely to survive and thrive if they are not overtopped by other unwanted vegetation. Side shading is beneficial and direct overhead sunlight a must. So, for example, if you spot a tiny oak tree in weeds, you can help it along by making sure that it doesn't have to compete for sunlight. I often use a hand-held weed chopper to cut down my tiny trees' oppressive neighbors. You may want to mark the presence of your chosen plants with flags (see ap-

The hand-held rototiller (top) and hand-held chopper (bottom) are handy tools to clear unwanted vegetation around a preferred seedling.

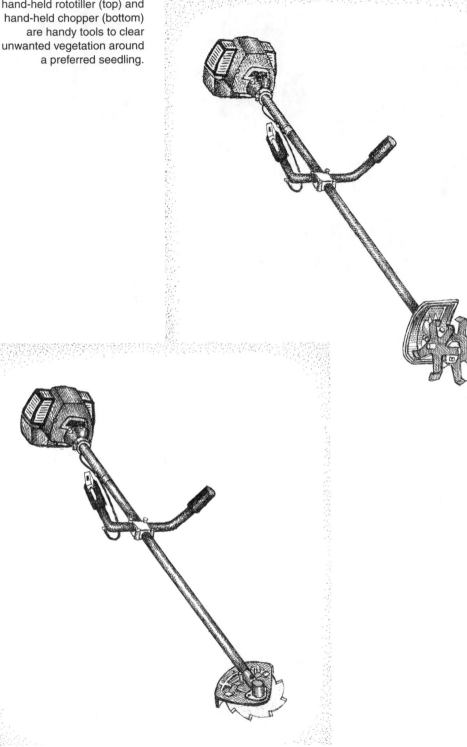

SEEDING ASPENS TO START SUCCESSION

I recently visited a quarry near my land and was amazed to see aspens flourishing there—amid gravel and poor soil. I am convinced that aspens are the key to starting a successional forest. Agricultural land set aside in the Conservation Reserve Program (CRP) could be easily and quickly forested if a convenient way were found to disturb the soil and distribute aspen seed. Aspen "seeds" are a dust with a density of five million seeds per pound, which makes harvesting difficult. A Wisconsin nursery supervisor I know uses a back-mounted vacuum machine to harvest aspen seeds. A friend suggested to me that I fell some seed-bearing trees and drag them over my field as a more effective way to distribute seeds. The trees could be hitched behind a chisel plow pulled by a tractor. The seeds would drop off, and the brushing action of the tree leaves could help cover the seeds. I was excited to try this technique, yet I found in two consecutive years that my aspens produced no seeds. What's more, my nursery consultant told me that even in a good year, the window of opportunity for trying this technique is only two days. Nonetheless, I am still eager to try it.

---

pendix B) or a plastic tube shelter. Once the trees have a share of the canopy, they will do wonderfully by themselves and will need no further attention for a long time.

The time required to start the successional process depends on the nature of the prevalent vegetation, the availability of ambient seeds, fertility, and your persistence. Generally, it is easiest to extend a forest into a field, using an adjacent forest as a base. As a practical matter, some trees, such as aspen and locusts, have an subterranean network of roots that gratuitously sprout trees in adjacent fields. If you encounter an influx of persistent, less-desirable vegetation, such as prickly ash or sumac, you should interplant more desirable trees or shrubs. Of course, you have to make sure that your seedling will retain access to the sun—if not it will die. Interplanting is fun work and will accelerate the establishment of your forest. If you're lucky, the succession to a forest can happen relatively fast. But as you will learn, nothing happens very fast in forestry, and patience is not only a virtue but a necessity for success.

You can measure your success at starting the successional process by the number of different species of plants that sprout in your plot. If you have brambles, shrubs, weeds, and some trees, that's an excellent beginning. If, on the other hand, you have a field of brome grass, sumac, or prickly ash, nothing may happen very fast. Monocultural weeds such as these will have to be disturbed by discing, chisel plowing, or scarification before the plot will attract a wider variety of plants. But even if you do nothing, sooner or later single plants such as an oak tree or an elm will manage to survive in a colony of sumac or prickly ash. You can further such invaders by making room for them to get some sun.

If you are an impatient sort of person, faster results can be obtained by planting your forest as described in the following chapter. This fast-track scheme is a bit deceptive because, as you will learn, some things in forestry take time to take root and grow. Planted seedlings may languish or even die in some instances. But do not be discouraged: Sometimes plants—both planted seedlings and volunteer trees—can grow rapidly. It is the art of forestry to anticipate what will work best and how to nurture struggling seedlings.

eight

ESTABLISHING A FOREST BY PLANTING SEEDLINGS

Planting seedlings is the most common way to establish a forest in an open field. Your choices are to plant by hand or to hire a contractor to plant rows of seedlings with a machine. Hand planting is a reasonable option if you are planting fewer than a thousand trees. If you plant an area larger than a couple of acres, you'll want to use a planting rig.

MACHINE PLANTING

If you're contemplating planting seedlings by machine, you'll need the cooperation of your DNR county forester or a consulting forester. Here's hoping that you have a competent one in your county. Your forester will help you order seedlings from the state or private nursery, find a planting contractor, and sign you up for cost-sharing funds (arranged by the DNR),* which will defray typically more than half of your costs. Traditionally, planting is done in the spring after the ground has thawed, although it is acceptable to plant deciduous seedlings—but not conifers—in the fall. (Conifers planted in fall may not establish

---

* Technically the DNR (a state agency) provides technical assistance only. The cost-share checks are issued by the sponsoring state agency.

their roots in the ground, and their needles often dry out.) Survival rates tend to be a bit higher with spring plantings.

On a cool early spring morning, a crew will appear with the appropriate equip-ment and big boxes of seedlings and expeditiously plant seedlings. You will do very little, except watch in amazement as something like a thousand seedlings per hour get inserted into the ground.

The planting process is speedy and efficient. A tractor pulls a planter manned by a person who inserts the plants into a furrow made by a large disc. Dirt is then firmly pushed together to secure the plant in the soil. A herbicide applicator, pulled behind the planting machine, spreads a band of herbicide about three feet wide. A third person readies the bundles of plants and trims the roots. It is important to make sure the root pruning is done properly and aggressively (see illustrations on pages 66 and 67).

I should note here that in rocky terrain, such as that frequently encountered in New England, machine planting may be impractical. The planting machine has a big thirty-six-inch disc, and when it hits rocks it loses its cutting edge (and jolts the operator). So if your land has a lot of rocks, hand planting may be necessary. I understand that there exist fairly rock-resistant planting machines with a smaller disc and a steel foot to open a slit in the soil, but frequently hand planting is the only alternative. This is also true for clearcut areas because of the tree stumps.

Your forester will probably suggest planting your seedlings in rows eight to ten feet apart and at linear intervals of six to eight feet. This spacing allows sufficient room for your tractor to maneuver between rows. (In a few years, however, lateral branches will have a tendency to smack you in the face as you drive your tractor between rows of trees. It's one of the many joys of tree farming!) The resulting density is about five hundred to eight hundred trees per acre. The cost of planting will vary according to the species you choose. At the low end, planting conifers currently costs $0.45 per tree. The seedling costs $0.15, planting it costs $0.20, and herbiciding it costs $0.10. At a density of 750 trees per acre, you will pay $300 per acre to plant white pines. The comparable cost of planting oaks is around $750. If you receive cost sharing (currently in Wisconsin the government pays 65 percent of the costs), your expenses are proportionately lower. If you consider that a single tree costing you less than a quarter could be sold for hundreds of dollars a century hence, this may sound like a great deal. But as you will learn in chapter 21, the realities of making money in forestry are less promising than you might think.

Planting on Grassy Land

A good forester will encourage you to prepare your site beforehand. You should apply herbicide to pernicious grasses, preferably the preceding fall, so that your seedlings have a better chance to thrive. But remember: The roots of some pernicious grasses reach down into the earth so deep that it is very difficult to apply enough herbicide to eradicate them completely. Also, an abundance of ambient seeds will sprout the following year. Still, an application of herbicide will retard the vigor of grass and will allow weeds to establish themselves. Remember that weeds are much more benign than established pernicious grasses.

As we saw in chapter 6, ambient grasses found in pastures and hay fields are more hostile to seedlings than vegetation on tilled fields. When I put down my first walnut plantation in 1978, herbicide applied during the planting process (this is still the most common method) did retard grasses just a bit. However, when the herbicide wore off, grasses re-emerged and stunted the walnut plants. Little did I know at the time that my trees were doomed to retardation by allelopathy and that this plantation would be just one of a series of humbling lessons on why not to trust the conventional wisdom of the forestry industry.

Planting on Land without Grasses

Planting seedlings on land after a clearcut, or on land where trees and brush have been cleared, will yield better results than planting on grassy land. Whether the previous vegetation has been herbicided or cleared mechanically, the newly planted seedlings will do relatively well because of a lack of grass competition. Grasses tend to absorb more moisture and nitrogen than shrubs or trees. Of course, emerging vegetation from sprouts and seeds will compete for space, but your seedlings should do well as long as they are not shaded out. As a matter of fact, side shading from other forms of vegetation should help the seedlings to grow straight with less maintenance.*

Selection of Tree Species

Your forester will suggest several species of trees appropriate for your site and make his own recommendations. An enlightened forester will suggest a few shrubs or pines along the edge of your plantation. Happily, many foresters in Wisconsin now recommend alternate rows of pine and mixed hardwoods.** Intuitively, I always felt that mixing different species of seedlings would make a more interesting forest. In 1978 my forester disagreed: "It's not done that way," he told me. "Pines grow best next to pines and walnuts next to walnuts. It simplifies maintenance and harvesting." He was dead wrong, but I suppose I can't fault him for following the customary procedures of the time. Learn from my experience: You should be firm in voicing your opinions on where and how dense you want your

---

* Mark Mittelstadt, a consulting forester, has very successfully planted on a site in Bear Valley, Richland County, Wisconsin, that he cleared by a combination of mechanical eradication and herbiciding. Because the cost of herbiciding is relatively high (about $300 per acre) and only minimally covered by a cost-share program, the scheme never became popular. Still, I very much recommend planting into existing vegetation, provided that the seedlings have access to the sun.

** A preferred planting may be two rows of pines (or other conifers) and one row of deciduous trees. Normally in the first thinning, one row of the conifers gets cut because they have commercial value for pulp. This would leave one row of conifers and one of deciduous trees, a better start for a mixed forest. Best, of course, is if you intermingle all plant species for planting, but the typical forester may consider this a strange idea.

seedlings to be planted. For diversity you may want to mix up a lot of different trees.

Tree seedlings, especially when planted by machine, will generally do well. Once, in an exceptionally dry year, most of my seedlings died, but in normal conditions you can expect a survival rate of over 95 percent. I should qualify that by saying that surviving and thriving are two different things. When my first plants leafed out, I felt the thrill of success. Little did I know about the problems to come. But that's a discussion we'll have in a moment. First, I'll explain other methods of planting.

HAND PLANTING NURSERY STOCK

If you intend to plant fewer than about a thousand trees, it does not pay to arrange for a planting rig. It makes more sense to use a spud (also known as a dibble or a planting bar), a spade-like planting tool designed to plant seedlings quickly and easily by hand (see illustration on page 218). Planting by hand is more work and generally not quite as successful as machine planting, but it is more suitable for smaller plots. I suggest the following pointers:

Where to buy your seedlings. You can buy seedlings through a state nursery (the DNR forester can help) or from a private nursery, which will typically charge you more. When planting by hand, it is best to get small seedlings (generally one year old). Alternatively, you can buy larger seedlings and prune them aggressively. One forester friend prunes the top to get a

more favorable root-to-crown ratio. If you intend to plant with a shovel and dig a big hole and shower a lot of love on your seedlings, you may buy larger plants (about three years old). Some geneticists recommend discarding the smallest 25 percent of the seedlings. I don't subscribe to this, because the weaker seedlings may have been crowded in the nursery and the smaller size may not necessarily be a sign of genetic inferiority.

Where to plant. If you have a large field, it makes sense to plant in straight lines. This simplifies the planting process and access for herbiciding, mowing, and pruning—or just getting around without stepping or driving on your seedlings. If you plant in small areas, there is no need to plant in a straight line. As a matter of fact, it may be more fun to plant in "cohorts," a term foresters use to designate a bunch of trees of the same species and age growing together. Planting in a cohort (inside a circle, for example) has the advantage that you can plant trees so close together that they will shade each other and grow straighter.

The literature on forestry typically advises against planting in areas smaller than a couple of acres or on the edge of forests. This oft-repeated factoid may be true for the Weyerhaeuser Company, but for you and me it's simply nonsense. In fact, the opposite is true. Trees grow best in company of other trees, and it is good to plant your seedlings into virtually any vegetation, provided you do the following: Make sure that all shade-intolerant plants have direct access to overhead sun, and avoid (or kill) grasses that stunt tree

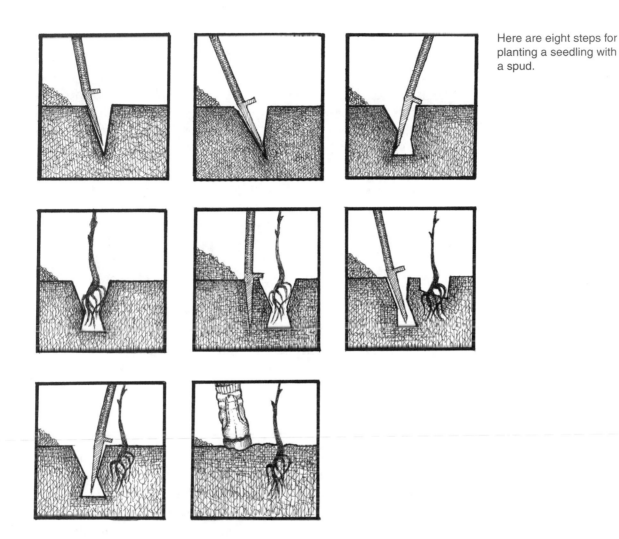

Here are eight steps for planting a seedling with a spud.

growth. If you do plant into pernicious grasses, remember to apply herbicide in coming years whenever the grasses reemerge.

Keep your seedlings moist and cool. If they're packaged in paper, soak them occasionally through the packaging. If you take them out of the package prior to planting, don't expose them to the sun and wind. To keep seedlings moist before planting, it used to be recommended that you dig a little ditch, stand the plants in it, and cover the roots with moist earth. This procedure, called "heeling-in," has been found to damage seedlings and is no longer recommended.

Trim the roots. When you get seedlings from the nursery, they typically

A typical oak seedling before trimming. Its roots are too long for spud planting.

have a long stringy beard of fine roots or long lateral roots. Don't be afraid to prune the roots: You want them to be a bit shorter than the depth of the planting hole (i.e., the same length as the blade of the spud, about ten inches). Root trimming is very important; it makes planting much easier, faster, and more successful. Root pruning minimizes the tangling of the roots that may cause a plant to become "rootbound," a situation where strands of roots choke each other. Rootbinding tends to be more of a problem with container-grown stock and with certain species, such as white ash. It is certainly more of a threat to your seedlings than any damage you may inflict by overpruning, so prune with confidence.

Plant the tree firmly. Step on the spud and wiggle it back and forth until you have a wedgelike hole (see the illustrations on page 65). Then pull out the spud and insert the plant, making sure that all of the root is in the planting hole. Plant to about the same depth as the seedlings were planted in the nursery (for ash you should plant a bit less deep). You can discern the depth by the change of color on the stem, which is darker below ground level. To anchor the baby tree in place, make another plunge with the spud about three to five inches away from your plant and pull the spud backward to fill the bottom of the hole and then push it forward toward the plant until the

The same seedling after root trimming. If necessary, keep pruning until it fits in a spud hole.

root collar is tightly secured. Remove the spud and close the top of the hole by pushing dirt into it with your boot. The tree should be planted so tightly that it resists being tugged out. This is very important because seedlings will die when the dirt is not securely compressed around them. Machine planting tends to be more successful than hand planting because the weight of the planting machine can pack the seedling tighter than you ever will. Planting is easier (and better) when the soil is moist, as the soil binds the seedling more tightly.

Make sure that the roots go straight into the hole. It is particularly bad if the ends of the roots make a U-turn and stick out above the surface after planting and critically important that none of the roots be visible after planting. A single exposed strand of root, acting like a wick, can cause moisture evaporation and adversely affect the well-being of the seedling. Also, try to make sure that the roots are not tangled or crossing each other.

Herbicide after planting. When you plant by hand you may want to spray manually. Be careful—you can kill trees by spraying too much.

TRANSPLANTING WILD-GROWN TREES

Choose a well-grown tree and plant it in an appropriate location, by which I mean: Do not plant an oak tree in the shade of a maple tree. The best time to plant is in spring before bud break. You can transplant in fall as well, but avoid planting after the new leaves have emerged. Before you unearth the seedling, dig a large hole to accommodate the transplant. Because most roots grow on the surface, make your hole wider to allow the roots to spread. The hole should be twice as wide as the root-and-soil ball of the transplant.

Before unearthing the seedling, sever the roots with a spade and carefully lift the tree out of the hole, keeping as much soil on the roots as possible. Use a tarp or bucket to wrap up the roots, avoid exposure to the elements (wind will dry your roots), and carry it to the new site. Plant as deep as it was growing in the wild. Fill in the soil gently and then give the tree a generous soaking. It is important that you water the tree periodically if there is no rain. Do not expect the tree to flourish immediately; it may take a couple of years for the tree to get accustomed to the new environment.

Mark the location of seedlings immediately after planting. When planting individual trees into vegetation, you may have a problem spotting your seedlings as they merge into the ambient plant life. To keep track of mine, I have used tree shelters—opaque plastic tubes (see page 201) you stake over your seedlings to protect them from browsing deer and weeds. That's what they're supposed to do—but they actually don't work for a variety of reasons. They fall over; deer use them to hone antlers; seedlings often die and disappear; and when you want to remove the shelters, the seedlings will be unable to withstand wind and tip over). I've stopped using them except as an aid to locate seedlings. Instead I use small plastic flags. I recommend getting the flags with a thirty-inch wire pole, which will make it easier to spot the seedlings.

PROBLEMS WITH PLANTING

How successful is planting? I have employed all the methods described above, but with only limited success. Whenever you plant into grasses, conifers are more likely to thrive than deciduous seedlings because they resist the toxicity of grasses. Among deciduous trees, ashes and cherries are the more resistant

PLANTING CHEEK BY JOWL

Some time ago, I surmised that I could establish an exciting mixed-species forest simply by planting as many seedlings of different varieties as I could fit in a given plot of land. As the stand matured, I could decide which trees to keep and which to cull, creating the mixture of trees I wanted. The stand would form an early canopy and the trees would side shade each other, meaning I'd never have to prune. Natural selection would favor the best trees to survive. They would become perfectly shaped veneer logs with little lateral branching.

To test my fantasy, I hired a planter and instructed him to mix randomly all available seedlings—including white pine, ash, walnut, black cherry, red oak, and white oak, and plant them three feet apart. Volunteer box elder, aspen, and hickory seedlings joined the party. This stand of forest is now four years old and about six feet high. (See color photo #8.) All species of trees are vigorously competing for sun and space, and it is not yet clear which will dominate. This stand of is the most exciting young forest I have ever encountered.

The downside is that this forest will never pay for itself. Planting five thousand trees per acre cost me a great deal—$2,500 per acre. Moreover, cost-share subsidies only defrayed the cost of the first eight hundred trees I planted (my DNR forester, to his credit, allowed me to try the scheme because he was himself curious how successful this plantation would be). By any reasonable standard of investment analysis, planting in this fashion is fiscal insanity. Yet this experimental plot promises to develop into a wonderful forest better than any other scheme I've witnessed for planting seedlings. It will require virtually no maintenance beyond thinning, which means it will flourish even if I do nothing. All I have to do is to lean back and enjoy the scene and to watch the wildlife, which undoubtedly will be attracted in abundance. If money is no object, I highly recommend you try one of these dense plantings on your own property.

---

to pernicious grasses.* Some other species of trees, such as walnuts and oaks, tend to be stressed by pernicious grass and at times wither away without a trace. So, it is not impossible to plant deciduous trees successfully into pernicious grasses, but you should beware of the drawbacks. I list a few below.

You may be herbiciding for years. As explained in chapter 6, many common grasses, such as brome and fescue, produce an allelopathic reaction in trees. Given the space between planted trees, you can pretty well count on pernicious grasses growing around them (and stunting them) until the trees

---

* I have observed that ash and cherry trees sometimes survive in pernicious grasses, while oak and walnut trees do not. Therefore, I have always thought that oak and walnut trees are more susceptible to the toxins in pernicious grasses. However, it also could be that the survival is just a matter of numbers, as birds excrete more cherry and ash seeds than walnuts or acorns.

form a canopy that shades out the grasses for good. As the canopy closes, weeds begin to establish themselves, which is very positive. In the meantime, you should be aware that a failure to control grasses may stress and stunt the trees. You will find that herbiciding is a complicated business, and it rarely yields the desired results, as the grass reappears much sooner than you expect.

You'll need to prune. Trees grow into the sun, and if the sun comes from all sides, a seedling may grow into a bush rather than a tree. While conifers have the wonderful propensity to grow straight, deciduous trees will branch out into available space. The typical open-field tree will develop much lower lateral branching—which makes it a great tree for your kids to climb, but not a great tree for lumber. The best way to avoid pruning duty on your deciduous trees is to grow them close together, so that they shade each other and thereby grow straight with fewer lateral branches. Dense planting is expensive, however, and cannot be justified economically. Some dreamers, such as myself, will do it for fun (see sidebar, page 69).

Monocultural plantations are more susceptible to diseases and other disturbances. German foresters accept as a fact that monocultural plantations are more susceptible to problems such as insect infestation and damage by windthrow. American foresters seem much less convinced of the correlation. (In this respect, I have not been naturalized to my adopted country.) Recent events make a strong case. For example, as a result of hurricanes in Germany in 1990, mixed forests incurred about one-third the damage inflicted on monocultural stands, and they recovered faster.

The success of hardwood plantations is spotty. I've mentioned a few reasons why you should think long and hard before planting hardwoods. Many plantations fail to live up to expectations, and it's not a mystery why this is so.* It is very rare to find a woodland owner who has the interest, commitment, time, and knowledge to spray, prune, and thin his plantation diligently. In fact, if such an owner could muster such energy and commitment, he would be better off, as I will argue shortly, planting seeds rather than seedlings.

If I have convinced you that planting seedlings is problematic, perhaps you will be interested in seeding, which I will explain in the next chapter. You

---

* It is my unscientific observation that many woodland owners do not care to nurture their plantations. There are others, however, who become absolute fanatics and go so far as to use a cherry picker to prune their trees to lofty heights. They often focus their efforts on timber value and do not regard their woodland as an ecologically viable entity. Woodland owners such as Larry Krotz (see chapter 16), who plant mixed stands of trees, are few. Some woodland owners are mere tree farmers, others are foresters. This is an important distinction: Tree farmers consider trees a crop, like a commodity, while foresters have a more holistic view of a forest. Foresters have more fun as well.

can plant seeds directly, with resources immediately at hand and without the cost of buying seedlings or hiring planters. On paper, at least, you will find direct seeding a financially more rewarding activity—as long as you don't put a premium on your labor. But, really, just forget about profit and think about what fun you'll have!

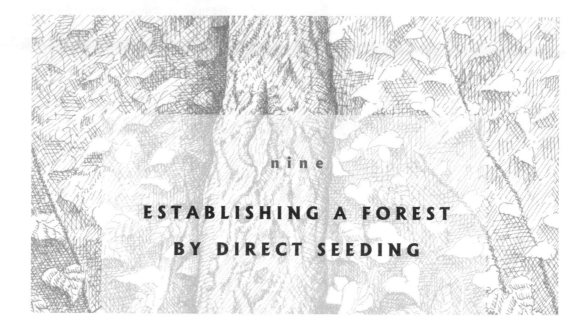

nine

ESTABLISHING A FOREST
BY DIRECT SEEDING

When harvesting a stand, foresters often leave some of the best mature trees as a source of seeds to establish a new rotation. The seeds of these trees fall on the exposed soil of what used to be the forest floor and, with luck, germinate. After young seedlings have gotten a start, the seed trees may be harvested. This natural seeding, known as the shelterwood method, mitigates some of the ill effects of clear-cutting.

The seeds from those seed trees will share soil space with zillions of competitors, seeds of hundreds of species. Which seeds will prevail? Most likely those of the trees that dominated the forest before it was harvested. The reason is instructive: The site has all the necessary attributes to raise another crop of the same species. Extraneous seeds may or may not like the site. Seeds will only germinate when the conditions are just right: the proper acidity, adequate access to sunlight, suitable soil chemistry with cooperating microorganisms, the right amount of moisture, and an appropriate miniclimate.

You can use the principle of the shelterwood method to establish a forest on a treeless plot of land. I call it direct seeding. You gather seeds, you prepare and expose the soil, you put the seed in the soil.

Direct seeding is an uncommon way to start a forest—most tree farmers plant seedlings along the lines described in the preceding chapter—but recently this practice has gained favor among some woodland owners at the cutting edge of forestry. While these foresters have achieved very encouraging results, direct seeding techniques are fraught with challenges—not the least of which is making sure that the site suits the seed.

Seeds will only germinate when the conditions are right. This truism explains a number of surprising phenomena you'll find in your woodland. Let me relate some examples from my own experience. In summer 2002, I had a new septic tank installed in back of my house, which required disturbing a lot of the soil. In one area, a solid cover of velvet leaf (a common weed in the Midwest) emerged. In the thirty years I have owned my place, I have never seen velvet leaf plants in the immediate area, so the seeds must have been there for some time. But how long? Some seeds can linger for decades and remain viable, just waiting for the proper conditions to emerge. You may also wonder why hardly any other plants emerged together with the velvet leaf? I do not have a good explanation; maybe the velvet leaf exudes a poison unfriendly to other plants, or maybe other seeds just did not like the conditions.

On other occasions, I have noticed that after discing or herbiciding, a new species is prone to dominate an area. A site I had prepared for walnuts suddenly was inundated by giant ragweed, which grew to twelve feet in a couple of weeks, totally smothering all my seeded walnuts and oaks. Elsewhere I disced ash seeds between the rows of a walnut plantation. The ashes never appeared, but an influx of Queen Anne's lace dominated the ground. Along a hedgerow of cedars I planted years ago, little cedars germinate in one particular spot and nowhere else. There must be something special about this spot (a "site-specific" condition, as ecologists and foresters say when they can't explain such a peculiarity). Similarly, on property I own miles away from my main farm, I see new white spruces popping up next to their parents, while I seem to be incapable of making them germinate on my farm. The pH is not low enough at my farm, and conifers prefer acid soil.

Whatever seeds are best suited for the prevailing conditions are the ones likely to emerge; others may lie dormant for years. Of the seeds you plant, some may not like the territory and so will fail to appear. Can one predict which seeds will emerge on a given plot? I can't, but I do know some things. For instance, larger seeds, such as acorns and nuts, are more likely than tiny seeds to tolerate less propitious conditions, because they have a lot of plant matter, giving the seedling a lot of initial strength and survivability. On the other hand, larger seeds are a favorite food for squirrels and turkeys, and the challenge in planting them is to prevent predation.

Throughout this book I make the case that direct seeding is the best way to establish a new forest on land without trees. And yet direct seeding is more complicated than it seems. I have had some instructive experience with it, which I will relate in this chapter. Before I do, let me outline the pros and cons of direct seeding as I see them.

ADVANTAGES OF DIRECT SEEDING

The advantages of direct seeding are both practical and inspirational.

An early canopy will control grasses. While it may take a decade or more for seedlings planted several feet apart to form a canopy, it may take only a few years in a densely seeded plot. Because of their large seeds, walnut trees, for example, can sprout vigorous seedlings capable of establishing a canopy in the first or second growing season. (See color photos #6 and #7.)

A seeded plot will require little or none of the maintenance required in the typical row plantation. Because seeded trees grow very close to each other, they are shaded by neighbors and will have a tendency to grow straight. As a result, trees in a seeded plot require little or no pruning. Mowing, too, is out of the question in a seeded plot.

Competition among seedlings will yield a quality stand of trees. You will put hundreds of seeds in a plot of soil that one day will be occupied by a single crop tree. That tree will be the one that grew most vigorously and straightest—the tree you never culled. In other words, it will have survived because it was the fittest.

Seeding is challenging and suspenseful. It is fun to collect seeds, determine what proportions of various species to mix, and then spread them. You never know for sure, unless you are very sophisticated, how many seedlings of each species you will get.

Seeding is relatively inexpensive. If you hire a contractor to gather and spread seeds on your land, it will cost about the same as planting seedlings. If you do the work yourself—and, remember, this sort of work is one of the joys of woodland ownership—seeding will cost less than planting.

DISADVANTAGES OF DIRECT SEEDING

Even though direct seeding is my preferred method, it does have disadvantages.

The results can be quite unpredictable. No matter how qualified you may be or how well you plan and execute, often your seeded plots will disappoint you. For example, many seeds may not be viable. In some years, hardly any of the seeds I planted have produced seedlings. In such cases, you have little choice but to try again the next year.

Seeds are difficult, even impossible, to find when needed. In some years seeds may be difficult to find. For example, 2000 was a bad seed year for many trees in my area. The aspens and cottonwoods were hailed out; there were but few acorns and walnuts and almost no maple seeds; the ash seeds were only on a few trees; and there were no cherries. Even in such circumstances, it is common that one species of tree will produce an abundant crop. In 2000 white spruce were so heavily laden with seeds that upper branches were more brown than green.

Critters, such as squirrels, mice, deer, and turkeys, may eat some or all of your seeds.

Seeding is a lot of work—and tricky. It may be wise not to seed large areas in any one year, and instead seed only a couple of acres at a time. You still need to control pernicious grasses. I do this by applying herbicide before seeding and again the following spring. However, herbiciding a seeded plot is especially tricky because small seeds are much more sensitive to herbicide than large seeds. This is important to remember with respect to plots of mixed seed: An overdose will kill the small seeds.

Seeding requires some expertise that may not be readily available. Academic forestry literature only discusses direct seeding techniques geared toward large commercial enterprises. Seeding techniques for the small-woodland owner are relatively new, and only a handful of seeding enthusiasts have been through the process. I am fortunate that a number of foresters operating in southwest Wisconsin and Iowa are eager to experiment with various techniques. Still, there are relatively few successful seeding projects to use as models.

Most states still do not endorse seeding as a cost-sharing practice. Wisconsin has not approved direct seeding for subsidy. Minnesota, on the other hand, is in the process of approving it. This, I suggest, is a cause that might usefully be championed by various state woodland-owner associations.

HOW TO SEED

First you must prepare the site. This may take a fair amount of forward planning. As you will recall from my earlier discussion of pernicious grasses, it is imperative that you eradicate grasses as much as possible, in particular when you have brome or fescue grasses. I recommend that you mow the field in late summer and, once the grass has grown back about six inches, apply two to three quarts of Roundup (glyphosate) per acre (see chapter 6). Roundup kills green vegetation on contact and works best when the plant is lusciously green and growing fast. In steep terrain, you should leave horizontal strips of vegetation to minimize erosion.

Collecting Seeds

Gathering seeds is difficult at first and always time-consuming, but you will do better with experience. Seeds native to your own soil are preferable to those from commercial sources. When it is practical, choose your seeds from beautiful, vigorous, and straight trees. While you should not pass up an opportunity to get seeds from a wonderful tree, I suggest you concentrate on quantity rather than quality. Again, it is also best to get your seeds from local trees—that is, from within fifty miles north or south of where you intend to plant. In the Midwest, seeds from more than one hundred fifty miles away may not do very well. There are good years and bad years for collecting seeds. Often seeds are scarce because an early frost or a hail storm may have killed blossoms or because an excessive rain hindered pollination. When seeds are plentiful, they are also better. Insects lay their eggs in any available blossoms or developing seeds, so when there are fewer seeds, a larger percentage will be wormy. Just as wormy apples drop off first, nuts that drop in early fall tend to have more worms. Wait until most of the nuts fall down (often after a frost) and then pick them up. Collect as many as you can, because a portion will be wormy.

Some seeds, white oak for example, start germinating as soon as they hit the ground. Others, called "dormant," refuse to germinate until conditions are just right. In some species, dormancy can be broken artificially, for example, by soaking the seeds one or two days before planting, or by scarification (which, in reference to seeds, means weakening the seed coat mechanically by such means as sanding it with an emery board). Many seeds are dormant for one or two seasons. Most seeds need to experience a winter before they germinate. For seeds kept in storage, winter can be simulated by maintaining them for a

period (generally between 60 and 120 days) at 100 percent humidity and at a temperature just above freezing. Techniques for breaking dormancy vary from seed to seed and are far too complicated to detail here, but with a little research you will be able to plant your favorite species in a timely manner. Again, by planting seeds soon after collecting them, deterioration problems can be held to a minimum.

The fact that some trees, such as walnut, produce seeds only in some years is a clever Darwinian scheme of nature. If, for example, walnuts had consistent crops every year, a stable squirrel population would thrive to consume nearly all of them, leaving but few for the next generation of walnut trees. But, given the cycle of lean years and abundant years, the squirrel population is held relatively low, meaning that a bumper crop feeds the squirrels and creates many new walnut seedlings.

Sometimes only a few trees bear seeds. One year almost none of my oaks had acorns, except for a single heavily laden white oak. Seeing that the tree had more seeds than I needed, I felt relieved, and in anticipation of the harvest, I cleared the brush under the tree. A week later I came back, intending to spread a tarp underneath to gather the seeds as they dropped, but when I got to the tree and looked up, much to my surprise, I saw no seeds; I found just a couple on the ground. The lesson I learned is that when fewer trees bear acorns, the remaining seeds are in higher demand. I should have anticipated this. I don't know whether it was squirrels, turkeys, or deer that ate my acorns; or whether they were picked off the tree or eaten on the ground. It did not matter—all

I knew was I had none. Similarly, an ash tree whose seeds I had "reserved" was suddenly barren. The culprits were most likely red squirrels.

I am told that one way to collect seeds is to rob a cache of seeds collected by squirrels. This may be great advice for folks younger and more nimble than I—and who are clever enough to know where to look. Only once did I accidentally find such a cache when I climbed a deer-hunting stand and found it full of nuts. Unfortunately the ground was already frozen, so I ate a few of the nuts and left the rest to the squirrels.

Collecting seeds is a science unto itself, and you should try to get help from a friendly manager of your state or commercial nursery. I cannot claim to be an expert, but I will pass on to you what I've learned from my own gathering forays:

Ash seeds should be picked in late fall and planted shortly thereafter. White ash seeds can be picked easily if you can get to them. The easiest way to get ash seeds is to cut down a tree, preferably one that needs to be thinned anyway. *A note of caution:* Ash seeds look a lot like those of the worthless and annoying box elder—confusing the two could be a sorry mistake.

Aspen seeds are very tiny, about eight thousand seeds per gram. Maturing in May and June, they generally last no more than two weeks unless expertly stored. If there are aspen trees nearby, there is a good chance ambient aspen seeds will establish themselves wherever they find exposed dirt. The same applies to cottonwoods. Given their small size, a number of innovative collection and dissemination schemes have been suggested to me.* I've considered collecting aspen seeds with a vacuum cleaner, but haven't yet tried it. A friend, David Mulcahey, suggested dragging a felled aspen behind the chisel plow. I planned to try last spring, but the hail had killed all blossoms. In any case, I have learned from a friend in the nursery business that the window of opportunity for this scheme—that is, the time when aspen seeds blow off the trees—is a couple of days a season.

Black cherries are best plucked off the branches. I know of only one other trick in picking them: My friend Larry Krotz (see chapter 16) told me that he recovers cherry pits from raccoon feces. I have never had the pleasure of duplicating this feat—nor have I tried very hard.

Cedars have small cones containing six to twelve scales, each bearing from one to five seeds. Seed dispersal starts in fall and extends to spring. The cones are easy to pick, since many are at breast height. As with most seeds in general, germination is best in plentiful years. Seeds are small, about a hundred seeds per gram. I have tried to plant the complete cone but never with success.

Conifer seeds are tiny. The white spruce seed is only as big as the period at the end of this sentence. Cones release the seeds, which are attached to a wing, beginning in early fall. It is important to

---

* It has occurred to me that millions of acres of idle CRP land could be forested quite easily with aspen. I have fantasized about mixing aspen seeds with water and spraying them on exposed soil.

harvest the seeds before the scales of the cones begin to open, releasing the seeds. (When cones are about to release their seeds they turn light brown.) You should pick the cones and leave them to dry. I put them in a gunny sack that I leave to dry in the sun on my patio. Tumble or shake them to release the seeds. An alternative to this method is to dry them in an oven at about 130 degrees until the cone flaps open and releases the seeds, prompted by a little shaking. Methods for extracting the seeds will vary. Some jack pine cones resist low heat and require the heat of a forest fire to release their seeds.

Maple seeds can be shaken off the tree (it helps to put a canvas tarp under the tree). Sugar maple seeds should be picked in early fall and, here again, it is convenient to collect seeds from a maple tree you're planning to thin out. Red and silver maple seeds develop just after the tree leafs out and typically should be harvested in May and then planted in spring or early summer. Interestingly, only one side of the paired maple seed wing contains a viable seed—the other is sterile and exists for aerodynamic purposes only.

Oak seeds (acorns) take a lot of work to pick up. You can test the viability of acorns by floating them—the good ones sink. However, I do not bother to float mine, because it takes time and I don't mind planting the good with the bad. Note that red oak and white oak acorns with their caps attached are usually wormy; even so, some wormy acorns may sprout. To gather acorns, it helps to mow or otherwise clear away brush below the trees. Mowed cemeteries and parks are a convenient source for acorns, as are parking lots.

The equipment manufacturer Goede sells an acorn-picker-upper for a couple hundred dollars that makes gathering a breeze (see illustration on page 79). The most convenient lode of acorns I've ever gathered was on a tennis court that had an overhanging black oak. I gave my son Paul a very compelling incentive to help me gather several buckets of acorns by promising to play a match when we were done. Others have told me it's easier to find acorns after using a gas-powered leaf blower to expose them.

Walnuts are best picked in the fall, from the tree or after they've fallen. You will often get a large number of black walnuts from a single tree; get as many as you can. It may be worthwhile to mow the area under prolific trees to make it easier to pick the nuts up when the time comes. If you have nimble offspring, have them climb trees and do some shaking, but be sure to step aside first! To test their viability float your walnuts in a tub of water; if they float, they have probably been eaten through by worms and are no longer viable, although this is not an infallible test (unhulled walnuts may float even if viable, but a hulled floater is always a dud).

Walnuts are easier to handle when they're hulled (and if you want to eat them, hulling is a necessity). Generally, however, I find hulling walnuts a lot of trouble, and it's a messy affair that will stain your hands black for days. There are legitimate reasons to hull: Goede, for example, makes a seeding machine that only works with hulled nuts. If you need to hull your walnuts there are any number of ways to do so. I use an old-fashioned corn husker. But you may roll them on the floor with

This clever contraption saves a lot of time collecting acorns.

your foot, drive over them with a car, or throw them in your barnyard and have the milk truck drive over them (advice from an Amish neighbor). You can even agitate them in a small cement mixer with gravel and water (works best when nuts are black—but it makes an inky mess).

A case study: Fall 2001

Before continuing my "how-to" instructions, let me give an example of a successful seeding. In fall 2001, I started collecting seeds for a new forest in what was recently a field. My friend Diamonds and I took my acorn picker upper to Jackson Park, a wonderful preserve by the Museum of Science and Industry in Chicago. Under just a few stately bur oaks we collected sacks of acorns by the dozen. I then purloined a few buckets of horse chestnuts from a neighbor's yard in Chicago. Later we visited a park in Cazenovia near my farm and gathered four or five garbage bags full of walnuts underneath a couple of trees. (I should note that my own walnuts were almost completely barren that year.) We hulled the walnuts in my antique cornhusker. I also collected cedar seeds by the thousands and spruce seeds by the hundreds of thousands (which is to say, several buckets full).

I kept the seeds around the farm until mid-November, hoping that an early frost or snow would make my seeds inaccessible to predators. That summer, I had mowed and herbicided the three-acre plot, and in early fall I hired a neighbor to chisel plow it. So in mid-November, the site was ready. On the appointed day, my wife and I hauled the sacks and sacks of seed to the site. I drove the Gator slowly while Kathy, sitting in the vehicle's bed, threw handfuls of seed on the exposed dirt. Once the seed was spread, we chisel plowed again and drove over the plot repeatedly to compact the soil. My city slicker friends thought it would be fun to make scarecrows to deter predatory turkeys.

In the spring, I sprayed the plot with Pendulum, a pre-emergence herbicide. As spring went into full bloom, things looked bad. No sign of seedlings among the few weeds that survived the poison. Did the squirrels get my seeds? Was there a problem with the seed, the soil? I felt pretty frustrated.

Then, suddenly in late June, there they were. Every square foot seemed to harbor two or three tiny trees, most bearing leaves in the distinctive shape of the bur oak. We looked for tiny walnuts, which were not as apparent to the eye, and sure enough, there were a few, but far fewer than the oaks. Searching further, we found even a few horse chestnuts. Significantly, no spruce or cedar emerged. Even more interesting, inspecting the plot a few months later I was astonished to find that the horse chestnut leaves had been nibbled away. (The oaks and walnuts were left alone, leaving me to wonder if horse chestnut leaves are some predator's special treat.)

This is merely one seeding trial, and I certainly can't draw scientific conclusions from it. But I will venture the following observation: The big seeds germinated and the small ones did not. Although I'm not going to give up yet, I believe my conifer seeding attempts are doomed to fail from the start. Gordy Christians, the superintendent of the Hayward Tree Nursery in Wisconsin, tells me that his outfit drills pine seeds into the soil with a machine, then covers the field with an opaque sheet of plastic for a whole year. Seeds and the field are treated with a variety of chemicals. I am not willing to go to that trouble, so maybe I should stick to big seeds. One further observation: The scarecrows totally freaked out Pooch, who attacked them upon discovering them. Their effect on turkeys is unknown, although a naturalist I know told me I had to shift them periodically to make them effective.

When and How Much to Seed

Storing seeds is complicated and prone to mishap, so it is best to spread seeds as they become available. It's Nature's way. If you do a lot of seeding and need to store seeds, or if you're dealing with seed that needs to experience a winter before germinating, ask staff people at a local nursery for information on how to do it successfully. Nurseries tend to store seeds that need cold treatment for several weeks.

I have never seen or heard of a seeding that resulted in too many trees. Experts suggest that about fifteen thousand seedlings an acre is a good number, which means about three seedlings per square foot. I suggest that you plant whatever seeds you have. It is difficult to guess how many seedlings will emerge. Several variables come into play, such as the germination rates of the various seeds in your mix, predation, and viability of the seeds.

How to Spread Seeds

Because seeds will only germinate when they come into contact with the soil and moisture, it is necessary to dig up the soil. Commercial timbermen often expose earth with an anchor chain, but for the small-scale forester this is a bit cumbersome. A more practical method of scarification is discing or chisel plowing. For a small area I recommend a rototiller, and for a tiny plot a shovel or a hoe will work. You may also use a hand-held rototiller (see page 58). In any case, it is best to agitate the soil thoroughly.

Spreading seeds is not always easy, and the method should be fitted to the seed. Larger seeds, such as acorns and nuts, can be flung from the back of a vehicle and then disced into the soil. Small seeds, like those of most conifers, should be mixed with a medium such as sawdust or sand for better distribution. Some seeds, such as ash, can be spread with a broadcast seeder or by hand. It is a good idea to soak small seeds in water for about twenty-four hours to facilitate germination.

Ideally, seeds should be planted at the proper depth: nuts about an inch deep and small seeds close to the surface. Small seeds planted too deep will not germinate, and large seeds on the surface may dry out. If you have a lot of seeds and you do not mind if many do not make it, the easy thing to do is to disc in the seeds. An alternative is to disc in the larger seeds, spread the smaller seeds on the surface, and drag a mattress or a chain over the whole thing. Finally, you should compact the soil. You can do this in any of several ways. Farmers use a compactor pulled by a tractor. You also can simply drive over the area with a vehicle of some sort. A forester friend of mine has had good results with his pickup truck.

FOLLOWING UP

When putting down large seeds (nuts and acorns), I recommend you apply a pre-emergent herbicide to the plot early the following spring. The method you use depends on the size of the plot. I use a rig mounted on my Gator. (See the illustration on page 49.) You needn't worry about driving a vehicle over the plot; the seeds (and, in subsequent years, seedlings) will not be damaged. It is very important to spray before the seedlings leaf out. You may or may not need to spray in subsequent years, depending on the severity of grass and weed competition, as well as the strength of your plants. (Also consider the species of the plants in question: For example, conifers are more susceptible to damage from early spring herbicide because their "leaves" are exposed, while deciduous seedlings are still dormant.)

With luck, your seeding will produce a dense cover of seedlings. Here is a handy way to count them: If you describe a circle by stretching out both arms and turning 360 degrees, the area covered will be roughly 1/1,000th of an acre. So if you count the seedlings in that circle and multiply by 1,000, you will get the approximate number of seedlings per acre. When calculating this figure, though, also consider that some seeds may not germinate until the following year.

One circumstance to look out for is weed competition on especially fertile sites. I have seen plots so fertile that seedlings, whether planted or directly seeded, are totally overcome by weeds. Some weeds, such as giant ragweed, can grow about ten feet in six weeks—so fast that unless you control them early and vigorously, they will dominate your tree seedlings. In a little valley on my farm, giant ragweed, pigweed, and burdock totally smothered every last seedling. One way to combat such a weed infestation is to brush herbicides with an applicator on the taller weeds, which avoids damaging the tree seedlings below. If the seedlings are small, you can Bush Hog the weeds at a setting higher than the seedlings. On my hyper-fertile site, as it happens, I gave up on planting seedlings and opted instead to plant larger orchard trees, which love the site.

I hope I have convinced you that starting a forest by direct seeding is a challenge. Nevertheless, it is the technique I like the best. We need more foresters, both professional and amateur, to experiment and share know-how. The rewards will be considerable. If you take me up on the direct seeding technique, you'll meet another enemy: squirrels. They're tougher to lick than you might think, as I'll explain in the next chapter.

SUMMARY OF SEEDING

Seeding is a natural process, and there is no reason not to help nature spread seeds. If you like to experiment and are not easily deterred by imperfect results, you should try seeding. Here's a summary of my recommendations and conclusions:

- Seeds should be spread as soon as you pick them.
- The denser your seedlings, the better your chances are for success.
- Large seeds, such as acorns and walnuts, grow stronger plants. However, the seeds are prone to be eaten by animals, especially when planted near a forest.
- Small seeds are more difficult to cultivate than larger seeds. I have never succeeded with a direct seeding of conifers. More information is needed about how to grow trees such as conifers and aspen from seeds.
- Pernicious grasses will kill some seedlings, especially oaks. I highly recommend herbiciding before seeding. Use a pre-emergence herbicide in early spring, but understand that it is very difficult to find the proper balance—that is, enough herbicide to kill the grass but not so much as to kill seedlings.

ten

THE TROUBLE WITH SQUIRRELS

The longer I devote myself to trees, the more convinced I become that seeding is the best way to cultivate a forest. But there is a very real problem with seeding that can be summed up in just three words: Squirrels love nuts. If you seed nuts within two hundred feet of a forest, the squirrels will love you and you will hate them.

I dream of a mixed forest plantation that forms a canopy the first year and looks like a cornfield the second. The trees fight for sunlight and are as straight as arrows. Every tree is destined to be veneer. They need no pruning, only thinning. This dream plantation would start with around fifteen thousand plants per acre, but because planting that many seedlings would cost a fortune, the only practical thing to do is to use seeds. Here my sweet dream ends sadly. Suddenly the plants are gone, and in their place are a bunch of happily socializing squirrels munching on a truckload of nuts.

Science has yet to produce a stealth walnut. For the tree farmer, the trick is to hide the nuts from the squirrels until they germinate in spring. Many substances have been used to make nuts unappetizing to squirrels, including fresh cow manure, rotten eggs, peanut butter, Tabasco sauce, human hair, fox urine, and diesel fuel. An Iowa forester claimed recently that he had achieved a high germination rate by painting the nuts with paraffin. A friend suggested a commercial product called Treeguard. I've conducted clinical trials of these methods and others of my own devising, and squirrels have yet to be fooled. Here are some of my findings:

• A squirrel will detect a nut hidden under a styrofoam cup and eat it immediately. Unhulled nuts must emit a stronger smell because they are detected first.

• Squirrels are smart. Once a squirrel associates styrofoam cups with nuts, it will poke a hole even in an empty cup.

• A squirrel will detect and eat a nut that has been soaked in Treeguard.

I have heard that birdseed is sometimes treated with pepper to make it unappetizing to squirrels. A couple years ago I received a tip on a concentrated form of hot pepper. A nut coated with this substance supposedly would be nearly lethal to any squirrel. The pepper is so hot, I was warned, that any contact to skin would cause extreme discomfort and would be particularly painful to careless men after urination. I handled the substance with extreme caution, diluting it with oil before soaking the nuts. But I stumbled on the way to the test site and dropped the nuts. I picked them up and then, inadvertently, I wiped the sweat off my face. In a few minutes it was painful and swollen. I was convinced that I had found a potent squirrel repellent. I planted the peppered nuts, along with some placebos, very hopefully. I watched the squirrels with anticipation, expecting them to drop dead. They didn't. In fact, all the nuts were eaten. Nonetheless, I still have some hope that

the pepper extract might deter the squirrels; I will have to do more experimenting to get the dosage and application right.

Of course, other ways exist to guard nuts from squirrel predation. Putting wire mesh over the planting area or planting the nuts in a jagged soda pop can are two ways. These methods work, but they are a lot of trouble (unless you are only planting a few trees). You can also plant seeds deeper (they will germinate up to five inches deep). You can also compact the soil over seeds to make it harder for the squirrels to unearth them. Dr. Larry Severeid, a Wisconsin walnut expert, has developed an interesting technique. He buries nuts in a milk crate in the fall. By early spring, practically all the nuts have grown a short root. Larry digs up the pre-germinated nuts, plants them under plastic tubes to minimize predation. The survival rate of his seeds is roughly the same as for planted seedlings.

It is widely reported that squirrels will pull out a seedling after germination to devour whatever is left of the nut, and I have read that squirrels will methodically dig up nuts buried in a straight line, one after another. It is difficult to think of an effective defense against such persistent predation. I am always amazed how genetically hearty squirrels are. Their fondness for "poisonous" mushrooms may be an indication that there are but few substances capable of repelling these critters. They are survivors. Still, I have not given up on finding a squirrel inhibitor. For me, it has become a point of honor. There has to be a squirrel-repellent substance that works, and hopefully someone will find it soon.

Another approach is, if you can't beat them, join them. As I have pointed out earlier, squirrels are quite capable of planting nuts for you, occasionally even in clever spots. So let them do the work. If you dump nuts near any forest, squirrels will bury most of them and forget quite a few. You can also try to eradicate them. I sometimes eat them; they taste as good as chicken. Another strategy for controlling squirrel populations is to provide convenient perches for hawks and other squirrel eaters. A friend once told me that the inquisitiveness of squirrels makes them "trap dumb." Next year, I plan to use no-kill traps and have my Amish neighbor empty them. He will feed the squirrels to his family. If you don't want to kill your captives, you can drive them a few miles away and release them. That is what my stepfather used to do at his home in Washington, D. C. Some returned to his house, however—he knew this because he spray painted them. A neighbor in Chicago puts his filled squirrel traps in a garbage can full of water. He assures me that none return to eat his birdseed.

A Wisconsin DNR forester, John Nielson, conducted an interesting experiment. He seeded walnuts in two equally sized fields in cut-over woods (let's call them Field A and Field B). On Field A he planted about a thousand nuts per acre, one and a half inches deep, and on the neighboring Field B he dumped twice as many nuts out in the open for the squirrels to pillage. More seedlings emerged on the Field B, because the squirrels did the planting for him when they buried their nuts. Using twice as many nuts was a cheap price for a better result, since the cost and trouble of planting is far greater than the cost of collecting more nuts. This "Nielson" test is revealing. I am inclined to try it the next time I plant nuts near a squirrel habitat. But the result may vary. Maybe the squirrel doing a lot of the planting got eaten by an owl, or maybe another squirrel forgot where the nuts were hidden. One lesson is clear: It is better to place more emphasis on having a lot of nuts than in planting them. Have the squirrels do the planting! I advise against trying the Nielson scheme with acorns, though, because it probably would not work. Squirrels can get to the meat of an acorn in seconds, but it takes close to ten minutes for them to crack a nut.

After having planted two fields next to a forest where squirrels stole every single nut in two successive years, I decided that I can live without walnut trees. They may produce the most wonderfully colored wood, but their leaves do not color as prettily in fall as maples do—and, anyway, their price has dropped. Consumers have taken a liking to the lighter maple wood. Maples are easier to grow, more colorful, and though squirrels do eat maple seeds, there still always appear to be lots left to germinate into seedlings.

THE ABCs OF PRUNING HARDWOODS

As I have maintained all along, forestry is not a science where all reasonable practitioners follow the same rules in the same way. It is more of an art where reasonable people may do things very differently. This is especially true with regard to pruning. Everybody seems to have his or her own pruning schemes. Forestry literature abounds with pruning guidelines. And pruning is frequently the subject of demonstrations at the field days held by woodland owners' associations. These provide an ideal opportunity to compare your practices with those of other plantation owners.

If you own a plantation of deciduous seedlings spaced at the typical eight-foot intervals, prepare for twenty years of never-ending pruning. As you have learned in earlier chapters, seedlings without neighbors to shade them will grow in all directions and become bushy—unless you prune them. Failure to do so will most significantly reduce the value of your trees. Moreover, you have to be judicious about how you prune your hardwoods. Pruning too many branches, or the wrong ones, or pruning at the wrong time or in the wrong way, could render your trees worthless.*

* Conifers, by contrast, need very little pruning; they grow straight by themselves. Occasionally you may want to cut out a fork, but even that is not necessary if your conifers are destined to become pulp wood. If your coniferous forest is intended for lumber trees, pruning the lower branches will make the trees more valuable. Pruning conifers is relatively easy work, because you do not have to puzzle with each tree over which branches to prune. It is more mechanical and mindless, but it is work just the same. See chapter 17.

Pruning can be an incredibly time-consuming task. And it's hardly a satisfying experience. After pruning, the remaining tree will be smaller and straighter, but it will also look pitifully unhappy and most certainly be full of scars. When my walnut plantation started to thrive (such as it could, that is, in meadows of stifling meadow grass), I discovered that pruning can be a nightmare. A few faithful companions and I spent numerous winter weekends pruning. I own about a hundred thousand walnut trees, so no matter how diligently I pruned, the task was never done. I always felt guilty for not doing more, and I did not learn for almost a decade that the excessive amount of pruning could have been avoided with better planning. I should have seeded a mixed forest rather than planting walnut trees monoculturally. Alas, it was too late.

HOW TO PRUNE

When cultivating trees for timber, pruning is important for the following reasons: (1) to make sure that the tree has a strong leader that will form the bole (the straight lower section of the tree trunk); (2) to cut off any branch which is so fat that it affects the value of the bole; (3) to prevent double headers, a situation common with conifers in which two competing boles develop; and (4) to maximize the remaining foliage so that the tree will continue to photosynthesize.

The maxims I will list below bear evidence that there is no unanimity on the rules of proper pruning. The technique of the pruning itself—that is, cutting off the unwanted growth—is less controversial. Simply put, you just cut off the unwanted part of a tree. But here, too, some guidance is appropriate.

In cutting off branches, it is important to minimize injury to the tree. The cut should be clean, and you should avoid damaging the bark of the tree. Sharp tools assure a clean cut, so do not use a hatchet to cut off branches, but a shear or a saw. If you do use a saw, make sure that you do not damage the bole. It is easy to touch the trunk and do serious damage. I found that the best saw for making clean cuts (in branches smaller than about three inches in diameter) is the Echo pole-mounted reciprocating saw. Just rest the blade in the crotch of the branch and cut the branch off. On the other hand, a pole-mounted chainsaw is better for cutting fat branches, but can cause damage unless you are very careful.

Another important matter is the location of the cut. All trees have branch collars where there is a visible difference in the surface texture of the branch where it connects to the bole (see illustration, page 89). Your cut should be just on the outside of the collar. A closer cut may result in a larger wound, which will take longer to heal and be more prone to infection.

Some books suggest that you should cut branches in two separate operations. First cut off the branch about a foot from the trunk and only then cut off the stub. The idea is to prevent the weight of the branch from peeling off the outer layer of the bark along the trunk. I have not found this technique necessary on my walnuts, but it might be advisable on tree species that have bark that peels easily.

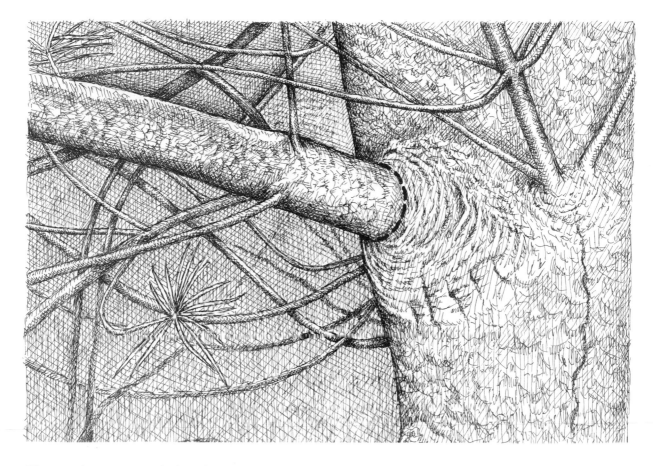

When pruning, cut next to the branch collar, the point where the branch meets the trunk.

The LaValley Method

If you are new to pruning or uncertain how to start, I urge you follow a simple set of precepts I've dubbed the LaValley rules. They're named after Rich LaValley, a former DNR forester in Richland County, Wisconsin. As you become more sophisticated at pruning, you may try some other principles. Here is the LaValley Method of Pruning:

1. Make sure the tree has a clear leader up to seventeen feet.
2. Prune off all lateral branches larger than an inch and a half, up to seventeen feet.
3. Prune only in the winter months (November to March).

I am confident that if you follow the LaValley method of pruning, you will achieve very acceptable results. Of course, all tree farmers will eventually develop their own pruning philosophy. It is part of the joy of tree farming. Remember, forestry is both an art and a science.

A Note on Equipment

The job of pruning is made easier if you have the appropriate tools. In addition to a chainsaw (a small one will do), you'll also need a pole pruner, of which there are different kinds on the market, and a remote motorized pruner—essentially a chainsaw on a stick. I feel strongly that a reciprocating pruner is best. It has a reciprocating blade, is much easier to handle, and does much less damage to the tree than a conventional chainsaw. (However, I have heard that Echo, the only manufacturer of this tool I know of, plans to discontinue making it.) It's also reliable and easy to use. For other necessary pruning equipment, consult Appendix B.

THE SUBTLETIES OF PRUNING

Over the years I have followed different pruning philosophies and procedures, and I vary my pruning regimen according to the individual needs of a tree or by my mood. Frankly, I have changed my mind so often on how to prune that I do not feel comfortable suggesting a given set of rules, but rather prefer to relate all the sensible maxims of pruning that I can think of and leave it to the reader to adopt rules that apply best for his or her situation. I know

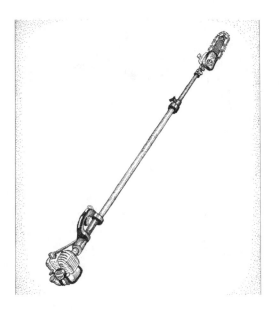

Motorized pole pruner.

some readers will find this confusing—especially considering that many maxims on the following list contradict others. It may help to consider an analogy between pruning and sex. It would be difficult to dictate strict procedures for sex, because such instructions would hardly be applicable to every reader alike—much less every reader's mate. Similarly, not all pruning instructions fit every plant—or, for that matter, your mood at a given moment. Too-strictly-defined pruning instructions may restrict you from responding to the unique situation of a given tree. Therefore, I think it much more prudent to make only suggestions. So, without further ado, these are the maxims of pruning:

Do not waste your time pruning an imperfect tree. In the long run, you will keep only the best trees. One forester rec-

This is an ideal walnut tree. It is very straight, it has a strong crown, and its lateral braches are too small to affect the value of the bole. I have not pruned the lower branches because they don't get in the way and are still photosynthesizing.

The effects of pruning. Above left, a tree before pruning; right, the tree after pruning; facing page, the same tree fifteen years later.

ommends never pruning more than one hundred fifty trees an acre. This means practically that you should only prune every sixth tree. That may sound like a burden off your shoulders, except it is hard to tell which of your trees will be among the chosen. I find it hard to ignore trees that need pruning. If you can, simply ignore imperfect trees but leave them to provide side shading for the "keepers."

Do not prune young trees. According to some foresters, a tree's early vitality and size are more important than its shape. Pruning too early will reduce a tree's ability to photosynthesize, the basis for growth. So, these foresters maintain, you should be patient and wait until the seedling is three or four feet tall. Trees thrive better once they are taller than the "browse line"—that is, taller than the height up to which deer can munch foliage—a height of about six feet. So holding off with the pruning gets you to that goal much sooner.

Start pruning your tree from infancy. Other foresters maintain that form is more important than height, and even a young tree must have a leader at all costs. (The leader is the main stem, ideally growing symmetrically in the center of the tree, with balanced lateral side branches.) The leader is the most important thing of all for a tree—without it, your tree will never become a good crop tree. Obviously, this conflicts with the preceding rule.

Do not always try to play God. The

tree may develop its leader independent of your interference. Some trees will do just fine if you leave them alone.

Prune only in the dormant season (November to March). Some foresters maintain that pruning in February and March is best because the pruning wounds are juicy and will grow over more quickly than those inflicted in late fall or early winter. I have pruned in spring and late fall with impunity, and I believe the prohibition against pruning walnut trees in warmer seasons is overstated. The exception may be in moister draws, where

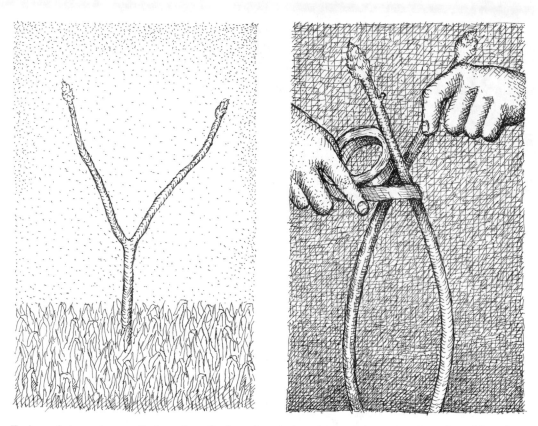

Taping a fork as shown will strengthen the branches. Later, you can remove one branch and the other will become the new leader.

cankers grow more readily. Still, I avoid pruning in summer, but I have chopped some branches occasionally without adverse affects. Interestingly, the French routinely prune in the summer. Quite possibly, people accept the rule against warm-season pruning only because it is so often repeated. Do not prune oaks in summer, when they are prone to oak wilt. Conifers can be pruned any time of the year.

Prune all lateral branches bigger than 1¹/₂ inches in diameter. Conceptually, if you cut off limbs larger than 1¹/₂ inches, the remaining tree should be tall and straight with only small branches. In practice, however, it is rare to have a tree thirty feet tall without larger lateral branching. The illustration on page 91 shows such an ideal tree.

Tape the ends of two branches of a fork together with masking tape so that one stem will become a straight leader. Leave the straight branch and cut off the other branch just above the tape. Remove the tape from the tree the following year.

Do not prune branches larger than two inches in diameter. This will do too much damage to the tree and is more likely to cause a canker. When faced with a decision about whether to give up on a tree or to prune aggressively, it makes more sense to chop away and see what happens.

I have left many a huge pruning scar that subsequently healed, saving a tree that otherwise would have become worthless. A tree has an incredible ability to overgrow a wound, given the opportunity. Sometimes the remaining tree will only have a ten-foot log, which at times is better than nothing. At the same time, I have taken the main branches off some trees only to discover that I've made them more susceptible to wind damage. What I believe happens is that by cutting the large branches, I've upset the balance of branches to roots, prompting the trees to grow more leaves on the remaining branches. The weight of these leaves, aided by a strong breeze, causes the branches to break off and hang down. Still, I endorse removing large branches, but suggest cutting one branch a season.

Remove all lower branches. Some foresters recommend pruning any foliage that is heavily shaded, since it does not contribute much to photosynthesis and may detract from the quality of the veneer log. Dead branches leave "black knots" that fall out when veneer is cut. Green branches fit tightly and do not fall out when lumber is cut. So if you plan to produce veneer logs, it seems desirable to cut off dead branches. On the other hand, knowledgeable foresters have told me there is no point in removing dead branches, because they eventually fall off on their own. I cut off lower branches only if they get in my way when I work on my trees.

Never remove more than a quarter of a tree's potential foliage at one time. Pruning too much will rob the plant of necessary foliage and may put it in a state of shock. While normally it is best not to prune too many branches off a tree, at times aggressive pruning yields the desired result. In one notable case on my farm, my friend James pruned away half the foliage of a walnut tree. As seen in the illustrations on pages 92 and 93, the tree is on its way to becoming a veneer tree, which would have been impossible had he not pruned it.

Do not prune the crown to be less than 60 to 75 percent of the tree height. The problem is, of course, that if you leave a lot of crown you will have branches that are thicker than one or two inches, which would violate a maxim given above.

Observe tree balance. Avoid pruning too much. After pruning, a tree should look balanced (not cockeyed) and not like a plucked chicken.

Keep in mind how the tree will develop. Try to anticipate how the plant will look after a few growing seasons. A skilled pruner can anticipate how lower branches will force a leader to grow in a desired direction. Certain lower branches can function as trainers and force the leader to grow straight.

Do not prune more than seventeen feet high. Eighty percent of the value of the tree is in the lower sixteen-foot log. Pruning higher than seventeen feet is not cost effective.*

You may tolerate a young crooked tree, because it might straighten itself out. Slight deformity in the trunk does not

---

* In a densely planted stand you may prune higher—for instance, removing forks up to thirty feet. I have a pruner with three six-foot extensions, and if I stand on the Gator I can reach thirty feet. It's a silly thing to do.

matter, since the tree will likely compensate for some crookedness by selectively adding tissue, making the tree rounder, as it ages. In any case, the core two to four inches of a tree is not used for veneer.

Trainer strategy is very successful. When you have multiple branches competing for the leader position, proceed as follows: Select the straightest branch as the leader and remove all competing branches growing on the opposite side near the top. Branches under the chosen leader will function as "trainers" and force the leader to grow straight, unimpeded by branches on the opposite side.

THE RUDY

When a tree refuses to do what you want, you may perform a "Rudy"—that is, cut it off close to the ground and start from scratch. The procedure is known in the trade as "coppicing," but our crew called it "Rudying" because our forester at the time, Rudy Nigl, introduced us to it. I used to make my Rudy cuts horizontally, but it has been recently suggested to me that a 45-degree angle will result in fewer sprouts. This is what I've learned from my Rudying experience:

Many foresters, including my county forester, perform the Rudy at ground level. I am not convinced that a low Rudy will produce a better tree than its neighbors. Cutting a tree at ground level will cause the root system to produce vigorous sprouts giving the tree a bushlike appearance. The theory assumes that you select one sprout by cutting off all others the following spring. This sprout with fewer side branches is a good candidate to become a super tree. Although we Rudied countless trees at ground level, hardly any developed into better trees than their non-Rudied neighbors. Remember, an apple does not fall far from the tree. A tree with poor genetics is unlikely to beget veneer-quality offspring. Moreover, a Rudied tree will tend to be overshadowed by neighboring trees and is not likely to catch up.

Rudying at a higher level can produce good results. When a tree decides to sprout in different directions and refuses to develop a straight leader, Rudying at a higher level (five to ten feet) is a viable alternative. There are many trees on my plantation that have been successfully Rudied—some more than once. After about ten years the tree will have a very smooth bole, and veneer buyers are unlikely to tell the difference thirty years hence (although one knowledgeable friend claims that a good buyer *can* tell the difference). And, again, defects near the core of the tree do not detract from the value of the bole. But the Rudy is not always successful. Sometimes the tree will refuse to produce a leader no matter what you do. And there is a danger that the scar tissue caused by the Rudy will become cankerous and kill the tree. Rudies higher than ten or fifteen feet tend to generate several strong shoots that are difficult to control, none of which is a clear leader.

Do not Rudy trees larger than three inches in diameter. It rarely works.

You may Rudy all trees that are unlikely to grow straight. There is no downside risk.

Rudying may just be a waste of time. Thinning a large stand of walnuts recently, I realized that none of the trees I

This shows the effect of Rudying after about ten years. The scar will heal and will not significantly reduce the value of the bole.

Rudied years ago graduated to the status of keepers. Truc, thc intermediate success of Rudying is impressive—the resulting sprout often is straighter than what you cut off. But neighboring trees tend to have better form and size.

I am sure that I have overlooked other equally valid rules. Indeed, all of the above rules have merit, even if they contradict others. Sometimes I look at a tree and have a precise vision on how it ought to be pruned. Then I step back and look at it from another angle, and a new perspective negates my previous decision. That's the nature of forestry in general. As we'll see in the next chapter, the same sort of judgment calls crop up when it comes time to thin your forest.

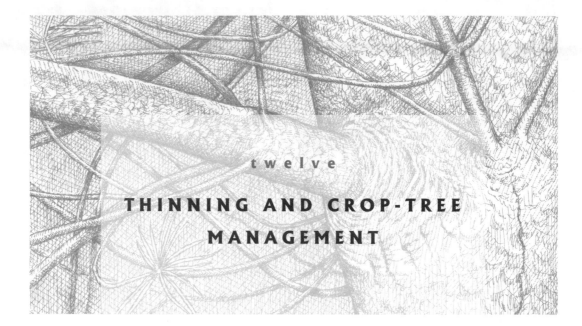

twelve

THINNING AND CROP-TREE MANAGEMENT

Any forest—whether planted, seeded, or natural—will require thinning sooner or later. When a stand is young and the seedlings are small, it's better for the trees to be planted densely so they can shade out grasses and force each other to grow straight. As they grow, they compete so intensely for crown and root space (see sidebar) that only the best and strongest will survive. Still, too many trees will survive, and a good forester will eliminate excess trees in order to enhance the growth potential of the best crop trees. A stand of trees may start out with thousands of little seedlings per acre, but there is only space for about twenty-five fully grown trees (depending on species). In the interim, which may be as long as a century, the stand will have to be periodically thinned.

A stand of trees is like a pond that can only support a given poundage of fish. When a pond is overpopulated, the fish become stunted. Similarly, trees planted too densely will remain weak and skinny. The solution is thinning. In general you will want to have fewer but bigger fish in your stand. One big fish is worth a lot more than dozens of runts.

SPREADING ROOTS

It may be useful to know something about the root size of your trees. The roots of a typical tree extend outward from its stem to a distance about equal to its height. Some trees, such as black walnuts and bur oaks, have a root spread twice their height. This means that a hundred-foot-tall walnut tree will have a root spread of four hundred feet (twice the height of the tree in all directions). This may help to explain why walnuts frequently tower over other trees in a mixed forest stand. The root depth varies according to soil porosity and species. Some trees have long taproots, such as walnuts (one to eight feet), locusts (five to twenty feet), oaks (one to nine feet), and apples (one to ten feet). The roots of most trees do not extend downward more than five feet.

FELLING TREES—AND LIVING TO TELL ABOUT IT

You can hire somebody to thin your forest or you can do it yourself. Learning to use a chain saw is not difficult, and small-diameter trees can be cut with little effort. Felling trees is fun, and there is considerable pleasure to be taken surveying the results of your efforts. Some of my city-slicker friends just love to cut down trees. But make no mistake: Felling trees is dangerous, and even experts are sometimes surprised by a close call. Trees do not always fall in the intended direction. Cutting down larger trees (especially hardwoods) is treacherous and best left to experienced woodcutters. The fall of a tree sometimes inexplicably shifts to the very spot where you are standing.

It is important that you remember that a chain saw is a potentially lethal instrument, and common sense dictates that you abide by a few simple rules: (1) work with a friend; (2) wear a hard hat; (3) wear chaps made of chainsaw-jamming material to protect your legs; (4) make sure that your chainsaw is sharp; (5) do not work when you are tired; and (6) do not attempt to fell large trees unless you are skilled.

When contemplating cutting down a tree, you should plan the tree's fall in a convenient direction, considering the natural lean of the tree, the wind, and the proximity to other trees that may block its fall. When a tree is less than six inches in diameter you can most likely muscle it to fall into any direction you want. However, it is not a good idea to try to fell a larger tree in any direction other than its natural lean.

When cutting down small trees (less than eight inches in diameter), stand at a right angle to the intended direction of fall. Then cut diagonally down (about 20 degrees) into the trunk until about 90 percent of the tree has been severed. If the tree has any lean, it will now fall by itself. If not, you will have

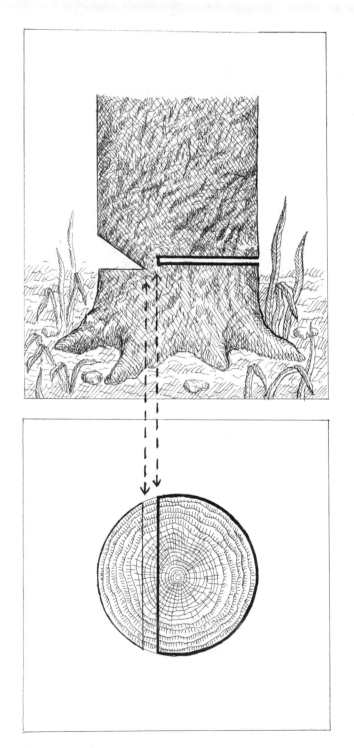

Standard cut for felling a large tree.

to push. The uncut portion, known as the hinge, should be big enough to minimize the chance of the tree falling backward, but small enough to allow the tree to fall. Sometimes the tree will tilt backward, clamping the bar of your chainsaw. If this happens, you may have to push the tree into the direction of the fall. Sometimes, on larger trees, the chain bar might be so securely clamped that you can't pull it out by yourself. In such cases, it helps to have a buddy and/or a second chainsaw to help liberate the first saw.

If the tree is larger than about eight inches, you should notch the tree on the fall side. First make a cut at a slight angle, maybe 15 degrees. Continue this cut until it reaches the height of the stump you wish to leave. Next make a horizontal cut at the stump height until the wedge drops out. Ideally, the wedge should be around four to six inches tall and about a quarter of the tree's diameter in depth. Try to have the two cuts meet at the inside edge of the wedge. Now go to the other side of the tree and make the felling cut at the same level as the original cut (some recommend a tad higher) and cut to within an inch or inch-and-a-half of the wedge. The uncut portion between the wedge and the felling cut is the hinge. Now the tree should fall. If not, push it, use a felling bar, or put a wedge into the cut. I have a small felling bar, which I can say is the only worthwhile purchase I ever made from a "yuppie" tool catalog.

I do my thinning cut at waist height for convenience. I don't mind the stumps, and cutting them so high makes them readily visible, which means they won't be a hazard for any vehicle or for walkers. But

This tool, called a fell bar, helps make a tree fall in the intended direction. It is my only useful purchase from a yuppie tool catalog.

if the stumps bother you, you may cut at ground level. If you do, be very careful not to get dirt into the chain saw, because doing so will dull it instantly. When a small tree gets hung up to a neighboring tree, you may pick up its butt end and drag it away from the hang-up.

As stated above, I would discourage you from felling large trees unless you have the advice and help of a skilled woodsman. You can learn to fell large trees, but I cannot impart to you the necessary knowledge to do so safely. It is imperative that you work with an expert before trying to do it on your own.

Using your chain saw in brush can be treacherous. It is easy to lose your footing, and the saw can get hung or jammed in brush. Always hold your saw firmly with both hands and work slowly. Do not wield your saw like a machete. Try to be cautious.

A SAFER OPTION: GIRDLING

When in doubt of your abilities with the chain saw, take the safe way out and girdle the tree. Girdling is simply cutting a one-inch deep slit all around the circumference of the tree trunk with a chain saw (see the illustration on page 54). It is important that the ring be complete and continuous, so that the cambium is severed all around. I girdle trees at about waist height, since it is easier than bending down. A girdled tree will generally die after a few growing seasons. Some trees are easier to girdle than others. If a tree refuses to die, you may consider a second girdle. Another advantage of girdling is that it can be done with a small chain saw without too much effort. There also is less damage done to neighboring trees, and the standing deadwood is good for wildlife. When the tree eventually does tip over, it will have lost most of its branches and most of its weight and is unlikely to inflict much damage to your neighboring crop trees. Standing dead trees also dry out very nicely and are a great source of firewood.

THINNING FOR BEGINNERS: THE ONE-TWO METHOD

There are different schemes for thinning.* If you are confident and knowledgeable, you can grab your chain saw, walk into your woods and start cutting. A friend does this, but he is a forester. We ordinary mortals really ought to do a little more planning and mark the trees to be culled. The process is referred to as "timber-stand improvement," or TSI. A forester uses a paint gun to mark trees to be culled (this service is typically performed by your county DNR forester, or you can choose to hire a consulting forester). I advise you to accompany him and question him about his decision making. You will learn a great deal. He mentally isolates a crop tree and then marks for extinction trees that interfere with the welfare of that crop tree.

---

* Forestry literature employs a thinning concept known as the crown competition factor. It is frightfully complicated, necessitating a tree count and diameter measurements and calculations with umpteen decimal points. It is difficult to understand, almost impossible to apply, and consumer-unfriendly. I just ignore it.

Many of these marked trees will be of an inferior species, such as birch, ironwood, box elder, or elm. Others may be desirable species but of poor quality. Some marked trees may be big enough to be sold for timber, but in general the point of TSI is to improve your crop trees; felling any merchandisable timber is incidental.

It may be helpful to mark the keepers rather than the trees selected for culling. That's how I do it in my monocultural walnuts groves. It makes it easier when I prune, so I don't have to contemplate (again) at every turn whether a given tree is a keeper or destined to be culled. Sometimes I also mark the keepers in a mixed forest with plastic tape. I find that it helps me visualize what my future forest will look like.

In a TSI operation, your forester typically will mark trees for extinction. In my forest, trees to be culled tend to be birches, elms, ironwoods, box elders, and shaggy bark hickories. Still, I preserve some of these inferior trees because I suspect that they may perform some biodiverse function in my forest.

TSI is cost-sharable in Wisconsin. As of 2002, the state pays $110 per acre; your 65 percent cost-share amounts up to $71.50 an acre. So if you do the work yourself, the state will pay you $71.50; if you choose to have a contractor do the work for $110, your cost is only the remaining $38.50. It is very much worth it, both as an investment and for the appearance of your forest.

Thinning decisions are based on many variables. Not only do you have to decide how many trees should remain, but also what species you favor. Somewhere along the line, you have to decide how close your crop trees can be to each other. There are various guidelines, which are often quite complicated. I have developed my own thinning formula, which I call one-two thinning. It is simple:

For trees up to eight inches in diameter: To determine how much space to clear around a particular crop tree, multiply the diameter of that tree in inches by one foot. Consider, for example, a tree measuring five inches in diameter at breast height (or, in the shorthand lingo of forestry, "five inches dbh"; breast height is four-and-a-half feet from the ground). You should thin all trees within a five-foot radius. This formula results in very tight spacing for young trees. Many arborists may feel uncomfortable with small-diameter trees so close to each other, but trust me, it has worked well in German forests. Your trees will be straight. At a diameter of about seven inches dbh, a typical tree should have developed a sixteen-foot clear log and will no longer need side shading. At that point wider spacing is beneficial.

For trees larger than eight inches in diameter: Use the above formula but multiply by a factor of two feet instead of one. So for a keeper measuring ten inches dbh, you should remove trees within a twenty-foot radius. Given the additional space, the released tree should respond by adding diameter girth. To minimize the danger of windthrow (when a strong wind topples a tree), you may not want to cut down all trees encroaching on your crop tree at once. It is best to do so over a period of several years.

Once a tree gets to be more than sixteen inches in diameter, thinning decisions should be made on an individual

WHY WE MUST THIN

In his book *Woodlands in Wisconsin,* S. A. Wilde wrote the following about the need for thinning for a pine plantation:

"Within the second or third decade after the establishment of a plantation, the trees will be crying out for living space and elbow room. This is especially true of closely spaced plantations. No other group of organisms provides more vivid illustration of the teaching of Malthus related to overpopulation. An overstocked thirty-year-old forest is usually a jungle of three-inch diameter fish poles, a community doomed to slow death by starvation. The only way that prevents wastage of time and energy in this unduly prolonged Darwinian process is a reduction of the population by thinning, eliminating weak and unwanted competitors."*

basis without applying a formula. If you are a rookie tree farmer, you probably should consult a forester; if you are a veteran, you will probably already have your own ideas. (Another method, the crown touching method, will described in a moment.) Thinning decisions in a stand of larger-diameter trees are often a matter of varying opinions, and even experts may reasonably disagree. (See color photo #1.)

If you use my one-two thinning formula, you are in safe territory. I must tell you, my one-two formula is a simplification but to my mind is more successful than other schemes. Personally, I no longer use my one-two thinning scheme because I prefer just to work by my intuition. However, after I am done thinning a stand of trees, I sometimes ask myself how my thinning decisions would have been different if I had applied my formula. Gen-

erally, I conclude that the differences would not be substantial. Therefore, I feel quite comfortable recommending this formula to neophyte woodland owners. If you are a perfectionist, you may want to use such methods as the crown competition factor, although I have yet to meet a woodland owner who does.

THE CRUEL ART OF THINNING

Thinning, like pruning, often admits of differing opinions and approaches. Your hunches may differ from your forester's, or you may have different objectives for one stand than for the next. However, unlike pruning, which one might regard as hygienic, thinning is ruthless. Painful decisions will be necessary that result in the demise of those beautiful objects upon

* S. A. Wilde. *Woodlands of Wisconsin* (Madison: University of Wisconsin Cooperative Extension Programs, 1977), p. 137.

which you've lavished years of love and care. It's a bit like slaughtering a favorite pig. Worse still, for the more sensitive woodland owner, the decision is heartlessly pecuniary.

You will have to ask yourself: Will I get more value from this tree by keeping it for a future sale or by culling it to benefit a neighboring crop tree? The number of trees that should be left in your stand is a function of tree diameter. When trees are small—say, one inch dbh—there might be as many as ten thousand trees in an acre stand (calculating according to the one-two thinning formula, about four square feet per tree). In the long run, you need fewer than a hundred crop trees per acre, so most trees will have to be eliminated over time either by natural selection or by thinning. If your ultimate goal is a stand of thirty trees per acre, the typical crop tree has no neighbors closer than twenty-three feet. As the trees get bigger, you will have to make some tough judgment calls whether or not to cut, for instance, a twelve-inch-diameter tree. The fewer the trees, the more stately the forest (and also the more understory).

To manage crop trees effectively, many factors need to be considered. I'll outline some below.

Choosing When to Thin

You should thin trees that impede keepers from developing into straight and vigorous trees. If neighboring trees serve a function of providing side shading, wind protection, or shading out pernicious grasses, they should be kept as long as they do not compete with the crop trees. In my mono-cultural plantations, which have been planted into pernicious grasses, the shading of the grasses is very important and I defer thinning until the canopy of the trees provides sufficient shade to weaken the grass. Once broadleaf weeds become more abundant, it is okay to thin. Even in my better groves, this may take more than a decade. It becomes a matter of judging when the benefits of shading out grasses are greater than the living space taken away from a neighboring crop tree.

Choosing among Species

If you have a homogeneous plantation, such as a stand of monocultural spruces, deciding which trees to keep is relatively uncomplicated. However, if you have a mixed forest with a lot of different trees, you will have to decide not only among individual trees but among different species. Some trees make wonderful lumber trees, such as oaks, maples, and walnuts. Other trees are particularly beautiful, and you may want to have them in your forest for aesthetic reasons. Still other trees are mast trees, which produce nuts and fruit to feed various animals. Some species are particularly well suited to attract certain animals. For instance, woodpeckers and grouse love aspens. Some trees are particularly good for firewood, such as hickory or ironwood. Maple trees can be tapped for syrup. In selecting preferred species, you may want to consider which trees do best on the particular site and which trees are favored by the timber market. You will have to decide which trees give you the most utility and whether you want to maximize monetary return, aesthetic ambiance, wildlife, or any other benefits. The more diversity in your tree population, the more options you will have to consider. This is what makes the perpetual mixed forest (PMF, described in the chapter 14) such an attractive forest.

My (generally mixed) forest has a lot of oaks. As they are harvested, maples, which are shade tolerant, tend to become dominant. I prefer oak trees because they are more valuable and beautiful, and their mast favors wildlife. So I have been cold-bloodedly liberating young oak trees to give them access to the sun, which means that I cut down competitive trees nearby. The best time to do this is in the winter, when you can very easily spot oak trees because they do not shed their leaves until spring.

Criteria for Selecting Crop Trees

It is very important that the specimens you select for crop trees be capable of good growth and have the potential to become good saw timber. In a young stand, most trees tend to be vigorous and have good potential. If a tree has been suppressed, however—that is, if it has lost its vitality in the race for light, water, and nutrients—it will likely never become a high-quality lumber tree, even if released. (A tree is "released" when all nearby competitors are cut down, leaving it alone to enjoy the sunshine and soil nutrients.) You should not release trees with dead branches in the crown, poor form (such as a low fork), a lack of vigor, or generally poor quality. You are better off starting your stand from scratch than trying to promote weak trees to future saw logs. The foresters for the Menominee tribe in Wisconsin remove all trees larger than one inch in diameter when creating canopy gaps. They reason

that many trees between one and six inches in diameter, despite the fact that they have survived (barely) in the shade, tend not to be viable and will probably never make good crop trees. It's better to let new trees take root in the canopy gap. Your forester can help you to predict which trees are most likely to respond favorably to being released. How well a tree responds to release depends both on the species and the individual specimen. For instance, cherry trees often do not develop healthy crowns when released.

Liberating Trees from Competition Using the Crown-touching Method

The one-two thinning formula provides a guideline for when to thin. A more sensitive approach is the crown-touching method. To give more space to your crop tree, eliminate trees whose crowns touch it. Crown release from all four sides can more than double the rate of diameter growth of crop trees. This is more significant than it may appear on the surface, in that a doubling of diameter growth translates into at least four times the wood volume growth. (There is, of course, a conflict between liberating a crop tree from all sides and the cohort theory, also mentioned later. My county forester recommends treating adjacent trees as one.)

Remember the potential damage of windthrow, though, and release trees gradually. In a stand prone to windthrow damage, it might be wise not to remove more than one touching tree every five years. Tap-rooted trees such as walnuts or oaks are sturdier and, therefore, less susceptible to windthrow. But be especially careful of thinning too aggressively in plots with damp and shallow soils because they provide less support. Another reason not to thin aggressively is that the penetrating sunlight may cause excessive epicormic sprouting, which decreases the value of some trees, particularly of oaks and walnuts (epicormic sprouts are small shoots, smaller than branches, caused by sunlight directly hitting the tree trunk). Released oaks are very prone to develop epicormic sprouts.

Overshadowed trees will die on their own and need not be thinned. However, if the overshadowed tree is of a shade-tolerant species, it will be more likely to compete with your keeper and therefore should be eliminated.

Choosing among Several Good Trees

Generally you should base thinning decisions on the quality of each tree and its distance from its neighbors. Here again, there are complications. If you have two wonderful trees standing close to each other, do you sacrifice one? In thinning my walnut stand, I frequently encounter such dilemmas. I used to be a cold-blooded adherent of the one-two thinning formula, because I knew that one fat tree would be worth much more than three or four slender trees, no matter how well grown. So out came the chain saw to cut off any tree that might impede the growth of my chosen keeper. There is much merit to this ruthless approach, but I have since changed my mind. The reasons are twofold: First, a forester told me that it is a good idea to treat two well-formed adjacent trees as one unit. Second, I have learned that the German adherents of the perpetual mixed forest (or *Dauerwald*, as they call it) follow this axiom: "Cut down any tree only if there is a same-species tree of greater quality in the stand."

If several perfect trees happen to be in the same spot, the Busse cohort theory may be of some assistance. In the 1930s, a German forester named Busse observed that trees frequently do better growing next to each other than they do further apart. We all know that redwoods, for example, grow very close to each other, often separated by less than the diameter of a tree. Busse called these groupings cohorts, and maintained that trees in a cohort will do better than uniformly spaced trees. He analyzed growth rings and showed that in their youth trees in a cohort often grow slower than more distant neighbors. But as they get older they outperform other trees in the stand. Somehow, they help each other grow stronger. So don't hesitate to save your best trees even if they seem to be too close to each other. Note, however, that the Busse cohort theory does not apply to clusters of trees of varied species. That is, a pine, oak, and maple growing close together do not make a cohort.

Thinning Conifers

In most planted conifer stands, the trees are so much alike that you can just cut out every other tree. Or just cull every other (or every third) row of trees. Generally a conifer forest should be thinned when the trees are about twenty years old and eight inches in diameter. The cultivation of conifers will be discussed in more detail in chapter 17.

Thinning Schedule

If you follow the crown-touching method, you can assume that the crown of a healthy tree will expand about one foot per year. The crown spread between two adjacent trees should, therefore, close at a rate of two feet per year. Consequently, a ten-foot space between two trees allows for crown expansion of five years. The frequency of thinning depends on the size of your woodland and the amount of time and effort you are willing and eager to devote to the task. If your holdings are small and you spend much time in your forest, you could thin a little every season. If, however, you own thousands of acres, you may choose to thin at five-year intervals.

Commercial Thinning

The principal purpose of thinning is to transfer growing energy (sunlight and soil space) to your crop trees. At first the culled trees have little or no value, but once the trees to be thinned are of a larger diameter (usually twelve inches or more), they can be sold. This procedure is known as a commercial thinning. It is discussed further in chapter 19. Thinned conifers, larger than eight inches dbh, can be marketed as pulpwood.

Thinning and Tree Height

While site fertility typically determines the height a tree will reach, neighboring trees generally determine its shape. Leaving a lot of space between trees will encourage lateral branching and lower crowns. Naturally, the reverse is true as well: If you do not thin, your trees will grow higher. Generally, long and slender trees with a clear bole are qualitatively and quantitatively preferable. There are, however, situations where stouter trees are desirable. French foresters often grow short hardwood trees (their formula: ninety trees per hectare, ninety centimeters in diameter, to be harvested in ninety years) that can be brought to market much sooner than a sixty-foot hardwood tree shaded from all sides. I have also talked to an Iowa walnut grower who did not allow his trees to grow taller than forty feet, lest they be blown over by a tornado. On the other hand, Germans love to grow their hardwood trees in excess of one hundred feet tall. Their trees look beautiful, but it takes a long time before they can be harvested. My Wisconsin DNR forester suggests that 80 percent of the value of a tree is in the lower sixteen feet of a tree and it does not pay to go much higher. Thinning will help determine the height of marketable timber.

Disposing of Culled Trees

The unavoidable by-products of a harvesting or thinning operation are the culled trees, branches, and other debris left behind, also known as "slash." Slash may be visually offensive for a few years until it is absorbed naturally by the forest. I leave the slash to lay where it falls, except when I use it for firewood. If you are a compulsively neat person, you can cut and pile the slash (rabbits like it) or you can buy a chipper and shred it into little pieces which will decay a little faster. Personally, I do not like chippers, and certainly the

Lord does not require the help of such a gadget to dispose of slash. I should add here that some foresters recommend the use of mulch around planted trees to suppress grasses. It is a lot of work to spread the mulch, though it undoubtedly benefits the seedlings. But you should also consider that decomposed slash is useful in the forest as well.

The Value of Understory Vegetation

Some people recommend that you remove understory vegetation such as shrubs and adolescent trees. I advise against this, since shade-intolerant trees will die on their own when they are overshadowed, and some understory vegetation is helpful to minimize epicormic sprouting, a major detractor of timber value. Furthermore, understory is good for wildlife and enriches the biodiversity of your forest. Besides, deer love stump sprouts because they have a higher sugar content—and you'd rather have deer nibble on stump sprouts than on your crop trees. So please do not fall prey to the advertising claims that herbiciding understory will be good for your forest. Using herbicides on the understory or on sprouting tree stumps diminishes biodiversity and may damage neighboring trees that share a common root system. (Some trees have root grafts with neighboring trees of the same species. Dutch elm disease and oak wilt are often transmitted through the root system to neighboring trees.) The only justifiable use of herbicide in your woodland is the suppression of pernicious grasses.

Thinning and Aesthetics

Even if you are not particularly interested in timber production, I still encourage you to thin. Once the trees in your stand are taller than you are, thinning is a good idea. Thinning will make it easier to see and walk through your forest, and it will enhance biodiversity (because thinning tends to introduce other species of vegetation). For example, if you own a dense stand of conifers, you would probably have a hard time even walking through your forest without getting totally scratched up. A stand of pole-sized deciduous trees, such as oaks or maples, will appear a lot more pleasing when thinned and will give deer little sustenance. Eliminating some trees allows rain and sunlight to penetrate to the forest floor, which greatly increases biodiversity. Felled or girdled trees generate dead wood, with its many benefits to your forest. You might also consider some aggressive thinning, such as the creation of canopy gaps, which always adds variety and excitement to any forest. Chances are that you will enjoy your woods more if you thin periodically.

There is no need to follow all my suggestions compulsively. Your forest is very resilient and will grow naturally all by itself. It is definitely more important for you to gain an appreciation and understanding of how trees grow and interact with each other. The joy of forestry is in observing the dynamics of nature, not in following instructions.

Forestry, but especially thinning, is an art. It is the forester's task to achieve, by skillful cutting, the optimal environmental conditions favoring quick recovery of the thinned stand and rapid diameter growth. A German forester summed it up a century and a half ago: "A good forester takes a high yield from the forest without deteriorating the soil. A poor forester neither obtains a high yield nor preserves soil fertility."*

* S. A. Wilde, *Woodlands of Wisconsin*, p. 141.

thirteen

MANAGING FOR BIODIVERSITY

I had originally intended to write separate chapters on aesthetics, wildlife, and environmental stewardship. But after reflection, I concluded that all three have a common denominator: biodiversity. By this I mean the presence and interactions of a wide variety of plants, beetles, bugs, fungi, lichens, trees, shrubs, mammals, birds, amphibians, insects, and an incredible variety of microscopic organisms. All these entities engage in relationships that are the basis of biodiversity. Human knowledge, even with sophisticated instruments, can only understand, explain, and document a fraction of these interrelationships. Over long periods of time, through mutation, adaptation, and experimentation, nature brings about biodiversity. By following the advice of this book (for example, by encouraging a healthy mix of domestic plant species) you can play a part in advancing biodiversity.

As a woodland owner, you can observe surface biodiversity in action on your land. However, much of the biological activity is subterranean. While some entities are huge—such as an aspen plant, which may weigh millions of pounds and extend over hundreds of acres—most subterranean activity is microscopic. There may be, for example, a billion bacteria in a cubic centimeter of your soil. Some microorganisms are decomposers: They break

---

* Technically the DNR (a state agency) provides technical assistance only. The cost-share checks are issued by the sponsoring state agency.

down chemicals into other forms, which then may be consumed by another critter or absorbed by a plant. Life-sustaining microbes called mycorrhizae, for example, form a mutual relationship in the roots of plants sucking up water and nutrients from the soil. There are numerous species of this fungus. Without it, our trees would die. Others species are predatorial. For example, a common single cell amoeba may consume more than a hundred thousand bacteria a day. The complexity of biodivesity is awesome, and most of the microorganisms have not been identified in spite of DNA analyses and the use of computers. Each entitiy attends to its assigned task and somehow the system works harmoniously—everything gets recycled.

Biodiversity is the basis of our ecology, and when left undisturbed, nature will produce all the tools necessary to keep the ecology in balance. As a woodland steward, you should recognize that ill-considered actions may damage your woodland. Clearcutting, soil compaction, monocultural plantings, exotic species, and chemicals are likely to disturb biodiversity. The balance is easily tilted. For example, if you plant only one species of tree, your forest will be more susceptible to damage from an infestation. The habitat of useful bacteria or insects—organisms key to defending your forest against maladies—may no longer exist or not in sufficient quantity. If you then try to use chemicals, you run a chance of destroying the natural enemy of the pest along with the pest. It is important to maintain your woodland's biodiversity. A healthy mixed forest works best.

Generally, the older and more varied a stand of trees, the more biodiversity it supports. The greater the variety of tree species, the greater the variety of critters that depend on them to live. The more insects and other small entities, the more food for larger animals. The more decay of trees (dead or alive) the more bacteria, beetles, fungi, and creatures feeding on them. The more variety in all kinds of living things, the more interaction and food sources. Noah could not have filled his ark from a monocultural pine forest; I am sure he searched for a biodiverse old-growth forest.

THE BENEFITS OF BIODIVERSITY

Aesthetics. Most woodland owners list aesthetics as one of their most important management objectives. We all know beauty is in the eye of the beholder, but if I had to say what makes a forest beautiful, it would be an interesting mix of tree species. The wider the variety of trees, the wider the range of colors. (See color photo #9.) A coniferous plantation might be nice to look at, but it will never astound you with its beauty. To enhance your woodland's visual appeal, you should vary the layout of your plantings and the age distribution of your trees, and allow your forest to develop naturally. There will be huge, medium-sized, and adolescent trees, and baby seedlings. Creating open vistas will add further visual appeal.

Wildlife. The variability of wildlife is directly related to habitat, which in turn is related to biodiversity. A biodiverse forest is more likely to provide food sources for a variety of animals. A varied rain forest offers habitats to a wider range of animals than a monocultural coniferous stand of trees or a pole-sized stand of northern hardwoods. On your own land, you can encourage your favorite wildlife by protecting or encouraging specific food sources, cover, water, nesting sites and breeding sites.

Water quality. Water quality can be adversely affected by pollution, silting, flooding, or changes in water temperature. Rich riparian vegetation (that is, shrubs and trees along the borders of creeks, ponds, and lakes) greatly benefits water quality and wildlife, including amphibians and reptiles.* Better still, a biodiverse watershed will greatly enhance the water quality of your creeks and ponds. A forest, with its tree litter, humus, and vegetative cover, acts like a giant blotter soaking up the rain and snow. Most of the water is stored in the ground and then is gradually filtered into lakes and streams. Gifford Pinchot, the originator of the USDA Forest Service under Teddy Roosevelt, said: "The connection between forests and rivers is like that between father and son. No forest, no rivers." The area from which water flows into your creek or pond is known as a watershed. My small four-acre lake has an eight-hundred-acre watershed, and because it is mostly wooded, my water is very clean.

Timber production. Generally, healthy and biodiverse forests will produce better crop trees than monocultural plantations. On paper some plantations, such as the pine forests in the southeastern United States, may have very high yields,

but when the higher probability of windthrow and insect infestations is factored into the equation, a mixed forest will produce competitive crops. A mixed forest will also provide the flexibility to shift harvesting to tree species that momentarily enjoy higher market prices.

A healthy forest. The myriad naturally occurring organisms make a biodiverse forest more able than a monocultural forest to defend against disease, pest infestations, and other disturbances.

METHODS FOR INCREASING AND FOSTERING BIODIVERSITY

Plant or seed a variety of plants. A variety of plants alone will not guarantee a biodiverse, ecologically sound forest, but it is a good start.

You should consider that each species of tree will attract all kinds of critters that add to the biodiversity of your forest. An oak tree, for example, will host a variety of birds, mammals, lizards, insects, worms, and fungi. Some are merely using the tree because it is handy, whereas others are fine-tuned to live in or about oaks exclusively. Some larvae eat only oak leaves or bore into its trunk, and these larvae may in turn attract mites, fungi, and predators. So a mix of trees attracts a mix of all kinds of organisms, which as a whole become part of the biodiversity of your forest. You should accept that the more biodiversity, the healthier your forest.

Maintain deadwood. Deadwood is a

---

* Wisconsin Best Management Practices (or "BMP," published by the University of Wisconsin Extension Service) calls for eliminating pasture and restricting tree harvesting along waterways.

YOU CAN'T FIGHT MOTHER NATURE

Some modern farmers grow clinically efficient crops in a sterile atmosphere, irrigated with a cocktail of herbicides, chemicals, and fertilizers. Their fields have but few insects and few birds, because there is little to eat and little biodiversity. Far from being Gardens of Eden, these are sterile environments run by folks with huge machines, guided by bioengineers, chemists, and satellites. I cannot argue with the bounty of industrial agriculture; it's how we feed the world. Yet it is important to keep in mind that maintaining biodiversity is essential to preserving our genetic inheritance. It is interesting to note that some crops resist the application of these modern agricultural methods. One is cocoa, which is grown in the shade of rain forests. Cultivated cocoa plantations tend to fail because plants are attacked by a fungus. Even vast research expenditures have failed to develop a more dependable source of cocoa than a biodiverse, shady jungle. By fostering biodiverse forests, woodland owners make an important contribution to our land and the world.

---

haven and source of food for countless insects, beetles, fungi, and microorganisms, and a wildlife condo for numerous animals. The simplest way to establish deadwood is to leave trees lying when they die naturally or after you've girdled them.

Minimize the use of fertilizers, herbicides, and insecticides. A healthy forest has no need for any of these. The web of biodiverse relationships is extremely intricate and delicate. The use of poison, fungicides, insecticides, and herbicides will most assuredly affect biodiverse relationships, and the ultimate damage done may be far greater than the problems the chemicals were applied to cure. Some chemical damage may not be immediately apparent and may only surface later. Still, I reluctantly endorse the use of herbicides to fight pernicious grasses when planting or seeding a forest. Without herbicides it can take generations to establish a biodiverse forest. However, I see no need to use fertilizers; academic forestry literature generally concurs that they are rarely cost effective. Rather than fertilizing, one may consider planting legumes (locust trees are an example), which fix nitrogen in the soil.

Chemicals often have disastrous affects on aquifers. The cost of removing chemicals from aquifers to make the water potable sometimes exceeds the benefit derived by spreading the chemicals in the first place.

Foster edge vegetation. Shrubs, trees, and brambles growing along the edge of your forest are important ingredients of your ecosystem and are particularly rich in wildlife. They take advantage of the more abundant sunlight and provide cover and nesting sites for many animals. Your forest-edge vegetation will be a hotbed of animal activity. Edge vegetation is also important to regulate the climate inside the forest. A healthy forest is cooler in the summer and warmer in the winter than the ambient temperature. Paths and vistas will naturally grow their own edge vegetation. Paths are wonderful for walking, jogging, gatoring, cross-country skiing, and snowmobiling, and are useful for logging. They should be mowed once or twice a year. It's a fun activity on a nice summer day.

Fight nonindigenous organisms. Any number of pests and blights—including the Asiatic long-horned beetle (which is attacking maple trees in Chicago), the gypsy moth (which is spreading from the East Coast), and Dutch elm disease—have been introduced by imported plants and lumber. Some plants, such as Kudzu, have been inadvisably introduced and now do extensive environmental damage. The Kudzu vine totally smothers forests. It's an incredible sight, the way it overtakes a landscape, as if taken from a bad movie. Various nonnative plants, such as black locust (once native only to Ohio but now spread throughout the Midwest), Russian or autumn olive, and multiflora rose, have become so common that we mistake them for plants that have been part of our ecosystem forever. The introduction of nonnative crop trees, such as the eucalyptus tree in Portugal and the ever-present teak plantations all over the world, often damage biodiverse ecologies for the sake of short-term profits.

Ecologists have very strong urges to expunge exotic vegetation. They feel as strongly about their mission as I do about stopping clear-cutting. The damage done by exotic species is that these species often spread very rapidly and displace native vegetation. In Wisconsin, some invasive plants are buckthorns, exotic bush honeysuckle, garlic mustard, Canada thistle, crown vetch, multiflora rose, and autumn olive.* I don't have any consistent feelings about nonnative species, pro or con. Consider autumn olive, which was introduced by the Wisconsin DNR. It appears a benign plant with lots of red berries that millions of migratory birds gobble up on their migrations south. I am not convinced that they do a lot of harm. Nor am I convinced that following the ecologists' suggestion and herbiciding the autumn olives would be any better for the environment. And even if I expunged the autumn olive from my land, and my neighbors did not follow suit, new plants would reestablish themselves on my land anyway. Autumn olives propagate by bird droppings, and it is hard to fight the pest single-handedly.

---

* The Wisconsin DNR sells a book, *Wisconsin Manual of Control Recommendations for Ecologically Invasive Plants*, published in May 1997.

It is interesting to speculate whether any invasive species is beneficial. I asked an ecologist friend in Wisconsin, who commented that pheasants are a nice addition to our biodiversity, as are some conifers transplanted from a great distance away but which are doing well.

I am not an ecologist, but I do agree that some pests should be eradicated when they establish themselves. Kudzu and the gypsy moth are among them. But it is totally impractical to set out to kill all the offending species. If you decided to methodically poison every invasive species, the damage done to your land would be as huge as the expense and the trouble. The exception is a concentrated colony, which may be relatively easy to exterminate. I am sympathetic to the concerns of ecologists, but I can see no practical way to act on their advice—with one exception: An ecologist friend suggested that I should wash the tires of any logging truck entering my forest. This is easy to do and worthwhile. The point was brought home to me when another friend told me that garlic mustard—a nonnative species—appeared in his forest after he logged his woodland.

I should mention here that controlled burning is effective in killing much invasive vegetation, since our domestic grasses often have well-developed root systems that make them immune to burnings.

As you may recall, the exotic plant giving me the most grief is smooth brome grass, a species imported from Europe in the 19th century. I would love to get even with that plant. However, the cost of eradication would be huge, requiring massive herbiciding for years at a large expense and unknown environmental consequences. The cure might be worse than the disease. The only practical way to defeat brome grass is to shade it out, and this is exactly what I am doing by planting trees. The unfortunate part is that this effort requires many decades to have the desired results.

I find most ecologists to be very knowledgeable folks, deeply concerned about the environment, and my instinct is to help them as much as possible. There is, however, a need for an overall program that will work to eradicate specific plants on a wider geographical scope. This requires organization and money. It would be money well spent. Recently, there have been workshops on invasive species. To date, however, the suggestions by ecologists have not been sufficiently clear and organized to prompt even willing woodland owners to act on them. There are some laws on the books forbidding harboring invasive species, but they concern agriculture and not forests.

Allow sunlight to hit the forest floor. In the early stages of your stand, you strive to have the trees shade out the grasses. Later, however, when you have a closed canopy, you should allow some sunlight and rain to penetrate to the forest floor to allow for the growth of brambles, shrubs, and other herbaceous vegetation desirable for a biodiverse environment. This can best

THE MOST INVASIVE SPECIES OF ALL

Ecologists would welcome your help in fighting a host of the most pernicious invasive species in the United States. The problem is that there are so many invasive organisms that you may want to zero in on the most destructive, pervasive, and stubborn species of all. This invading species decimated and displaced natives and is indirectly responsible for the introduction of numerous plants and animals into our ecology. Further, this particular pest endangers our forests, almost eliminated the ubiquitous buffalo, and killed every last passenger pigeon.

It is too late to reverse the European settlement of this continent. Since eradication of this species would be a masochistic endeavor, we can only try to modify its behavior. Being a good steward of your woodland is a good start.

---

be done by creating canopy gaps. Please remember that mowing is inimical to biodiversity.

Maintain equilibrium among species of plants and animals. An overabundance of any one species will effect the living conditions in the ecology of a forest. An example of this is deer.* Because humans have done away with many natural predators, deer have become a serious problem. There are only two ways to effectively exclude deer from your land: predation (including hunting) and fencing. In Germany young forest stands are routinely fenced. This would be prohibitively expensive in North America, since our white-tail deer are much larger than their German cousins, the *reh*, which only weigh thirty pounds and cannot jump higher than six or seven feet. While our whitetails do not normally jump higher than eight feet, I have seen a buck pursued by bow hunters negotiate a ten foot fence topped by barbed wire.

There is abundant literature on how to discourage deer without killing them. You can help minimize deer damage by providing them with lots of varied forage, which may make them less likely to munch on your tender crop tree seedlings. Sometimes thorny brambles, which often establish themselves in decaying wood, can protect the trees that grow next to them. I was recently

---

* Recently, the chronic wasting disease has spread from Colorado to deer in the Midwest. It is related to the mad-cow disease and is a real threat to the Wisconsin deer population. It generally affects local deer populations, which gives some hope for control. Hunters are very concerned. Though some foresters, like Larry Krotz (see chapter 16), hate deer, I have not come across anybody expressing glee in the spread of this malady.

acquainted with a new technique: crimp a small sheet of foil paper over the end of the leader of the tree. This has effectively kept deer away from my oak seedlings. Put foil on each tree. There is also a deer repellent called Durapel on the market. Friends have used it with some success, but if you have a lot of trees, protecting individual plants from deer is just too much trouble. Unless you have a rather small farm, or if you want to just protect a few chosen plants, the most essential approach is aggressive hunting.

Deer browse most readily on trees nicely spaced on a manicured lawn. If weeds and shrubs are intermingled with your seedlings, however, damage will be much less. You may request an out-of-season hunting license from the DNR. In Wisconsin, this is possible, although regulations are cumbersome.

Maintain a small natural forest. If your woodland is large, consider setting aside a small area where you allow nature to govern without interference. This is a practice followed in some progressive German forests. I have segregated about three acres for this purpose.

Do not clear-cut.

Treat your woodlot gently. Harvest tenderly. Do not clear-cut and avoid compaction by heavy equipment.

STRATEGIES TO ENHANCE WILDLIFE

A biodiverse forest will have a much greater variety of animals than a monocultural plantation. A German study in Wilhelm Bode's *Waldwende* found twenty-five species of birds in a coniferous mono-cultural plantation but fifty-five species in a more biodiverse forest. Even in a mixed forest there are a few things you can do to encourage wildlife. Some suggestions are:

Leave many mast trees. Mast trees bear large seeds, such as nuts and acorns, that provide a lot of sustenance for larger animals. Acorns feed turkeys, squirrels, deer, raccoons, mice, and many others, while the smaller seeds of the cherry, pine, and ash are eaten by smaller animals.

Leave brush piles. Brush piles have multiple functions: nest sites, habitats for insects and small mammals, and refuge from predators and the cold.

Delay logging. Mature stands provide habitat for many more animals than younger forests. For example a pole-sized stand provides very little habitat, while older trees tend to be an animal-diverse paradise.

Prune gently. Aggressive pruning may affect the habitat of some animals. I pruned a stand of white pines for timber quality and thereby severely reduced the population of red squirrels. They may have migrated, but more likely they were eaten by owls. I miss the squirrels. (I also miss the needly green wall the lower branches made for the "Hidden Passage," as we called the Gator path the passed through the rows of pines.) I now wish I had not bothered to prune the white pines, an activity which will only have a minor effect on future harvest values. Whenever you work in your woods, you will affect the balance of different organisms. A good forester should anticipate the changes.

Encourage deer—in moderation. While it is more common for woodland owners to discourage deer, some folks ac-

1. Which trees should be kept? In this threesome, the black cherry tree on the left is the straightest and has great potential to become fat and valuable. The larger trees on the right are mature basswoods, a species with less commercial value. So my decision was easy: I cut down the basswoods. Without competition for sunlight, the cherry tree should double its rate of diameter growth. After I cut the basswoods, my county forester opined that I had made a mistake. He doubted that the cherry tree had sufficient vitality to respond to the improved growing conditions. He was wrong. The cherry tree's foliage increased immensely. Unfortunately, at about fifty feet up, the trunk developed a profusion of epicormic sprouts, which will make the upper part of the bole less valuable. Nonetheless, the lower logs should add girth.

It can be argued that I would have done better to leave the trees alone, but it is too early to tell. This example shows that two savvy foresters can have very different opinions on a given situation, and only time will tell who is right. The learning curve in forestry is steep, which is one reason that it is so exciting and rewarding.

2 and 3. Two beautiful walnut trees on my farm. The tree in the center of the lefthand photo, a walnut, I call a "hidden tree" because it grew hidden among other trees. Crowded by its neighbors, the tree developed a small crown and a long stem. In nature such trees are frequently planted by squirrels, but in this case I can take credit. The two elm trees provide side shading and have forced the walnut to stretch toward the sun to survive. It has a beautiful shape and a long trunk and is destined to become a valuable veneer tree. The adjacent elms will be removed (I girdled the one on the right already), allowing the hidden tree to add girth.

The walnut tree on the right is a beautiful free-standing specimen with a large crown and a heavy trunk. An elm used to shade it, but I cut the elm down to give my walnut more living space. I have pruned the walnut meticulously, in part because I gaze at it many a morning from my bedroom and give it a lot of thought. This tree will continue to add girth. But because I will not prune any higher, its bole will not become longer. It would not be cost-effective to do more pruning (and, remember that 80 percent of the value is in the bottom sixteen feet).

In the long run, the hidden tree will develop a larger crown and become stronger. It will have a longer, cleaner, and more marketable bole than its free-standing cousin. Forest-grown trees are generally better than plantation-grown trees.

4. Pernicious grass carpet. This benign-looking meadow is actually a pernicious grass carpet that tolerates no competition. It has remained essentially unchanged for the thirty years I have owned the farm. The prevalent smooth brome grass produces a phytotoxic ("plant-poisoning") chemical that keeps competing trees and other vegetation away. The process is known as allelopathy. Smooth brome is an exotic grass imported from Europe, and its only natural enemy—on my farm, anyway—appears to be me. The most likely plants to succeed in colonizing a brome meadow are trees from adjoining forests. Trees that propagate through suckers (sprouts from a large root system), such as black locust and aspen, have no problem invading a meadow from the edge of a forest. (On the other hand, if you were to plant a single aspen, lacking the support of large root system, it would most likely die.) Occasionally a lone cherry or hickory may manage to establish itself. I have hand planted many oaks on similar sites, and none has ever survived.

5. Some deciduous trees grow better next to pines. All the trees in this photograph were planted on the same day in 1978 (except the red pine in the left foreground, which was planted in 1994). Notice that the stunted, leafless walnut trees in the foreground have started hibernating (this picture was taken in September), while their cousins in the rear are still photosynthesizing and growing. In spring, the larger walnut trees get their leaves long before the stressed smaller trees. There is a simple reason for the difference: The walnuts in the rear were planted next to a row of white pines (you can barely make out the tips of some of the pines peeking over the walnut canopy).

Some experts have doubted my contention that pines can invigorate hardwoods grown nearby. A visit to my farm would confirm my point of view, although I can offer no tested theory of why pines help nearby walnuts. Different foresters have offered different explanations; the academic literature of forestry, unfortunately, has no guidance to offer.

In any case, sickly trees like those in the foreground will present a challenge to the woodland owner. Herbiciding the surrounding pernicious grass might seem to be a reasonable way to restore the trees' vitality. As a matter of fact, I applied a fair amount of herbicide around the trees pictured, but apparently not enough to make a real difference. I have since decided to try interplanting red pines between rows of distressed walnuts in the hope that they will somehow invigorate the walnuts. It is too early to determine whether this scheme works.

6. A three-year-old walnut seeding. These walnuts are in their third growing season on a fertile site. They actually formed a canopy in their first season. But since walnuts leaf out late in spring, the grass surrounding them will survive for a few more years, before being gradually replaced by more shade-tolerant weeds. These trees are a wonderful beginning for a trouble-free forest requiring little maintenance. As it happens, I seeded oaks on this site at the same time. Since they germinate from a smaller seed, the oaks will take more time to establish themselves. If I want some oaks to survive, I will have to find them and give them access to the sun.

7. A successful seeding. These seedlings (mostly oaks, along with a few walnuts) are about six years old and are grown from seeds. Because of shading by neighbors, these saplings will grow into straight timber without any large lateral branching. They will require no maintenance, unlike planted seedlings. Since I bought acorns by the bushel from neighboring Amish farmers without specifying the species, you will notice several different kinds of oak trees.

8. A very expensive forest. A diverse mix of trees, grown very densely, seems to solve a lot of problems for the tree farmer. Shaded from all sides, the seedlings will have minimal lateral branching, which means less (or no) pruning down the road.
The young trees will compete with neighbors, assuring a process of natural selection. When the time comes to thin the stand, the tree farmer can choose the most desired species. All in all, the scheme requires minimal maintenance. As an experiment, I instructed a contractor to plant a random mix of all available tree species. The result is a very appealing multi-species forest. The cost of this close planting—several thousand dollars per acre—will never be recovered financially. So I would not recommend this scheme to you as an investment. However, it works if you want an instant forest and are willing to pay for it.

It may be possible to obtain similar results more inexpensively by direct seeding. I have experimented with that, too. While trees with big nuts, such as oaks, walnuts, and chestnuts, come up, trees with small seeds—pines, cherries, and ashes—have not. I will continue to experiment.

9. A mixed forest. Besides observing that the fall colors are pleasing, a woodsman might deduce a variety of conclusions about this Wisconsin landscape. He'd note that it's a mixed forest of deciduous and coniferous trees. Given that mixed forests are rare, he might conclude that the conifers were planted.

He'd also note the anomalous presence of a birch tree (actually, there were more birches in this stand before the picture was taken, but they were felled in a TSI operation). The birch, an intolerant tree, does not thrive in a mature forest. Its presence here suggests the possibility of a disturbance in the past (such as a fire or pasturing).

Our woodsman would recognize in the different leaf colors the presence of various species of trees. The holes in the canopy would indicate that some tree release or a harvest has taken place. The shrubs at the front edge of the forest were probably planted, since there are only a couple trees among them. Finally, the bare walnut tree in the foreground bears clear marks of having been aggressively pruned—otherwise it would have lower lateral branches.

It is easy for me to make these observations; having owned the land for thirty years, I know that they are correct.

10. A sustainable forest.
This photo shows one of the many charming spots on my farm. This mixed forest has a wide variety of trees: oaks, white pines, aspens, ashes, birches, ironwood, basswood, and a few walnut trees. It is a bio-diverse forest with lots of deadwood, wildlife, and understory vegetation. Twenty years ago, we used red oak from this site for booths and tables in one of my restaurants. Is it a sustainable forest? That is a complicated question and you will find an answer in chapter 23.

11. "The Hidden Passage" is the center lane in four rows of white pines planted on my farm. We called it the Hidden Passage because we could travel on it with the Gator without being seen. Two years ago we did some thinning and felled some trees to the left and right. We didn't fell enough trees to bother selling them for pulp, so we just let them lay. In a pure pine forest letting thinned trees lay is dangerous because the deadwood is highly susceptible to insect infestation and fires. In a small stand these dangers are minimal.

tually try to encourage them. I did, when I was a rookie. If you want more deer, plant oaks (deer love acorns), provide some dense thickets (conifers work well), preferably on a southern facing slope, for protection against winter winds, and leave grassy areas for pasture. And, of course, provide plenty of small trees, stump sprouts, and shrubs for forage. Deer density is difficult to determine, and it has been suggested that even DNR estimates are unreliable. Wildlife biologists in Pennsylvania suggest a maximum density of thirty per square mile. A forester friend in Wisconsin is suffering deer damage from a population of around fifty deer per square mile.

Hunt undesirable animals. Ideally, a biodiverse environment will maintain a balance between predators and prey. If, however, there are too many of one kind of animal, there is no reason you shouldn't join the ranks of the predators yourself. In some states, the law allows you to shoot beavers, raccoons, foxes, coyotes, and crows on sight. If you like to hunt turkey, grouse, or pheasant, you may want to do away with some of the competition. You should know that coyotes, contrary to general opinion, are omnivorous, eating berries as well as birds. Beavers can do remarkable damage to low-lying trees in a short period of time. Crows can do great damage to song birds and your eardrums but are difficult to shoot and are unfortunately inedible. Wisconsin law allows you to shoot cowbirds (they lay eggs in nests of other birds), starlings, and red-winged blackbirds. If you entertain hopes of including nut trees in a seeded mixed forest, near any stand of trees, you had better have

your shotgun ready to take care of a few squirrels.

Don't poison pests. I know of woodland owners who poison mice to keep them from girdling seedlings, but I advise against the practice because poisoned animals may poison the predators as well. (If you are determined to poison mice, put the poison in a small diameter pipe around the seedling so larger animals don't eat it instead.) In the long run you are better off with healthy predators. You can set up perches on your land to help hawks and owls spot mice and rabbits. Insecticides can cause harm for unintended victims, the best known example being the use of DDT, which weakened the egg shells of eagles and other prey animals.

Build nesting and shelter sites. If you are energetic, you can build all sorts of boxes for wildlife to nest and sleep in. I have had good luck with bluebirds and wood ducks, but my purple martin house remains empty and no bat has found my bat house. One easy way to help wildlife is to leave snags (standing deadwood) alone, especially oak or basswood. If you want to be especially accommodating, you could cut off some larger branches from a snag, and the resulting knot hole in the tree will form holes for critters. In Germany, foresters often stencil a woodpecker image on trees that have holes suitable for wildlife. These trees in many forests are never cut (in some German states the government will pay the landowner the timber value of such trees which are then left standing). Such a scheme would remove about 10 percent of my trees from timber production. On the other hand, girdled trees frequently generate nesting sites, so

CAUSE AND EFFECT

A forester tried poisoning squirrels in order to leave more seeds to germinate. For a while the scheme seemed to have worked, but eventually most of his seedlings died. It turns out that flying squirrels spread the spores of mycorrhizal fungi, which help trees absorb minerals, and that without the squirrels the seedlings were unable to establish their necessary fungal connections.

---

there may be no need to sacrifice timber trees for that purpose. Some woodland owners stack loose branches and felled trees in piles for rabbit and bird habitat.

Enhance aesthetics. A mixed, uneven-aged, biodiverse, and healthy forest will always be pleasing to your eyes. Just the same, I can think of three ways to improve aesthetics. One is to allow multistem trees (in other words do not insist that all your trees have valuable long and clear boles. Another is to allow some trees to grow lateral branches (don't cut off lower branches to get better lumber). The third strategy is to allow some trees to grow beyond harvestable age. Some oak or maple trees can look stunningly beautiful with great foliage, even though they are hollow and have no lumber value. Such trees are also great for wildlife condominiums.

DOES BIODIVERSITY MAKE SENSE—AND SHOULD WE CARE?

There are extra costs involved in following my recommendations. Indeed, the folks who do short-rotation forestry would consider my methods inefficient, because I do not focus every bit of land, capital, and effort on maximizing timber production. It's not clear, though, that the cost of being a good steward is all that great—nor is it known how many rotations of monocultural plantation a piece of land may support. One glance at a monocultural pulp forest makes it clear that such enterprises are unnatural and uninteresting. I trust you understand the trade-off. For me, the benefits of biodiversity—pleasure, pride, and the satisfaction of your own natural paradise—add up to a very important sum: sustainable vitality of one of our most important natural resources.

This hawk perch is a marvel of rustic engineering. The hawks express their admiration by never perching on it. Such perches are recommended by foresters, however.

fourteen

MANAGING A PERPETUAL MIXED FOREST

German foresters have developed a sustainable forest model known as the Dauerwald, a term which I translate as meaning a perpetual mixed forest, or PMF. Such a forest has a variety of native tree species and is ageless, which means that it has young, adolescent, mature, dying, and dead trees. An ageless forest is different from an even-aged forest where all trees are harvested at the same time. There are three basic rules to be followed in the cultivation of a PMF: no (or very limited) clear-cuts, the presence of trees of all ages and varieties, and ongoing care for selected trees until they are harvested.

There is no blueprint on what a PMF should look like, because by its very nature it is varied and difficult to define. It's a multifaceted, beautiful, and productive forest which may evolve in a variety of ways. If a thousand foresters were to set out to establish a PMF on a bare piece of land, the results would differ in a thousand ways. It is a little bit like an instructor in an art class giving students a blank canvas and a box of paint tubes to paint a picture. The designs will vary a lot, but if the students have learned the basics of design, color, and texture, most results should turn out well. If you apply the recipes given in the previous chapters, your PMF should turn out well. Better yet, it will have your personal imprint. Though planting a variety of trees does not by itself create an ecologically sound biodiverse forest, it is a good beginning.

This description may be a bit idealistic since it assumes that there is a fertile piece of land suited for a mixed forest. Very commonly we find situations offering but limited options to develop a forest. If, for instance, you have dry and sandy soil, your strategic possibilities may be limited, and the site may make planting conifers a good choice. Still, you should always try to vary age classes and species as much as possible. Even with land that on first sight may appear to provide limited options, you may accomplish a lot with a little imagination. Remember the gravel pit described in chapter 4.

THE ATTRIBUTES OF A PMF AND HOW TO NURTURE THEM

Limit clear-cuts. For reasons given throughout this book, clear-cutting should be limited and avoided altogether where practicable.

Favor the best crop trees. When thinning a stand, especially in a commercial thinning, remember this maxim: "Never cut down any tree unless there is a better one of the same species in your stand." (The procedures for crop tree selection and thinning are as laid out in chapter 12.)

Promote an ageless forest. If you preserve your best trees until they are mature, you will almost certainly foster a multiaged forest of young, adolescent, mature, and dead vegetation. Different species mature at different times.

Encourage many species of trees. I warmly endorse the maintenance of many tree species in your forest. Tree species diversity should be one of your selection criteria. In my forest, I even keep a few junk trees such as box elders and ironwood for diversity. It is also a good idea to encourage some nitrogen fixing trees such as black locust.* Having many kinds of trees assures you will always have some timber that the market favors. Further, mixing species of different root configurations tends to maximize utilization of the soil.

In the course of natural succession, shade-intolerant species (such as oak) give way eventually to shade-tolerant species (such as maple). When you thin a stand, however, you create an opportunity for regeneration in the gap created in the forest canopy. If you vary the species in a stand, and vary thinning and harvesting, you can maintain a diversity both of the species and the ages of your trees.

Harvest trees gently. Harvested logs should be removed gently when the ground is frozen or dry, always with the wide end in front. The use of horses is ideal as it minimizes damage to remaining trees. Alternatively, a skidder with a winch is also a nature-friendly harvesting method. Please note that the use of farm tractors can be dangerous. Harvests should take place about every five years (see chapter 19).

---

* Some purists consider the black locust an exotic species to be eliminated in our area. It is so widespread that I have accepted it as a native. It is a nitrogen fixer in the legume family and in the pioneer days its hardness made it ideal for wooden nails. In the South it was harvested so much that some old-timers complain that it is hard to find anymore.

Only mature trees are harvested.* Care should be taken that there are always young trees to take the place of harvested trees. It is difficult to arrange for adolescent trees to be ready to become crop trees after a harvest. This takes planning and thought.

Leave empty spaces in your forested area. You should plan for at least 10 percent of your woodland to become open space such as paths, grassy areas, open vistas, and canopy gaps. This will promote wildlife and make your woodland visually appealing.

Foster biodiveristy. Leave deadwood, encourage a great variety of plants and wildlife, avoid chemicals to the extent possible, and eschew nonnative species. Entrust pest control to nature.

Encourage miniclimates. By encouraging different-sized trees, healthy rim vegetation (the hedges on the edges of the forest), and leaving some areas open, there will be miniclimates throughout your forest. The edge vegetation will block the wind, which furthers the absorption of particulate matter and gaseous impurities from the air. A healthy forest will be cooler in the summer than ambient temperatures and warmer in the winter.

Allow light and rain to penetrate to the forest floor. The forest floor should not be totally shaded. The intermittent harvest of trees allows sunlight to penetrate and encourage vegetation. Ideally your forest floor should have a rich, moist, spongy, nutritious texture with enough sunlight to encourage ground vegetation. Light and rain help in the decomposition of deadwood and leaves. The absorption of water in the forest is very important to nature. Understory vegetation is rich in biodiversity and animal life and useful in the reduction of epicormic sprouting. (Epicormic sprouts are suckers growing out of the bole. They reduce log quality.)

Encourage shade-intolerant trees. The succession of species of trees over time may result in a forest of shade-tolerant trees to the exclusion of others. These shade-tolerant trees, such as basswood, ironwood, and maple, are known as "climax" trees. This can be a serious problem because the climax shade-tolerant trees are not always the most valuable trees and may diminish biodiversity. For instance, deer will have a hard time surviving in a maple forest that offers little forage. There are several ways to encourage shade-intolerant trees such as oak and walnut, including:

(a) Clear-cutting. I am against clear-cutting, but you do clear-cut, keep them small, preferably less than two acres.

(b) Canopy gaps. As you harvest trees, there will be canopy gaps that allow you some latitude to promote the growth of shade-intolerant trees. You can plant or seed or just encourage ambient seedlings. Remember that shade-intolerant trees will grow only if they have direct access to the sun, and it will take some care on your part

---

* Tree maturity is an elusive term. Probably the best definition I encountered is by Molly Beattie, *Working with Your Woodland*, page 123. "A tree is considered biologically mature when, despite adequate growing space, the diameter growth added each year is consistently less than the average growth to date."

to liberate them from oppressing vege-tation. Unless you manage thousands of acres, you should be able to encourage enough intolerant trees to assure a biodi-verse mix of tree species. As pointed out earlier, forestry literature suggests that shade-intolerant seedlings should be planted in an area no smaller than two acres. My forest is living proof that this is nonsense.

(c) Encouraging shade-intolerant trees on the edges of your forest where they will grow naturally.

(d) Employing shelterwood or seed-tree reforestation techniques, that is, al-lowing some seed trees to remain on the site after a harvest to be cut down only after new seedlings have established them-selves.

(e) Liberating desirable shade-intol-erant trees growing in your forest by killing competition. I liberate oaks in late fall and early winter, when they are more visible because they retain their foliage. When you spot an oakling struggling in the shade of taller trees, take your chainsaw to the competitors and make an opening for the oak to have direct access to the sun.

As succession favors the dominance of shade-tolerant trees in large forests, some foresters spend their careers trying to prevent natural succession from occurring. While this may be a problem for large stands, with reasonable care, a small-woodland owner should always be able to make sure that there will be a desired mix of tree species. The fact that succession does not always result in pure maple and basswood forests suggests that nature has a way to maintain a healthy mix of tree species. Does this mean that a small-woodland owner is becoming a part of the successional equilibrium? Well, if our skills as forest owners help in the estab-lishment of a PMF, so much the better!

THE PROBLEMS WITH A PMF

German foresters have grown PMFs since the middle of the last century with great success. Though there are American woodland owners[*] who experiment with sustainable forestry, there are few ad-herents of the Dauerwald philosophy in the United States. American foresters maintain that a clear-cut after each ro-tation is necessary and customary, while my German forestry friends would con-sider such a statement blasphemous. American foresters need to learn to foster a mixed-age-distribution forest where ado-lescent trees are ready and prepared to claim a place in the canopy after a mature tree is harvested. I know of no intrinsic reason why a PMF should not work in this country. And yet:

1. Many American foresters and much of the academic literature think that clear-cutting is a lot more efficient than selective cutting. Clear-cutting is simple, requiring

---

[*] Hans J. Burkhardt, Mendocino County, California, suggests a self-sustaining scheme that would limit harvest in his coniferous forest to 2 percent of the inventory, which approximates annual growth. His ex-tensive study is privately printed.

no great decisions and logs are cut and loaded in record time. But I believe that the benefits of a PMF are so great that it pays to go to a little more trouble and harvest individual trees. Admittedly, prices may be lower because fewer loggers may bid on trees to be selectively cut. On the other hand, you save reforestation expenses. Certainly, for a small-woodland owner, selective cutting should be no problem.

2. When encouraging subcanopy trees to take the place of a harvested crop tree, there is a tendency for shade-tolerant trees, such as maples, ironwood, and basswood, to become dominant. With a little care, this should be a manageable problem, as explained earlier.

3. Commercial U.S. timber operators who are trained in commercial monoculture cannot muster the necessary care to nurture a PMF. In Europe, on the other hand, where the environmental benefits are deemed as important as timber production, there is a tradition of more ecologically sound silviculture. In central Europe wonderful forests based on the Dauerwald principle have been profitable for generations.

Small woodland owners are uniquely qualified to further a PMF by following the suggestions provided in this book. Commercial forests, on the other hand, have cost and time limitations, and those operating them cannot give them the loving care that a small-woodland owner would. For example, large forests are prone to being taken over by shade-tolerant trees that limit tree variety. A small woodland owner, however, can further intolerant plants and thereby foster a PMF. So do not let any academician or commercial forester tell you that clear-cutting is essential to good forest management. This does not apply to you, unless you own thousands of acres (and even then it is a matter of some controversy).

HEDGEROWS

Permit me to stray a bit from the main message of this book to tell you about a subject close to my heart: hedgerows. Besides looking pretty, rows of shrubs or trees growing along the edge of a field, like a PMF, foster biodiversity and improve overall conditions for cultivation. Common in many civilizations, hedgerows were grown in England before the Roman occupation. How do we know? Because the Romans built roads cutting through existing fields, and at some places the hedgerows cut by the road are still in the same alignment.

The type of plants used in a hedgerow does not matter; any shrub or tree will do. Traditionally, native plants are used for hedgerows. The most important thing is to generate a vegetation mass to block the wind. As hedgerows age, they will attract more species of plants. Indeed, British hedgerow enthusiasts date hedgerows by counting the number of plant species they contain. In Britain, hedgerows are often used as fences, and the weaving of plants together ("hedging") has developed into an art form.

I became enthusiastic about hedgerows on a trip to England. Struck by the unaccustomed beauty of the English countryside, it did not take long for me to figure out that the hedgerows were one reason why. And so I set out to learn more about them and found an expert, Jim Brandle, at the University of Nebraska, who maintains that hedgerows, or windbreaks as they are known in the United States, increase the yield of crops. He maintains that you can grow more crops on a field with hedgerows, even when making an allowance for the space they take up, because hedgerows block the wind, which reduces surface moisture evaporation in summer and binds the snow in the winter. They also reduce wind and water erosion; some experts argue that hedgerows would have reduced soil loss by about a third in the Mississippi flood of 1993. They could also filter the agricultural effluent that now pollutes rivers and maritime fishing grounds. As preserves of biodiversity, hedgerows foster many organisms critical to the biological health of crops. These are awesome benefits at a relatively low cost.

I was convinced that America should have hedgerows, so I started the Hedgerow Foundation in 1989. I knew farmers were unabatedly tearing out whatever hedgerows remain in the United States, because they get in the way of their equipment. Farmers have bulldozed thousands of miles of shelterbelts (large hedgerows planted in the 1930s to reduce the damage caused by dust storms). Even the English are starting to uproot their hedgerows (among other reasons, they blame hedgerows for taking away parking spaces along roads). Still, I believed there was a way to convince farmers of the benefits of hedgerows. I was dead wrong. The Hedgerow Foundation could not persuade farmers to plant hedgerows. The only enthusiasts were hunters eager to preserve game bird habitat.

When I set out to find likely candidates for hedgerows, I naively targeted the Allerton Park, a large expanse of farms and parkland in central Illinois governed by an independent foundation for the benefit of the University of Illinois. Generously conceived by a cultured Chicago philanthropist, Allerton Park boasts a pleasant sculpture garden and broad, green spaces. The farms, however, are operated strictly for profit and, perhaps as a consequence, form an unlovely industrial expanse of soybeans and corn that allows no room for other plants or animals in the landscape. The farms' waterways have been straightened and look like sewage ditches and presumably contain a soup of herbicides, insecticides, and fertilizer. I thought nonetheless that Allerton might serve as a demonstration project for the benefits of hedgerows. It could be administered with the help of the University of Illinois's highly regarded school of agriculture and become a model for surrounding farmers. Hedgerows would beautify the landscape and increase crop yields. Paths could be laid out along the hedgerows to attract strolling and bicycling students. I had high hopes that Allerton's board of directors, allied as it was to an academic institution, would embrace such a progressive scheme. I offered to draw up plans at my foundation's expense and to make a presentation to the board. But the board wasn't interested. Perhaps the directors chuckled a bit at this outlandish proposal by an amateur and a dreamer.

When I acquired some agricultural land in Minnesota of my own, nobody was going to stop me from creating a demonstration site to show surrounding farmers that hedgerows work. When I bought the land, I told my share-cropping farmer about my plans. He warned me that it would be impossible for him to maneuver his huge equipment between my hedges, and he produced a letter from a friend in the real-estate business claiming that the presence of hedgerows would reduce the value of my land by half. Furthermore, I was told, my shrubs were certain to plug up tile lines, which would render my fertile fields swampy (tile lines are underground perforated pipes that drain extra water into sewage-type ditches). I was also told that herbicide sprayed on row crops would drift into my hedgerow plants and kill them. I would be a damn fool to insist on hedgerows. But I did. Then a new surprise destroyer of hedgerows surfaced. The Interstate Power Company, which has an easement to traverse my property, sensed an immediate threat and herbicided my ten-inch-high dogwood plants. (I have yet to resolve my conflict with the Interstate Power Company.) Meanwhile, the township road-maintenance crews that apply herbicide to ditches along the roads sometimes aim their poisonous spray beyond the allotted thirty-two feet from the center of the road. It is country ethics that all nongrass vegetation bordering crop land should be destroyed. To hear my tenant, my neighbors, and the local authorities tell it, the beauty of hedgerows is an affectation of city slickers who know nothing about farming. (This is all the more reason to stray from the "proper" path!)

When you travel through the United States and you see vast stretches of agricultural (or should I say industrial?) grain fields without any trees or shrubs, you may rightly surmise that country folk do not much care for environmental niceties such as hedgerows. In Turner County, South Dakota, where I own a small parcel of land, I was surprised that the beautiful cottonwoods, just about the only trees that thrive in the area, had been cut. It turns out that the presence of the cottonwoods increased the township's liability insurance premiums (they tend to shade the road, preventing the sun from thawing snow and ice on the pavement). So they had to go. To say that a massive cottonwood, but not a corn stalk, could pose a threat to vehicles is uncontestable. Yet the notion that the beautiful cottonwoods have to go to save a little on insurance premiums is awful.

It is easy to convince environmentalists that hedgerows are beneficial and aesthetically pleasing. And, surprisingly, even the government is on my side. In Spring 2000, the United States Department of Agriculture (USDA) announced a major initiative to subsidize buffer zones (vegetation along streams) and windbreaks. But no matter how well financed and glossy the brochures, it is difficult to induce farmers to plant hedgerows. For some time, the Farm Ser-vice Agency has provided considerable incentives to grow hedgerows that would emphasize streams meandering through the country. The government pays a hefty rent ($150 per acre, per year) plus a signing bonus. At any rate, it is encouraging that the USDA is promoting hedgerows. However, as I write this, in early 2002, the Bush administration seems intent to cut environmental subsidies, including cost-share funds applicable to hedgerows.

THE HEDGEROW EFFECT ON YOUR TREES

Hedgerows will make any adjacent crop do better. Trees, too, will do much better when growing next to hedgerows. Hedgerows on my farm in Wisconsin had a huge impact on my walnut plantation. I always

Hedgerows are useful and pretty. Common in England, they are rarely seen in the United States.

envisioned having a mixed forest, and in my initial walnut planting on my farm in Wisconsin I planted mostly walnuts, but also pines and wildlife shrubs. I wanted to mix the trees and shrubs randomly for variety—but my forester objected. He said it was just not done that way: "Pines grow next to other pines, and all walnuts are planted together to simplify pruning and harvesting." I succeeded in negotiating a compromise: We planted rows of pines throughout the walnut plantation. This turned out to be a happy solution, because over time the rows of pines functioned as hedgerows. The walnuts next to the pines did much better than the walnuts a few yards away. Today, twenty years later, walnuts planted next to pines are doing extremely well, often towering over them, while walnuts a few rows away look puny. (See color section photo #5.)

My very knowledgeable forester believes that much of my plantation suffers from an eroded soil condition. At one time he suggested abandoning walnuts in favor of other hardwoods or pines. The advantage of growing next to pines may have offset the disadvantage of poor soil. The disparity is particularly striking in the early fall, when walnuts not growing near the pines have lost their leaves, while the walnuts next to the pines are dark green and still photosynthesizing. Similarly, in the spring, walnuts next to pines leaf out weeks before walnuts just a few rows away.

I have asked experts why my walnuts grow better next to the pine hedgerows, and they have offered the following explanations: The fast-growing pines protect the walnuts from the wind (particularly if the hedgerows run north to south, blocking the prevailing west winds). As a result, the walnuts benefit from increased soil-moisture levels because the wind absorbs less moisture on the lee side of hedgerows. (It is noteworthy, however, that my walnuts do better on both sides of the rows of pines, not just the lee side.) Pines may kill grass, allowing walnut roots to spread. Pine litter may disrupt the dispersal of anthracnose, a spore capable of damaging walnut foliage. Finally, the pines create a microclimate that accelerates plant growth. Whatever the reasons for the wonderful benefits of hedgerows, your trees will do better when intermingled with other trees, such as pines.*

I hope you see underlying connections between hedgerows and a mixed forest. Trees love company, and a community of diverse plants increases the health of a forest and produces better trees. Hedge rows at the edges of a forest greatly increase forest life. Hedges are full of birds and insects, and they create a cooler microclimate in the summer and a slightly warmer one in the winter. Hedgerows, along with the mixed forests, provide more biodiversity, resistance to disturbances, abundant wild-life, excitement, and beauty.

---

* It is accepted in the literature that juglone (an allelotoxin released by some nut trees, including walnuts) will eventually retard the growth of nearby pines. On my farm, however, pines and walnuts are essentially the same height and doing well. A knowledgeable friend, Jerry Van Sambeek, theorizes that my experience is a site-specific exception.

sixteen

MAVERICKS OF FORESTRY

Forestry, like any field of endeavor, is indebted to the contribution of creative individuals who have had the imagination and persistence to stand athwart the conventional ways of doing things. Often such innovators figured things out on their own, free from the constraints of academic or industrial consensus. In writing this book, I crossed paths with three unusual foresters. All three share one thing in common: They all pursue their forestry in unusual, but very practical and sensible ways. They do what works best for them, and it seems as though they are on a right track.

WILHELM BODE: A CIVIL SERVANT IN CONFLICT WITH THE ESTABLISHMENT

German foresters are engaged in a hot debate on how to grow trees, with conservatives advocating monocultural pine production and the opposition, largely members of the very large Naturschutz Verein (Society for the Preservation of Nature, a sympathetic do-gooder organization), favoring mixed forests.

Wilhelm Bode's book *Waldwende* is the bible for mixed forests, providing information on the one-hundred-fifty-year-old tradition of growing mixed forests. Interestingly, the practitioners of this philosophy were not foresters but independent, amateur woodland owners (the most famous German mixed forest was owned and managed by a surgeon). They were interested in lowering production costs of wood and less concerned with biodiversity and sustainability (I don't know if these words even had been invented yet). Their main interest was to produce the most wood with the least effort. The basic philosophy of mixed forest rests in a conviction that a naturally occurring, indigenous forest will continuously produce great trees and require relatively little direction.

Wilhelm Bode.

Wilhelm Bode was recruited to reintroduce mixed forests in the Saarland, a state in the southwest of the German Republic. As chief forester, he helped to get laws passed outlawing clear-cutting and helped to reintroduce mixed forests. Thanks to his reforms the Saarland is known for the success in rejuvenating its forests. He did not accomplish this, however, without alienating certain people. He asserted himself against forestry academics and also insisted that his workers be allowed to hunt in public forests, an unheard-of proposition at the time, much resented by the hunting establishment.

Bode's natural scheme of establishing a forest is called the three Gs: *Gatter, Geduld, und Gewehr*, which translates to "fence, patience, and gun." To establish a forest you fence in an area to keep the deer out, you allow nature to take its course, and you shoot any deer that threaten the scheme.

Bode was happily and successfully doing his job when he became inconvenient to the minister-president of the Saarland and was excused from his duties. The strict German civil-service laws make it impossible for the government to dismiss a bureaucrat as long as he does not steal or sexually harass his subordinates. So Bode still "works" for the government. He maintains an office and a secretary but has nothing official to do.

Wilhelm Bode is not idly occupying his office. For seven years he turned out a steady stream of literature, generally critical of the establishment. His latest book, *Jagdwende*, is a frontal attack on the hunting establishment. From feudal times to the present, the hunting lobby has dominated German forestry. Because of political pressure from hunters, German foresters have had to tolerate a very high population of huntable animals on their land. Deer are so plentiful that they make it difficult to grow trees without fencing all emerging young forest stands. Luckily, the German deer is smaller than the white-tail of North America and does not jump nearly as high.

The situation is absurd. There are nearly ten times more huntable animals in Germany now than a century ago. They increase the cost of wood production, reduce biodiversity, and cause thousands of car accidents. Politically, it is difficult to fight the status quo. Hunters are well represented, and the German populace likes to see animals on their walks. German farmers and landowners have been conditioned to tolerate the nuisance of deer overpopulation. The fact that most deer are undernourished and unhappy does not seem to matter.

In the United States, a widely published intellectual of Bode's stature might be offered a forestry faculty appointment at a prestigious university. This is not an option in Germany's state-run universities, where only academics with PhDs and who have advanced through the academic ranks are considered for faculty positions. Wil-

helm's academic training is primarily in law, although he does have the equivalent of a masters of science in forestry.

Through all his professional trials, Wilhelm Bode has maintained his sensible policy positions with conviction. Much to the distress of Oskar LaFontaine, a famous German politician who sparred with Bode until recently stepping down as the minister-president of the Saarland, Bode enjoys tremendous popularity with environmental organizations, students, and the press. *Der Spiegel*, the largest German weekly, recently published a feature article on Bode. Bode also has been assigned to the Environmental Section for Nature and Humanity (Leitender Ministerialrat, Leiter der Abteilung Natur und Mensch). He is still a very active speaker and a prolific author on environmental matters in Germany. He will busily continue writing about the imperfections of German forestry management and foster his sensible positions. He is energetic, young, and tough.

LARRY KROTZ: A HERETICAL TREE FARMER

Larry Krotz, a retired Air Force fighter pilot, has a remarkable tree plantation in southeastern Iowa. On sixty-five acres, he grows an abundance of mostly deciduous trees very close together and very straight. His rules are: (1) plant seeds densely; (2) do very little thinning; and (3) do very little pruning.

The results are extraordinary. His trees, as close as a few inches apart, are extremely straight and very tall. Larry's walnut trees reach a height of nine feet in their third growing season. As for pruning, Larry says: "Don't worry about it, nature will take care of the problem. The weaker trees will die." How about forks? "That matters not a bit. In a few decades, you won't be able to tell the difference. Anyway, whenever I prune a tree, I find I do more damage than good. Let nature do it." How about thinning the trees to give the better trees more space? Larry Krotz wants no space between trees. When sunlight hits the bole, the quality of the veneer wood is jeopardized. When a tree considers developing epicormic sprouts (sprouts, or suckers, grow from dormant buds beneath the bark on a larger branch or stem of the tree), damage is done to the log internally, regardless of whether a sprout appears or not. Larry claims that a good log buyer can tell the difference. When his trees become big, he interplants basswood, ironwood, and maple (they all grow in the shade) to make sure that no sunbeam hits his bole. This is extreme heresy!

Larry clears some understory vegetation for one reason only: to kill deer. He kills all the deer he can, regardless

Larry Krotz.

of the season, and makes no secret of it. He has lost hundreds of thousands of trees to the animals and has declared war. He does not eat the venison—"that would be poaching"—and apparently nobody takes offense at his "Bambian" wars. The problem is that Larry's farm is an oasis surrounded by thousands of acres of grain land. So when it gets cold, deer like to hang out at Larry's for cover and to nibble on his trees. After all, there is not much else to eat. "The DNR sets deer hunting quotas so low they endanger my woodland operation," Larry says. You might expect Larry to invite hunters to help solve the problem, but he doesn't want their stray bullets to ruin the veneer quality of his trees. What about Larry's bullets? "I never miss. Also an element of surprise is in my favor since I shoot out of season." Larry's not worried about getting arrested. He is convinced that justice is on his side. Apparently the DNR, which normally takes a dim view of such behavior, has avoided the challenge.

While in the military, Larry spent some time in Germany. He visited the forests south of Frankfurt, where the Bavarian state grows oak trees on a three-hundred-year cycle. Initially, the raison d'etre of the oaks was to feed acorns to the boars that the noblemen loved to hunt. The trees grow very slowly, adding rings of about one millimeter per year, and produce the best veneer wood anywhere. A good tree will bring $30,000 at an auction. The seeded stand area is fenced to keep wildlife out, and by the time the fence breaks down, the trees are big enough to survive. Larry believes that these trees are the most perfect trees cultivated anywhere, rivaling the quality of original hardwood stands in North America. Larry wants to duplicate the feat.

Larry Krotz's seeding philosophy is very straightforward: Seed many. Larry believes in mixing up all kinds of trees, just as they grow in nature. If you mimic nature, you cannot go wrong. To plant walnuts he recommends this method: Stick a shovel into the dirt, push it forward, toss in two nuts under the shovel, pull out the shovel and close the hole with your boot. He is not at all worried that the two seeds will produce two plants that will fight each other for survival. The better will prevail. Larry talks about matching a

dream tree, cut in New York in 1829. It was two hundred feet tall with a diameter of eleven feet and no lateral branching for sixty feet.

It is practically impossible to plant just a few trees per acre and expect to get quality veneer trees. It took me years to assimilate the simple fact that trees, no matter how tender and lovingly cared for, will not grow like Krotz's two-hundred-foot wonder. It would be very hard to cultivate such a tree and, unfortunately, there is no financial incentive to grow a tree this tall. As a financial analyst, I figure that the prospect of a harvest three hundred years hence is too remote to make it an interesting investment. It will be difficult to find owners with the discipline not to harvest such trees long before their prime. Still, the Germans have been doing it. But unless your objective is to harvest trees sometime around A.D. 2300, I propose not using Larry's scheme.*

I much enjoyed visiting the Krotz plantation, although I must admit that I was itching to do a little pruning. Some of Larry's trees have multiple stems (in particular the silver maples), and Larry maintains that in a few decades all but one stem will die. Expert tree farmers, and even we amateurs, can learn a lot from Larry. There is no doubt in my mind that his densely planted walnuts, up to pole size, are unrivaled. While our walnut trees will be chopped and forgotten, the Krotz trees will tower over the countryside, a monument to a farsighted tree farmer.

Larry loves his tree farm and readily

---

* Employing the analysis procedure explained in Chapter 21, the present value of a perfect 300-year-old oak tree is 32 cents.

relates his philosophy to interested parties. Two years ago he was elected president of the Walnut Council. It speaks well for this traditionally stodgy organization to choose a leader with such novel ways of growing trees.

DAVE JOHNSON: DOING THINGS SENSIBLY BUT DIFFERENTLY

As I state repeatedly, forestry is an art: There are few right answers, and reasonable people may do things very differently. So if you think that you have mastered the basics, you may come across someone who violates all the rules and surprisingly still maintains a nature-friendly forest.

A case in point is Dave Johnson. Dave and his wife, Marcia, devised a very smooth technique of harvesting logs on their red-pine plantation. They work as a team, a dream of economy and efficiency. Every motion and every detail is rationalized, starting with

Dave Johnson.

calorie intake, the girth of his chain saw, the type of fuel, and the division of labor.

The Johnsons own a large plantation of red pines established about sixty years ago on sandy land. Once all their pines have been cut, they intend to clear-cut and replant a new rotation. Now they are engaged in commercial harvesting, thinning the stand of twelve-inch-diameter trees. Marcia selects the tree to be cut, and Dave fells it. When necessary, Marcia inserts a felling bar to assure that the tree falls in the intended direction. Once felled, the tree is limbed and cut into twelve-foot sticks. (Dave uses a tape with a tack at the end to measure the twelve-foot sections.) I timed the process—it took ninety seconds. The pace is steady, but not rushed. They sell their logs by the ton, and Dave is proud that he gets more for them than anybody else.

The Johnsons work three hours per day, nine months per year, and earn about $40,000 on their 441 acres. They are happy: They love working together, and they work together well. It is a good and healthy life. The Johnsons have been very active in the Wisconsin Woodland Owners Association in the past but no longer attend meetings. Dave wrote a useful and highly readable book, *The Good Woodcutter's Guide*, published by Chelsea Green.

Dave and Marcia Johnson are aware that they could sell their land (the current price is expensive—around $3,000 an acre—since it is only 70 miles north of Madison) and the sale of about 100 acres would allow them not to do any work for the rest of their lives and still maintain the style of living to which they are accustomed. "We are not interested in doing that," Dave says. He is not the couch-potato type.

Dave considers himself an environmentally concerned woodland owner who practices sustainable forestry. Yet he is clearly in violation with what "environmentally correct" authors (like me) consider the rules of forest management. Consider Dave's "violations" according to my principles:

He plants red pines, a nonnative species. They are well suited for the Johnsons' sandy soil, but they are not native to the area, hailing from northern Wisconsin.

He practices monocultural silviculture. This is said to be nature unfriendly and prone to disturbance such as disease, fire, and windthrow.

He doesn't foster biodiversity. There are only three kinds of trees on the Johnson farm. Primarily, there are red pines, Dave's money tree. Then there are some white pines, which do not do as well because of tip weevils and a lack of soil fertility. On the positive side, Dave encourages white pines, being more shade tolerant, to establish themselves naturally

among his scrub oaks. His farm has relatively little wildlife.

His harvesting method is tantamount to clear-cutting.

The question is, can one fault Dave's management scheme? What is the alternative? Before the red pines were planted, there was a lot of sand and scrub oaks. I presume that the oaks provided a better wildlife habitat than pines, and there probably was more biodiversity, certainly more deer. Either way, over time more soil should accumulate through the decay of trees, and the land will become a bit more fertile in the future.

On the positive side, the land produces timber useful to society and it provides the Johnsons with an enjoyable existence. I cannot find fault with what Dave is doing. I might recommend that he put more emphasis on natural tree generation, and I suspect that he really doesn't need to clear-cut and replant. I believe that natural regeneration would produce a more nature-friendly forest than a clear-cut. But I like the fact that he encourages white pines to grow among his scrub oaks. He is not enthused about natural regeneration of pines because he believes that thinning would be quite labor intensive (notice the contradiction to Larry Krotz's philosophy).

Strangely, Dave says that he is the only landowner in the area engaged in cutting and marketing his own trees. His commercial thinning will produce good red pines. The Johnson's thinned stand is more beautiful than any other stand I have seen in the area. Neighboring landowners tend to have their timber harvested by commercial loggers, and the result is bound to be less gratifying and frequently injurious to the forest. Furthermore, Dave probably gets better prices than his neighbors, because his buyer knows that the Johnson logs are consistently cut to size (six inches at the small end), freshly cut, and neatly piled up for an easy pick up. The Johnsons are caring and responsible woodland owners.

The question then becomes, what about all the rules I postulate in this book? How can I stand by what I write and still like Dave Johnson's operation? It boils down to the dictum on first page of this book. "The only general rule in silviculture is there are no rules."

Much of the acreage surrounding the Johnsons is devoted to potato production. It turns out that the sandy soil is ideal for that crop, particularly when irrigated. Potato farmers love irrigation because it makes it easy to administer their myriad chemicals efficiently. Dave tells me that potato farmers hate rain because it interferes with the application of the prescribed chemical cocktail. Interestingly, a friend of mine has seen the following sign in a local grocery store: "These potatoes are not from around here." Sadly, most of the chemicals end up in the aquifer. So while Dave's forest is producing clean water, his neighboring potato farmers are polluting the aquifers. Then why are the feds subsidizing aquifer-polluting farmers, while a subsidy for woodland owners is not even under consideration?

CONIFERS

There is an extensive body of knowledge on commercial coniferous plantations: how close to plant them, when to thin them, how fast they grow, and how much income they provide. Most commercial tree plantations in the United States and Europe tend to be coniferous monocultures, lacking in biodiversity. I encourage small-woodland owners to interplant deciduous trees amid their conifers whenever possible, but there are situations where soil and climate conditions make a purely coniferous stand the best option. For example, scotch pine will grow on dry sandy soil where it would be difficult to establish a mixed forest. In light of just these situations, and since cultivating conifers requires different procedures than cultivating hardwood, I want to make the following points:

Conifers are relatively easy to establish and to care for. They are easy to plant because the seedlings are small and straight and have simple root structures, not prone to rootbinding. More importantly, conifers grow on virtually any type of soil and are relatively immune to pernicious grasses—a huge advantage. One application of a herbicide as part of the planting operation will generally suffice to establish the seedlings even amid hostile vegetation. Conifer seedlings are sensitive to overspray with herbicide, so never apply more than the minimum recommended doses. The survival rates for conifer seedlings is high.

And since they grow very straight on their own they require only minimal corrective pruning. Occasionally they become "doubleheaders," but that can be corrected quite easily by cutting off one of the stems. If your trees are destined for a paper mill, you need not prune them at all. If they are destined to become lumber, you should plan two lateral prunings, one at age fifteen (when you should prune up to eight feet), and another at age thirty (prune up to sixteen feet). As a rule, you should not prune more than one-half of the height of the tree. Pruning is an elementary, straightforward task, done quickly and with relatively little effort. It's fun and satisfying because the result of your labor is readily apparent and dramatic. I should add that Dave Johnson, who owns a red-pine plantation (see chapter 16), does not view pruning as a cost-effective activity.

Coniferous forests tend to offer relatively limited biodiversity. The forest floor of a coniferous forest is totally shaded out and almost devoid of vegetation. An acidic floor of needles inhibits the growth of all but a few shrubs and weeds. Deer find little to eat, though conifers provide shelter from the cold. There will be squirrels and some birds, but fewer species of birds than in a mixed forest. If you ever have occasion to fly over Georgia, the Carolinas, or northern Florida, you will be astonished to observe huge expanses of coniferous plantations, laid out in squares and periodically clear-cut and herbicided to keep out deciduous vegetation (which is considered a weed to be exterminated). Owning such a forest would most likely give you little pleasure.

Thinning a coniferous forest is easy—and should be profitable. In general you should cull about one-third of the stand at each thinning. Of course, you should always thin the most inferior trees and leave the best. But as a practical matter, most conifers are much alike, and the easiest way to thin is to eliminate whole rows of trees. Most growers either eliminate every third row or every other row in the first thinning. If your pines are destined solely for pulp in a paper mill, you may not need to thin at all. If you intend to produce timber trees, you should thin first when your stand is about twenty years old. You may sell the culled trees for pulp. Your second thinning will produce either pulp or timber trees; the time to thin is a judgment call, depending on your aims. Pulp trees should be at least ten inches in diameter. You may reasonably expect to do the second thinning within forty years of planting.

The remaining trees should become stately and make excellent lumber. If you have a chance, allow other trees to invade your coniferous stand. At times I find elm trees invading a stand of pines. I used to cut them down, but now I keep them for diversity. The third thinning—which really varies in timing according to a number of factors, such as the market for various timber products and soil fertility—should be selective, which means that you choose the trees to be cut or left standing based on any criteria you deem appropriate. Your county forester may offer good suggestions, but be open to a second opinion. It's best if you base the cutting opinion on your fancy, and generally there are no right or wrong answers. Right after thinning is a good time to introduce some other species to start your PMF. Often different species will appear on their own without your doing anything. Remember that any new species of tree in your monocultural stand could be a beginning to a PMF forest. It won't flourish in your lifetime, but it will be on its way.

Conifers are highly combustible. Especially in dry years, conifers are a fire hazard because they contain a combustible petroleum-related resin that acts as a sort of antifreeze to prevent freezing of plant tissue in winter. This tarlike resin was used for the manufacture of turpentine and pitch, staple commodities until the Industrial Revolution. Its presence explains why coniferous wood makes great kindling. Once conifers catch fire, the flames spread from tree to tree, often at a frightening speed, and even your fire department can do little about it. The best way to guard against this is to build a firebreak somewhere downwind. Conifers interspersed in a mixed forest do not constitute as great a fire hazard, and such stands resist forest fires.

Conifers have a beneficial effect on deciduous plantations. Although monocultural deciduous plantations often do not work out as well as your forester may have promised, deciduous trees will grow much better next to conifers. If you have an underperforming plantation, like my walnut trees, you may consider interplanting pines.* The pines may help other trees to grow better. I call this the hedgerow effect. I am proud to be one of the early pioneers of this technique in southern Wisconsin.

It pays to know the value of different kinds of conifers. The market value differs for different species of conifers. For pulp, currently jack pine is high in demand, and red pine is more valuable than white pine. For timber white pine is best. It would make sense to plant a mixture of red pine and white pine, harvest the red pine for pulp, and retain the white pines for timber. The woodland owner could eventually add some deciduous trees and enjoy a mixed forest while the white pines grow tall, towering over everything.

Blister rust is a threat to white pine, but a treatable one. Since I lack the expertise of a plant physiologist, I can say very little about the health problems of trees. I do know that there is no effective treatment for many diseases. For instance, butternuts, elms, and American chestnuts die even with the best of care. However, at least one exception—blister rust—is very treatable. It afflicts white pines, and its primary symptom is a dead branch, which

---

* I used red pines, but white pines would have been better because some walnut trees, as if sensing competition, are threatening to overshadow some of the red pines, which are less shade-tolerant than white pines. I have also heard of other foresters successfully using aggressively managed silver maples as a nurse tree.

takes on a rust color that stands out from the green, healthy branches of the tree. If you see a dead, rusty branch on a white pine, cut it off. Once the blisters spread to the main stem, the tree is doomed and eventually may also infect its neighbors. I cut down diseased trees, which appears to prevent the spread of blister rust to neighboring trees. There is no need to burn or otherwise dispose of the affected tree.

It is not an exaggeration to say that it requires virtually no skill to grow conifers. They grow with little maintenance, and if a woodland owner does nothing more than call the woodcutters at appropriate times, his stands should show some profit. The shorter the growing rotation, the higher the profit. Pulpwood in Georgia is grown in twenty-year rotations. Of course, such "industrial" stands are relatively poor in diversity and wildlife. Can a forest sustain many rotations of coniferous harvests forever? I do not have the answer. Critics maintain that repeated cycles of clear-cutting—and that is usually how coniferous forests are harvested—diminish the fertility of the land. Others maintain that coniferous monocultures inflict no observable ill effects on the ecosystem. I side with the critics, but in any event the small-woodland owner will do best who treats his forest not as a source from which to extract pulp, but as a rich and delicate resource to be husbanded.

eighteen

HIRING A CONSULTING FORESTER

Throughout this book, I have recommended that you develop a good relationship with your county forester. The quality and time commitment of your county forester varies with local conditions. Richland County, Wisconsin, where my farm is, has good county foresters who really love their work. It's not surprising: The surrounding country is pretty, and woodland owners there care about their forests and are interesting to work with. Over the years, I have enjoyed working with all my county foresters. I think they enjoyed working with me, since I always picked their brains and was willing to try new things. Even though I've worked on my land for thirty years and written a book about it, I still know that the DNR foresters are more knowledgeable than I am. That doesn't mean I have not disagreed with them on occasion.

County foresters typically take care of hundreds of landowners, and they have to divide their time and effort among them. Consequently, your county forester will probably devote less time to your woodland than you wish. If you want more professional attention, you should consider hiring a consulting forester. Your DNR forester will be glad to give you a list of consulting foresters (generally all have forestry degrees). Your DNR forester is not supposed to recommend a specific consultant, but with a little probing you can often sense whom he likes best.

Consulting foresters charge about $50–60 an hour—well worth the money if you can afford it. Of course a consulting forester's fees may not add to your bottom line, but this is true with any expenditure in your woodland. Nonetheless, a consulting forester will help you enjoy your land and enhance your forestry skills, which is more important.

Consulting foresters make the most money when helping you arrange for a timber sale because they customarily receive a commission of about 10 percent of harvest proceeds. So be suspicious of consulting foresters too intent on conducting timber sales. A more productive use of a consultant is to walk your land with her, rather than giving her clerical tasks, such as taking inventories. You will learn a lot by just talking to a competent forester and working with her on projects. It should add significantly to your enjoyment of your woodland.

A consulting forester might work with you on the following projects:

Assist you in planning and executing a timber sale. The charge is generally 10 percent, and the task constitutes a relatively lucrative proposition for a consulting forester. Since the exposure to being taken advantage of by timber buyers is considerable, the services of a forester may be a good idea.

Walk with you on your land. A forester will see a lot of things you likely won't notice on your own. She might, for instance, point out wildlife activity and help you identify trees. It is fun to listen to her and pick her brain.

Help you buy and sell land. Though consulting foresters are rarely real-estate brokers, they often know woodland owners interested in buying or selling. Chances are that they have a pretty good idea of the price at which woodlands are selling. They are also good people to consult before you commit yourself to buying any woodland.

Write a management plan. Your county forester will draw up a management plan, but in Wisconsin and some other states, the DNR will under certain conditions accept a management plan from a consulting forester. In some states, such as Vermont, a consulting forester, and not the county forester, writes management plans at the woodland owner's expense. One reason to use a consulting forester for this purpose is that her plan will typically be more detailed and comprehensive, integrating your special interests and wishes.

Help you sign up for cost-shared practices. The nature of these programs changes a lot, and it is good to have a consulting forester to tell you what programs are available.

Establish a forest. A consulting forester can help you plan a seeding or planting. She can analyze your soil profile, point out indicator plants, and advise you what kind of trees will be suitable for your site.

Help you buy supplies and equipment and show you how to operate it safely. If you are a novice, for example, it is a good idea to have somebody show you how to safely operate and maintain your chain saw.

Work on special problems and projects. A consulting forester should be able to advise you on how to convert a sumac field or a prickly ash plot into a forest, or how to get vegetation going in a gravel pit. Suppose you have a forested ridge, and you want to cut down some trees to make a vista. A consulting forester can help you plan it. Or, if you want to establish a prairie-grass field, she can put you in contact with a prairie-grass expert and plan the kind of grasses and flowers you desire.

Lay out paths on your land. Good paths are absolutely essential for maintenance and for pleasure. You will enjoy your land more if you have nice paths for walking, gatoring, snowmobiling, cross-country skiing, or running. A good consulting forester can lay out an arrangement for you and find somebody to implement the plan. (See color section photo #11.)

Help you maintain your roads. It is important that your roads resist erosion.

Burn. Burning is useful and fun. But it can also be tricky, especially around conifers. It helps to have a consulting forester present to guide and help you.

Help you with thinning, timber stand improvement, and other silvicultural practices.

Help you attract wildlife. It is nice to install nesting boxes for birds, or bat houses. Some silvicultural practices will attract wildlife.

Help you fight pests. Are there too many ladybugs, too much ragweed, too many coyotes, too many deer, too many mice, too many trespassers on your land? Your consulting forester can give you some idea on how to address these problems.

Define your borders. Sometimes the borders between your land and your neighbor's are not well defined. A consulting forester can help you to determine your property line.

Get an aerial photo of your land. It is fun to see your land from the perspective of a pilot, and it is not too expensive. Having an aerial photo of your property can also be very useful for planning and making maps. I would like to have a fun rendering of my land that I can give to guests. I have not found a consulting forester willing and able to produce a map for me; I'll have to find someone else for that. Having an aerial photo is a start. You may also obtain an old aerial photo, which gives you some idea on how your land has changed in preceding decades.

Introduce you to other landowners who share your interests.

Take inventory of your timber stands.

Help you prepare Schedule C of your federal tax return.

Plan and build a pond on your land. It's getting more difficult to get clearance from the government to build a pond (generally you are only allowed to dam water that originates on your land), but if you do get permission, a consulting forester can help you do it right.

Landscape around your buildings.

Determine the profitability of your forestry operation.

All in all, I encourage you to hire a consulting forester. She will help you to learn more about your land, which in turn will help you enjoy your woodland more.

nineteen

HARVESTING

If you are an average woodland owner, you will own your property for around twenty years and may never conduct a timber sale. Bearing this in mind, I will limit myself to high-lighting the basic issues regarding harvesting.

In conducting a sale on your property, you have to trust somebody for advice. I used to think that sawmill buyers, who have to preserve their reputation to do business in a local market, could be trusted. I have attended meetings of foresters and woodland owners where any suggestion of trusting a timber buyer elicited smiles. Nor can you count on the reputation of timber buyers as a reference. A local consulting forester, Mark Mittelstadt, stated that "the sleaziest ones are still in business and often do financially better than the decent buyers. . . . The typical landowner in a do-it-yourself sale will get high-graded [see pages 148 and 149], will receive about half of the market value of the timber, and will get some screwy misadvice about management." Personally, I have dealt with timber buyers on small TSI harvests and I have no idea whether I got an acceptable deal. However, TSI harvests are generally small in volume and do not generate much interest from buyers. I have conducted sales with the county forester with good results. In Wisconsin, however, the county forester is limited in the volume of sales he can conduct for any one landowner.

You should make sure that you get an honest count on your trees, and that only marked trees are harvested. Though most sawmills' log buyers will be happy to mark the trees for you, it's a better idea to do it yourself or to have a forester do it. (You should keep in mind, however, that your consulting forester's pay goes up in proportion to the number of trees he marks.) Once the trees are marked, you or your forester has to prepare a fact sheet to announce the sale to log buyers. The information provided should give the size of the harvest (so many thousands of board feet), the species of trees, location, and any other particulars. You will have to determine whether the timber is to be sold on the stump (in other words, standing) or whether somebody else will cut the logs and bring them to a landing (i.e., a staging area) for buyers to bid on.

You should also be aware that the men felling trees and operating skidders (the machines that drag logs to a landing) get paid by the sawmill by the volume they cut—not by the care they take to minimize the damage to trees they leave standing. Careless loggers can inflict serious damage to your land and trees, and you'll want to protect yourself against that.

MANAGING THE HARVESTING PROCESS

Keep in mind that all harvesting decisions ultimately rest with you, even if you have sought the counsel of a forester. Loggers will typically recommend harvesting merchandisable trees as small as sixteen inches in diameter. Don't be swayed. Cutting immature trees of little value is a bad idea. Trees show their most vigorous growth when they are between fifteen and twenty inches in diameter, at which point their growth can exceed 12 percent per year. A fifteen-inch oak tree now worth $100 could be worth $500 twenty years from now. So do not cut trees in the teens (between 13 and 19 inches) unless you need to make room for a superior tree nearby, or unless they are on a poor site where they will not grow much more.

Trees can be felled any time, but skidding (dragging the logs to the landing site) does the least damage to your land when the ground is frozen. So, the middle of the winter is an ideal time for harvesting, although it is also acceptable to harvest at other times as long as the ground is dry, such as in late summer or fall. Harvesting when it is wet greatly increases the likelihood of erosion, since a skidder pulling heavy logs can cause incredible ruts in muddy terrain. Another timing consideration is the availability of seeds. If you expect oak seedlings to reforest the holes left by a timber harvest, it is best to harvest after a plentiful crop of seeds. Finally, if you harvest oaks in late spring and summer, you need to be careful to minimize scraping the trees left standing because of a possibility of oak wilt infection. For that reason some foresters discourage logging oaks before August.

When selecting the trees to be harvested, you're the boss. Beware that timber buyers are most interested in fat and straight timber trees. If you let them, they will often cut all trees above a certain diameter ("taking the best and leaving the rest"). This is called "high-grading," and you should avoid it. The problem with high-grading is that you tend to be left with a stand of trees of inferior shapes and species, such as aspens, birches, ironwood, box elders, and elms. If left unattended, the stand will degenerate into a low-quality forest.

You should also remember a suggestion I made earlier: Always cut the most inferior tree before cutting your best. You should upgrade your forest so as to maintain large, well-formed trees for future harvests. I urge you to be personally involved in deciding which trees are to be cut.

Set the price for your logs in the way most advantageous to you. You can sell your logs by the board foot or by the log on the stump. Selling on the stump is the easiest, the most straightforward, and requires the least difficulties in negotiating. You mark the trees and a buyer decides how much they are worth. A large sale will attract several interested buyers. If you only sell a few logs (for instance, if you're doing TSI) you may have difficulty finding a buyer willing to bid, and you may have to sell cheaply (not that it really matters—the point of TSI is to remove trees and improve your stand). Timber is most commonly sold on the stump. Rudy Nigl, my former county forester, maintains that you'll get a higher price selling on the stump. Other foresters have different ideas. If your logs are good, they say, you get more after they have been assembled at a landing. The reason is that it is difficult for a timber-buyer to look at a stately oak tree and determine whether it's solid or hollow. A conservative timber buyer may assume that large trees are

hollow and not attach any value to them. As with so many decisions in forestry, you are faced with an unknown. Whatever the method of sale you choose, says Rudy, under no circumstances should you let your logs leave the premises until you have been paid.

Mark your harvest trees carefully. Most commonly trees to be harvested are marked with a paint gun by you or a forester. It is best to mark two spots on the tree: one at eye level to be seen by the logger and a second spot at the base to assure that only designated trees are harvested.

Insist on sustainable harvesting methods. As you have read, I discourage clear-cuts because they tend to be ecologically damaging to your land. If you do any clear-cutting, try to limit its size to an area not much larger than a few acres. I favor selective cutting of mature timber, leaving enough younger trees to assure harvests in subsequent years. Selective harvesting is better for your land, but it will increase harvesting costs. Another alternative technique is "shelter wood management," where you leave seed trees to be harvested after new seedlings are established.

It may be efficient to mark inferior trees for removal at the time of harvest. It is not uncommon that all trees over four inches in diameter are removed. I think such a scheme is extreme and that more thought should be given in the selection of future crop trees beyond the categorical removal of trees of any given size.

Be careful building roads. To get at a stand that you're harvesting you may have to build logging roads, which generally means using a bulldozer. Road-building is a major cause of erosion, so you'll need to be careful. Above all, you should not allow your logging road to become a waterway. Roads should be pitched to the downhill (outsloped) side to allow water runoff, and where necessary you should include open ducts to let water flow across the road or culverts to let it flow underneath. The diversion channel (pictured on page 151) is on the road leading to my house. It works quite well and has solved an annoying erosion problem. You can also build water bars every twenty-five to a hundred feet to channel water downhill off the road. Water bars are bumps in the road high enough to divert water downhill. They are easy to build and effective. After logging, it is a good idea to spread some grass seed to minimize further erosion. If there is a creek to be crossed, you need to decide who will build a bridge—you or the loggers—as well as how much it will cost and whether it will remain in place after the harvest. Typically, a logger will chain some logs together to serve as a temporary bridge.

Extract your logs as unobtrusively as possible. An environmentally friendly method of getting logs to the logging roads is a system of winches and cables. Extracting logs by suspending them from cables does less damage to the forest than the use of heavy equipment.* German foresters don't allow skidders to move about in the woods, so all logs are dragged by cable to a logging road. Unfortunately, this is not customary in the United States. In general, the larger the skidding equip-

ment, the longer the distance to the landing area, and the sloppier the operator, the more damage is done to your land. Large logging equipment compacts your soil and puts deep ruts in your roads (compaction is considerably mitigated when the ground is frozen). Using access roads when they are wet can cause serious erosion.

The least harmful way to extract logs is with horses. This method will increase the cost of harvesting, and you'll have to cut the logs shorter because they might be too bulky and heavy to be handled by horses. This may be undesirable for some buyers. Moreover, horses are hard to find in some areas. I am fortunate to have Amish neighbors with lots of horses.

Leave trees for mast, seeds, wild-life, and aesthetics. It's your forest, and you should decide what emphasis to put on nonmonetary considerations. Very often, harvested areas look like a moonscape and can put you (and your land) in a deep state of shock. Harvesting selectively and leaving some trees standing is a good idea to minimize the visual impact. The remaining trees in the harvested area will form the future forest. I always leave some senior citizen oak trees, which look beautiful, provide lots of acorns for wildlife, and function as wildlife condos.

Don't be obsessed with removing the slash. When settlers decimated the beautiful Wisconsin forests, the debris (slash) was just left in the woods, where it became a fire hazard in dry years. History books tell of huge fires that often killed scores of people. I doubt you will have to worry about a fire in your forest, unless

* Research by the U.S. Forest Service found that forests logged by cable yarding are less susceptible to erosion than forests logged by tractor yarding (*Forest Magazine*, January 2001).

I built this water-drainage channel with black locust logs, modeled after a Bavarian design. It has eliminated an erosion problem on my access road.

you clear-cut hundreds of acres. Note, however, that slash left around conifers is more of a fire hazard. Generally, nature is very adept at recycling slash and does not need your help or that of a chipper. Slash is wonderful for wildlife, and it helps to maintain a forest climate and adds nutrients to the soil. There are, as usual, potential downsides: The slash will get in the way of scarification, and the slash of some conifers may attract insect pests that subsequently attack healthy trees. Nonetheless, I would recommend that you leave slash lying unless you notice a problem. You can tell when harmful bugs are present because they produce visible saw dust. If you cultivate a PMF, and you harvest by individual tree selection, infestation is unlikely.

Get new seedlings started. To encourage the natural seeding of a new forest in a harvested stand, you'll have to prepare the site, and you should do so right after the harvest. Remember that seeds grow best when they fall on exposed dirt. The process of roughing up the dirt is known as scarification, and it is generally done by dragging an anchor chain over the area or roughing up the dirt with a chisel plow or a disc. In *Finding the Forest*, Peter P. Bundy maintains that scraping the forest floor with a bulldozer produces extraordinary results for oak regeneration. Oak seedlings develop rather slowly and will do much better if competing vegetation is reduced. On the downside, a bulldozer will likely cause considerable soil compaction, and the stumps will undoubtedly get in the way. No matter what you do to prepare your site for a new forest, understand that you will be more or less at the mercy of unpredictable mishaps. A flock of hungry turkeys may scratch up and devour all your carefully placed acorns. This is one of the many reasons why forestry can seem more an art than a science.

Put all the details in a sales contract. No contract can replace the component of trust in the relationship between you and the buyer. Nonetheless, you should still have a contract summarizing the final understanding between the parties. This is more important than its potential use in a case of law. Provisions should include the price, a description of log roads, creek crossings to be built, an assurance that the employees are covered by insurance, payment terms (again, get paid before the logs leave your property), and a small guarantee (10 percent of the sale) that the area will be left as agreed upon.

Sensible harvesting is the foundation for the remaining forest. It is the future. To preserve this future, it is essential that you resist the temptation to succumb to the short-term economies of clear-cutting, which can never repay the damage done to your forest, your person, and humanity. The evils of clear-cutting are the subject of the next chapter.

twenty

ARE CLEAR-CUTS EVIL?

Many progressive foresters consider clear-cutting akin to a crime against humanity. Clear-cutting is a major disturbance, and its manifestations are all too visible to a traveler driving through Idaho, Oregon, Montana, Washington, or British Columbia. Vast tracts of denuded mountainsides stretch alongside lushly green patches of forest. You do not have to be a rocket scientist to figure out that clear-cutting with heavy harvesting equipment on steep mountainsides will cause massive soil erosion.

AN ECOLOGICAL DISASTER

Road construction and the arrival of huge timber-harvesting machines signal the destruction of the forest. The resilient, spongy forest floor cannot tolerate the compaction and deep depressions caused by the heavy equipment.* The forest's ecological system loses its ability to absorb water, especially after being scorched by

---

* Compaction is detrimental to the forest because it greatly reduces the subterranean ecosystem. The top layer of the forest soils contains millipedes, worms, and bacteria that digest wood and leaves. Their excretions (called frass) are consumed by fungi, bacteria, and algae, whose excretions are in turn consumed by smaller bacteria that convert the second generation frass into particles that can be absorbed by the roots of trees. Standard logging equipment compacts the soil and no practical method exists to reverse compaction. Only the freezing and thawing action and burrowing creatures can do that. The absence of frost makes compaction much more serious in the tropics than in our climatic zones.

THE EMPEROR'S NEW CLEAR-CUTS

I have wondered a lot about how forestry academicians and timber industry experts could still condone and promote clear-cutting in the face of the incredible aesthetic and environmental damage it has done to our land. I am not thinking of DNR foresters, who may do limited clear-cutting as the best way to generate a stand of shade-intolerant trees; I am referring to experts beholden to big government and the timber industry, who have left vast stretches of denuded and barren land where pristine forests once were. I believe, albeit cynically, that the reason can be found by reflecting whence these forestry "experts" derive their incomes.

Consider a parallel in the finance industry. A few years ago stock analysts talked the investing public—both the greedy and the greenhorns—into heavily investing in Internet stocks. Even primitive financial analysis showed that most of these Internet companies could not possibly generate enough income to justify their high stock prices. Eventually, the predictable happened: Somebody saw that the emperor had no clothes, and the market collapsed.

So why were these "analysts" so wrong? To answer that question you must consider who pays them. They were cheerleaders whose sole purpose was to push high-tech stocks on the unsuspecting public. The big firms got their tech-market bubble, the public was left holding the bag, and the analysts were quite handsomely compensated.

The conclusion is that whoever pays for expert advice gets the desired result. Do forest experts, both academic and corporate, really regard clear-cutting as a commendable procedure? Did stock analysts sincerely believed that the tech stocks were undervalued? Perhaps, but this much is clear: The capacity for self-delusion is enormous when large amounts of money—or prestige or job security—are at stake.

When the timber industry commits its misdeeds, the general public does not feel it in the wallet. But more and more citizens are rightfully outraged over the rape of the few remaining old-growth forests. Clear-cutting has been restricted in many countries and outlawed in some. Europeans have done much to end the barbaric practice of clear-cutting on their continent. In Switzerland clear-cutting is forbidden because trees impede snow slides. A movement to restrict clear-cutting is also gaining steam in the United States and Canada.

---

direct sunlight. Ruts form and with a little bit of rain turn into gullies that wash soil downhill. When the forest floor stops absorbing water, precipitation runs more quickly and directly into the rivers. Even a slight incline is enough to start the erosion process. Naturally, the steeper the slope the faster the erosion, but even level ground is susceptible to a phenomenon called sheet erosion. The rivers, not accustomed to handling the greater volume of water, flood downstream.* Dissolved forest soil mixed with agricultural runoff (fertilizers, chemicals, and topsoil) support the growth of algae, which reduce oxygen levels in the water, killing fish. Silt and a higher water temperature reduce spawning activity. As this soup empties into the ocean, gigantic algae vegetation forms. As the nutrients get used up, algae die, decompose (this decreases oxygen dissolved in the water), and become a toxic pollutant that endangers oceanic fisheries. This is what happens in the Mississippi basin and the Gulf of Mexico. It is an ugly business. Though some partisans of clear-cutting maintain that agriculture, and not their own forestry practices, is the main culprit, it is obvious that topsoil washed away from clear-cut areas has a devastating effect on ecological processes downstream (not to mention the ecological damage done in horrible, massive landslides).

After clear-cutting, land is typically converted into a monocultural stand—unless the erosion has been so complete as to preclude the growth of trees altogether. Thus a once-thriving old-growth forest community becomes a monocultural stand, losing most of its biodiversity. A healthy mixed forest contains a wide variety of weeds, grasses, herbs, beetles, bugs, fungi, trees, shrubs, mammals, birds, insects, and an incredible variety of microscopic organisms. The interaction of all of these entities constitutes biodiversity. Clear-cutting greatly diminishes this biodiversity, and even under the best of circumstances, it will take nature many human generations to regenerate the land to the kind of a forest climate that existed there before.

Clear-cutting persists because it makes economic sense. Financially, the money to be made from clear-cutting a stand of trees may be greater than any other form of woodland management. The present value of future harvests on clear cut land is so small that virtually no timber man would spend money to cultivate it.** In such cases, the woodland owner who clear-cuts is acting rationally, at least as we conventionally understand the term. Humanity, however, is deprived in some part of such ecological benefits as a steady climate, clean water, and clean air—not to mention aesthetic benefits. What makes sense for the businessman does not necessarily make sense for society.

* It is interesting to note that the Chinese government initiated a huge reforestation program right after the devastating 1998 Yangtze River floods. At the same time, logging of primary forests was severely restricted.

** Timber companies in the southeastern United States have developed methods of short-rotation production of pulpwood. It's a purportedly sustainable regime, but the forests lack biodiversity and aesthetic appeal. Most of the clear-cut land in the Northwest is not suitable for fast rotation pulp wood.

You might think that forestry academics would caution their students about the blight of clear-cutting. You might also reckon that the USDA Forest Service, being entrusted with preserving public lands, would do everything in its power to prevent blatant abuse of our forest lands. You might imagine that Congress, which approves huge expenditures to allow timber companies easy access to pristine forests, would suffer some backlash from voters. Sadly, none of this is the case. The forestry establishment carries on the American tradition of exploiting resources to the fullest, regardless of long-term consequences. For generations, the timber industry, in cahoots with politicians, has extracted as much timber as possible as cheaply as possible. Damage done to ecology, wildlife, or water supply has never mattered. Nor has there been much interest in reforestation. Clear-cutting has destroyed most of our old-growth forest, often leaving a moonscape in its wake.

CLEAR-CUTTING IN THE MIDWEST

Midwestern foresters, when pressed, may concede that clear-cutting damage done in the Northwest is unfortunate, but they consider clear-cutting an important procedure in forest management. In the Midwest, clear-cuts account for 40 percent of all timber harvests. Foresters regard clear-cuts as essential to regenerate shade-intolerant species (such as oaks), to produce even-aged stands, to regenerate commercial aspen and jack-pine stands, or to convert a stand to another species. I own a stand of primarily oaks with an understory of primarily maples where a partial clear-cut could be justified to allow acorns to help generate a new oak stand. I must concede that some of these uses have merit—though similar results can be obtained with canopy gaps (which are very small clear-cuts). I have seen instances where a clear-cut helped to turn abused land into a beautiful and biodiverse forest. It is wonderful to see, and I would not condemn such a clear-cut. For example, clear-cutting a stand of elms, destined to die, and then planting hardwoods on the site (using emerging elm tree suckers as nursing trees) is a good strategy. But there is vastly more clear-cutting than necessary or desirable. Most clear-cuts are succeeded by the environmentally objectionable monocultural plantations, generally accompanied by a hefty dose of herbicides and other chemicals. Pulpwood rotations, as short as twenty years apart, produce boring forests lacking in biodiversity and beauty. The typical Midwestern practice of clear-cutting and regenerating aspen or jack-pine stands provides only marginal income for woodland owners.

When I circulated this manuscript for comment among forestry professionals, their most frequent criticism was what they considered my radical position and extreme aversion to clear-cutting. Midwestern foresters regard clear-cutting as a sound practice. My advice: Do not be swayed. The small-woodland owner has strategies at his disposal (such as the seed-tree system or the shelterwood system) much superior both ecologically and aesthetically.

PRESCRIBED BURNINGS OF GRASS-LANDS AND WOODLANDS

Some foresters maintain that clear-cutting is functionally equivalent to the traditional prairie burning and, therefore, not at all offensive. I never bought this argument because clear-cuts are generally followed by monocultural forests that have nothing in common with the ecosystems that resulted from American Indian prairie burning.

Historically, the American Indians burned prairie, savannah, and some forests periodically to drive game, improve habitat, and reduce the accumulation of flammable matter. Some plants have adapted to the practice. For example, oak trees have developed a flame-resistant bark and jack pines have cones that shed seeds after the heat of a fire. Fire tends to favor plants with large root systems, such as prairie grasses, and is more punishing to above-ground vegetation.

Prescribed burnings, generally undertaken in spring or fall, are accepted as a means to control wooden vegetation and to fight nonnative species that generally are vulnerable to burnings. The ashes of burnings absorb the sun, thus increasing the soil temperature in spring, stimulating early plant growth and increased forage for animals. Environmental organizations, such as the Nature Conservancy and the Sierra Club, conduct prescribed burnings. The objective of burning is to recreate the original savannah vegetation, but it is difficult to recreate the savannah ecology. When the Native Americans stopped burning the savannah, a sparse oak population grew into oak forests, and over time other deciduous trees settled to generate the forests of today. Some land has been set aside to recreate the original savannah vegetation, and some folks, like me, have a small prairie flower plot. Mine is about two acres, and quite young, so as of yet I have not seen many flowers, but the little plants are there busily developing their root systems before blooming.

I think the tide is turning. I suspect that many forestry academicians abhor the abuses of clear-cuts but find it politically unwise to say so. When will they begin to tell their students about the pitfalls of clear-cutting? When will the evils of clear-cuts be discussed in forestry textbooks? Maybe we have to wait until environmental organizations gain enough power and money to hire forest professionals. Still, there is hope. The state of Vermont has passed a law regulating clear-cuts larger than forty acres.* It's not a perfect law, but it is a beginning.

It may not be fair to liken the damage done by huge clear-cuts in the Northwest to current forestry practices in the Midwest. Still, I would welcome a change in our clear-cutting practices, especially in the cases of small-woodland owners, who hardly ever have justification or incentive to clear-cut.

---

* The enforcement of this law, known as Act 15, is described in the Spring 2001 issue of *Northern Woodlands*.

OUT OF THE ASHES

I have had one interesting experience with trees damaged by burnings. In 2001, I harvested a stand of oak trees, where the winning bidder was surprised to find that most trees had a rotten core due to fire damage inflicted about a century ago. He had not detected the defects from the outside, although a knowledgeable friend opined that a skilled buyer would have noticed the imperfection. An experienced sawmill owner familiar with the territory told me that local dairy farmers often burned woods in the area to enhance forage for their animals. It is probable that a denser stand of trees increased the intensity of the fire and thereby caused the damage. In contrast, a fire set in a savannah setting, where tree coverage is less dense, would not have caused damage, since the oak bark can resist moderate, but not severe, fire temperatures.

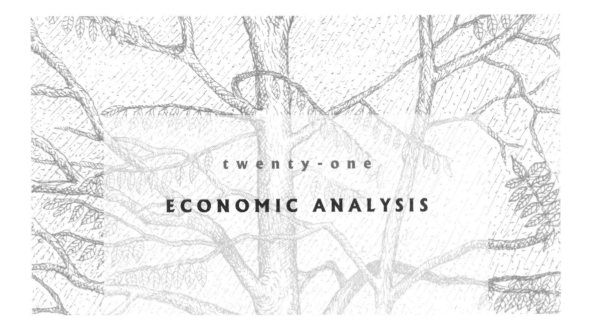

twenty-one

ECONOMIC ANALYSIS

In my twenty-five years of woodland ownership, I have never come across a useful economic analysis of the sort of small-scale silviculture that I do. Oddly enough, for a businessman with an M.B.A. from the University of Chicago, I jumped into my venture without running the numbers first. I took my forester's word that I'd make a pile of money. I also figured that since huge lumber companies have made money planting and harvesting lumber trees for generations, I could do it, too.

To be honest, I attempted to do a financial analysis of my woodlands only when I started writing this book. I have always suspected, however, that my management style was not going to make me a fortune. For one thing, there are government subsidies I haven't taken full advantage of, such as the Conservation Reserve Program.* I have also planted on unsuitable land, with the result of many thousands of stunted walnut trees. In addition, I have blown a great deal of money accumulating a barnful of equipment: a tractor, a bush hog, a mower, a Gator, a sprayer, several chain saws and pole pruners, hand tools too numerous to

---

* This program, sponsored by the USDA, pays you for not growing a crop on agricultural land. In order to qualify, the land must have been planted with annual crops for at least two of the last five years. It might have been planted one year with corn, one year with oats, and three years with hay. Further, the land in question must be deemed to be in danger of erosion. As a practical matter, much land is considered erodible, because the program's primary purpose is to reduce grain production. The amount of subsidy varies.

mention, plus miscellaneous goodies from a yuppie catalog. Finally, I have employed a lot of outside help. In general, I have spared no expense to take very good care of my trees.

But rarely have I pondered the economic sense of what I spend my money on. I'll wager this is true for most woodland owners. I have attended many meetings of the Walnut Council, an association of woodland owners like myself who believe that our beloved *Juglans nigra* is just the most wonderful tree anywhere. Because walnut trees have historically commanded very high lumber prices, we take our investments in our forests very seriously. To be worth the trouble, our trees have to be straight and of veneer quality. We consider it an unforgivable sin not to prune our trees religiously. After all, failure to snip away a little fork today could cost our unborn grandchild a thousand dollars a century from now. Strangely, given all the time and effort my colleagues and I sink into our forests, we hardly discuss the economics of growing walnut trees at our Walnut Council meetings. In fact, an assumption underlies our discussions of the matter—that if you are not making money growing walnuts, it must be your fault. Nobody dares to find fault with the Lord's chosen tree!

Worse, I have cross-examined the experts who occasionally show up at these meetings to speak on the subject of economic analysis, but their answers have varied so much that I doubt their accuracy.* Nor does the literature circulated by the USDA and the state university extension services shed much light on profitability. I have yet to find a lucid model of economic analysis in the academic literature, though I dearly hope one exists somewhere. I have discussed woodland profitability with younger foresters, and my impression is that neither their college curriculum nor their professional training prepares them to comment usefully on the subject. Why is this crucial subject ignored? I cannot answer that question, but it is abundantly clear that woodland owners, woodland associations, and forestry academicians avoid discussing profitability and for the most part are ignorant of the facts.

ANALYZING PROFITABILITY

Analyzing the profitability of growing trees is indeed a difficult proposition, because there are more variables than you can shake a stick at. There is variability in soil fertility, in climate, in aspect of the land, in the characteristics of different species of trees, in the age when timber is harvested, in the anticipated rate of inflation, in the prospects for marketability of a given kind of wood at the time of harvest, in the availability of cost-sharing programs, in the value you put on your own labor, the level of real-estate taxes, in

---

* At a recent meeting, one expert maintained that hardwood plantations in Wisconsin can yield a rate of return as high as 30 percent. When I expressed my doubts, based on hard experience, another expert surmised that an average rate of return was closer to 12 percent. When I again expressed doubt, a third person, a forester himself, offered that the figure is probably closer to 4 percent. I wasn't convinced, but he certainly was getting closer to the truth.

the quality of timber, in the symbiosis of different species of trees growing on the land, in the accessibility of harvesting machinery, in the proximity to the buyer, in the quantity of timber, and in the resources spent on cultivation. In addition to these is the risk associated with major disturbances. Tornadoes, ice storms, fires, severe droughts, severe frosts, and chronic and severe pollution are statistically significant events. In the past several years, ice storms have struck in New England and Wisconsin, awesome hurricanes devastated forests in Europe, and infestations have decimated elms, butternuts, and the American chestnut tree. A European scientist told me that major disturbances damage on an average 30 percent of crop trees. All these factors impose awesome obstacles to any reliable analysis of profitability. I suppose one could assign probability factors to all of the aforementioned variables and arrive at neat tables with a rate of return figured to several decimal places. One might even employ sophisticated statistical tools, such as regression analysis. But, in reality, one small-woodland owner is bound to have different results from the next.

Nonetheless, one should not forgo economic analysis altogether, as even simple analyses reveal interesting facts. In the following examples, I have purposely ignored several cost inputs (such as herbiciding, pruning, thinning, etc.) and unpredictable disturbances (such as poor growth, catastrophic disturbances, etc.) in order to make a simple point. That is, assuming even the best results, money sunk into tree cultivation is less attractive than many safer investments. Before getting to the examples, let me introduce an analytical tool of the finance trade: present value (PV). In the examples below I will cite figures for the "present value of future revenue." By this I mean the value of future proceeds from timber sales, discounted back to today's dollars using the interest rate of a benchmark investment. The benchmark I have chosen is the U.S. treasury bond, which yields a safe and pedestrian return of 5.8 percent.* To illustrate this analysis, please look at example 1 below. Discounting the anticipated proceeds of $7.1 million in the year 2302 to the present, we arrive at a PV of $0.32. An alternative way of interpreting the PV is that if you put $0.32 into a government bond now, it will be worth $7.1 million in 300 years. This may seem surprising, but the figures do not lie. Because the cost of planting a white oak is more than $0.32, you may conclude that it does not pay to do so. So let's consider the investment potential of a few woodland scenarios.

---

* More specifically, I use the Office of Management and Budget's 2002 estimate of the discount rate to be applied to nominal cash flows with horizons larger than thirty years, namely 5.8 percent.

Example 1: White oaks planted in a 300-year rotation

White oaks were planted about 300 years ago in Germany to feed wild boar, which noblemen loved to hunt. These trees grow quite slowly and are probably the most spectacular and valuable cultivated trees anywhere. They are huge, fat, of wonderful veneer quality. Today some of these trees sell for more than $25,000.

*Yield**: $7.1 million per tree in 2302 dollars

PV: $0.32

Planting Cost: The method used in establishing the oak plantation was labor intensive, since the stand of trees is fenced to protect against deer. Figuring any cost, the resulting profitability would be even more disastrous, in that it would be a great deal more than $0.32.

Evaluation: The present value of such a tree tells the whole story. It explains why this sort of tree management would only ever happen in state forests. I presume that if you were very lucky, you might kick an acorn into the dirt and it might be worth millions at some future date. There is no harm in trying, but if you plant nursery stock, it is certain to be a money-losing proposition.

Example 2: Oak trees commercially thinned after 60 years, harvested after 140 years

In this example, we will suppose you have established a plantation of oaks at a cost of $750 per acre, or $263 after cost share. After sixty years, you will do a commercial thinning, in which the culled timber will have some lumber value. (Actually, you will thin the stand earlier, but these early thinnings will not yield any value.) Your thinning will yield about 250 trees at a value of $12 apiece, totaling $3,000 (in 2002 dollars).

Yield from thinning: $9,281 per acre (i.e., $3,000 inflated over sixty years)

Present value (PV) of future revenue from thinning: $315 per acre

Let's assume that after thinning, the remaining oaks will grow for the most part into merchandisable veneer trees. I have chosen a harvest point of 140 years because a German forester suggested that age for his forest. We will assume in this example that the harvested trees yield high-quality logs that would sell for $800 apiece in today's market. At the Office of Management and Budget's (OMB) projected inflation rate, such a log will fetch $11,155 in 2142 dollars. We will assume that thirty such trees will be harvested per acre.

---

* I am inflating the $25,000 using the rate of 1.9 percent implied by the Office of Management and Budget.

Yield from final harvest: $334,650 per acre after 140 years

PV of future revenue from harvest: $125

Take a good look at these figures, because they reveal why so many woodland owners are misled into thinking their plantations are a pot of gold. In our example, you (or more accurately, you and your heirs) will make money at only two points: when you conduct a commercial thinning and when you finally harvest. The present value of all revenues you can expect, per acre, will be the sum of these.

PV of all expected future revenue: $440 per acre ($315 + $125)

An interesting fact should be noted: The real money to be made in this example is from the commercial thinning sale—not from harvesting the stately crop trees. This nicely illustrates an argument I make elsewhere: It does not pay to grow trees to maturity. In general, the shorter the rotation, the higher the yield.* This is unfortunate, because older trees have greater ecological value.

But what about that return of $335,000 in 140 years? It sounds like such an impressive sum. To see whether it lives up to its allure, we need to compare its present value to your investment. That investment is essentially the cost of planting.

It only costs about a dollar to plant a little seedling mechanically, and generally you will plant at least 750 seedlings in an acre. Net planting cost will be reduced to $263 if you qualify for 65 percent cost-share.

Planting/seeding cost per acre (no subsidy): $750

Planting/seeding cost per acre (subsidized): $263 at maximum cost-share subsidy of 65 percent

Evaluation: When you compare the present value of all your expected future revenue, $440, to your investment in each of these cost scenarios, you come up with starkly different conclusions. The calculation suggests that you would have been better off harvesting the trees long before the suggested 140 years, which is an unfortunate fact. But the conclusion is clear that there is no money in growing oak trees.

Example 3 : Jack pine harvested on a sixty-year rotation

Suppose you own some sandy property and want to put a cheap and low-maintenance plantation on it. Pines are your crop, here. An acre of sixty-year-old jack pines will yield about twenty-two cords of pulp wood. You may wonder why planting jack pines is less expensive than planting oaks: Jack pine seedlings cost only about a dime each, and planting them is relatively easy.

---

* Not surprisingly, commercial timber operations harvest coniferous forests with predictable growth and short rotations.

Today a cord of jack pine pulp will get you about $50. In our example, we inflate the revenue to 2062 dollars.

Yield: $3,403

PV: $116

Planting cost per acre: $250

Planting cost per acre (subsidized): $88 at maximum cost-share of 65 percent

Evaluation: As with example 2, this investment doesn't approach being attractive unless it is subsidized. With the cost-sharing subsidy, your investment yields a return only slightly more attractive than a treasury bond. Maintenance costs are much lower for jack pines than for hardwoods, but they will affect your return nonetheless. Considering that a jack pine plantation is aesthetically boring and not good for wildlife or biodiversity, this scenario has little to recommend it.

Example 4: Aspen harvested on a forty-five-year rotation

Elsewhere in this book, I've described how decades of woodland management experience have convinced me that doing nothing to your land may be the best way to establish a forest. In this example, we'll consider how such an approach might work out as an investment.

On my farm in Wisconsin, aspens are plentiful volunteer trees. A stand of aspens may in fact be a single plant, the trunks you see above ground sprouting from a vast root system. They spread easily into open fields, and the trees grow fast. So lets consider an acre of aspen established in just this way: by doing nothing and letting it grow on its own. At forty-five years old, an acre of aspen will yield 22 cords of pulp wood, which at $50 per cord amounts to $1,100. Such a stand may be clear-cut (though I don't recommend this) and it will almost always regenerate automatically. In this example, the yield expressed in 2047 dollars is $2,566.

Yield: About $2,566

PV: $203

Planting cost: None beyond the cost of land and taxes*

Evaluation: There is a little money in it. A young aspen stand may be good for wildlife, but it is not exciting aesthetically. After ten years of growth, your stand will be boring and give you little pleasure. Your best bet would be to allow succession to take its course and to encourage other hardwood trees to establish themselves. Anyway, you will do much better selling your land and buying a certificate of deposit.

---

* The cost of land is significant in determining the attractiveness of this investment. At this time, spring of 2002, the land value is $1,500 per acre paid by hunters.

Example 5: Plant nothing (but take the Conservation Reserve Program money)*

CRP payments: ten annual payments of $65 per acre

PV: $532 per acre

Evaluation: If you are happy to rake in the money and not have trees, this is the deal for you! The CRP payments essentially serve to reduce the cost of your land. In order to qualify, the land must have been planted with annual crops for at least two of the last five years. It could be one year corn, one year oats, and three years hay. The CRP program allows you to seed or plant a forest, and you may even get cost sharing from the federal government. In all, not a bad deal.

I used to wonder why more owners of CRP land do not grow trees. If you plant trees, you can collect CRP payments for fifteen years and if you do not grow trees, payments are limited to ten years. Of course, growing trees would be better environmentally. It would be nice if the USDA would pay a farmer something like $35 per hour to do a bit of soil agitation, which would have a huge impact on Midwestern farmland over a relatively short period of time. The disturbed soil would attract weeds and in the successional cycle would produce forests, increasing wildlife substantially. The results would be huge in terms of wildlife, appearance, and environmental benefits.

Example 6: A sustainable forest

Only the quantity of timber is harvested periodically equal to natural growth (about 2 or 3 percent of standing timber per year) If the value of your stand of trees is $20,000 and you harvest 2 percent a year, your annual yield will be $400.

Annual yield: $400 per acre per year

Planting cost: Nothing, assuming that the forest already exists. If, however, you have to invest time and money to increase the quality and quantity of your forest to a desired level (and some nature-friendly woodland owners do that), your costs will be higher. There will be some minor maintenance costs, but total costs should be lower than in most other timber growing methods.

Evaluation: You harvest periodically an amount roughly equal to growth—about 2 percent of the inventory (the total value of all the trees in the stand). In essence, you are getting about 2 percent per year of your investment in your trees. You maintain a biodiverse ecological environment,

---

* The Bush administration has suspended the CRP program for 2002. It is unclear when and if it will be resumed.

and your trees sequester carbon and release oxygen. Your forest is beautiful and fun. It is your Dauerwald. It is relatively easy to maintain, and it provides a steady stream of income in perpetuity. So what is wrong with this scheme? Nothing, if you are rich and you love woodland. But if you need money, you'll be much better off cutting all the trees and putting the money in the bank. You'll get about 5 percent interest with less trouble.

The upshot is that the PMF does not pay. As I argue in chapter 23, the government should subsidize the PMF, which would show huge dividends for the environment: clean and plentiful water, better air, more recreational use of forests, more carbon sequestration, and more biodiversity.

SUMMARY AND CONCLUSION

In evaluating the six scenarios just presented, you should be aware that the examples are simplified. Certain factors, such as the expected inflation rate or the amount of labor you put in as the woodland owner, will yield different conclusions. This is the case with almost anything in this book. I encourage you to expand this analysis to reflect your own situation.

It is noteworthy that the cost-share subsidy you receive from the state can make the difference between a good and a mediocre investment, especially because most cost-share funds are received early in the rotation and therefore have a sizable impact. I encourage you to take advantage of any cost-share program available. As a conscientious woodland owner you are entitled to every penny available—as a matter of fact your contribution to biodiversity and climate control is huge and deserves much more support.

It is clear that there is very little money in woodland ownership. In order to do even marginally well, you have to be very knowledgeable and disciplined, attributes not always associated with new woodland owners. Furthermore, you must not expect to be compensated for your labor. It is much more likely for you to make money in land appreciation than in silviculture. Just having any kind of tree will increase the value of your land. But in general it is apparent that spending a lot of effort on your trees does not pay. The love and care I showered on my walnut plantation has been financially imprudent.

I have excluded the use of land as a cost of production because it is most likely recreational land much more valuable than that typically used by timber companies. However, it could also be argued that you own and enjoy your land regardless of whether you generate a little income on it. Obviously, assuming that the cost of using the land is zero could lead you to the erroneous conclusion that you can make money from your trees. In growing trees on your land, profit from the sale of timber should come second to your primary interest in increasing the beauty and value of your land. Because the supply of land is fixed and the demand for it is increasing, you will probably show sizable appreciation on your land. For example, in southwest Wisconsin the value of land has gone up at the rate of 10–12 percent per year over the last twenty-five years, and more if you grew an appealing forest on your land. In a way, inflation is paying for your land, but be forewarned, land prices have been known to decline for several years at a time, as they did about thirty years ago.

The message of this chapter is that you should not expect to make money on your woodland operation. So why do commercial timber companies make money? There are several reasons: First, there are economies of scale. By buying thousands of acres at a time, they acquire land much more cheaply than you or I. Timber companies also clear-cut and use chemicals heavily. They grow monocultural plantations in short rotations. These practices, though they may make commercial forestry profitable, hurt the land and appear not to be sustainable. I also believe they are inimical to the interests of the average woodland owner.

You may ask why wood is selling below replacement value. The reason is the availability of untouched forests ready for exploitation. Will it change when Canadian, Malaysian, Siberian, and Brazilian virgin forests are depleted? I do not have the answer.

I realize that my conclusions in this chapter will be hotly contested. Some sophisticated managers have figured out how to squeeze out a little profit on their woodlands. In truth, some may make a little money, but it is unlikely that you will. If you seek to make money, pastures are greener elsewhere. But do remember that the principle rewards of growing trees lie in your personal enjoyment and your concern for the environment.

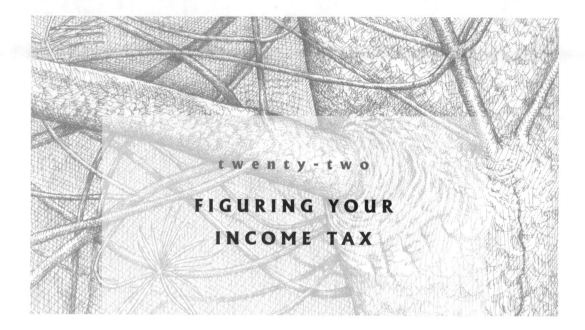

twenty-two

FIGURING YOUR
INCOME TAX

If you are cultivating woodland with the intention of eventually selling some timber, you will need to learn how to keep records and how to file your income tax return. Figuring out the taxes you owe on your woodland operation should be simple, but like many things in forestry, it can get complicated. Matters are often made worse by the experts who speak to woodland-owner groups on tax issues. I have sat through seminars where experts, rather than focusing on the basics, droned on at length about subtle changes in the tax code or extraneous matters such as trusts. Or, when they kept to the basics, they advised woodland owners to undertake a lot of unnecessary record keeping. So I will try to keep it as simple as I can. Don't worry, I know nothing about trusts.

The form on which you have to submit the financial activity of your woodland operation is Schedule C, a subsidiary form to your 1040 federal income tax return. Schedule C is used for any kind of noncorporate business activity, including a woodland operation.*

---

* You could also use Schedule F instead of Schedule C. It makes no difference, though my accountant thinks that Schedule C is a bit easier to use for a tree-farm operation. Stay away from Schedule T (T stands for timber), a six-page nightmare devised by an IRS bureaucrat with a sadistic streak. It contains instructions such as: "Briefly give the provisions of the purchase or lease agreement, including the number of years from the effective date to the expiration date, annual minimum cut or payment, and the payment rates for different kinds of timber and forest products. Follow the format . . ."

ESTABLISHING THE COST BASIS OF TIMBER SOLD

The sale of timber is taxed as a capital gain—in other words, at the current relatively benign rate of 20 percent—unless you harvest within a year of purchase, in which case the proceeds would be taxed as ordinary income. This occurs rarely, since most woodland owners recognize the considerable tax benefits of waiting a year to harvest.

Before I tell you how to fill out your tax return, I want to explain a rather complex matter, the cost basis of the timber you plan to sell. (If you do not plan to do any harvesting, skip this section.) Simply put, the cost basis of your timber is the cost you incurred to buy it. (Strictly speaking, the costs of cultivation and maintenance are also included in the cost basis. However, these costs typically have been amortized long before a harvest, and are therefore not a part of the cost basis at the time of harvest.) Determining your cost basis is an important part of figuring out how much tax you will pay on a given timber sale. The formula for determining your taxable gain is as follows:

Proceeds of sale – cost basis = taxable capital gain

When you bought your woodland, you were buying land (perhaps some was wooded and some was not), whatever timber was standing on it, and perhaps some buildings as well. To figure the cost basis of the timber, you need to answer this question: How much did the timber cost you when you acquired the property? This is the most confusing and complicated matter in this chapter. It is virtually impossible to determine your cost precisely.

One way for you to determine the cost basis is to engage a consulting forester when you buy the property to break down the purchase price into different components. This is often recommended by experts, but don't do it. The cost of this expert advice (around $60 an hour in my neck of the woods, adding up to as much as $1,000, depending on circumstances) is much greater than any benefit you could ever derive from the information. Furthermore, the average owner holds a small woodland about twenty years, and most never sell timber. To my mind, no good case can be made for spending money to appraise timber at the time of purchase if the sole purpose is establishing the cost basis. Of course, you could delay hiring a consulting forester to establish a cost basis until you actually harvest timber. But even then it is not a good deal.

Using my own experience as an example, let me illustrate the difficulty of determining your cost basis. I acquired two hundred acres of woodland in 1974 for $45,000. In 2001, I had a contractor harvest timber on a twelve-acre stand. My proceeds were $18,750. In order to determine my cost basis, I would have to deduct from that $45,000 purchase price:

- the cost of the land;
- the cost of the buildings on the property;
- the cost, at time of purchase, of the timber on twelve stands other than the one I harvested (this requires taking a complete inventory of all twelve stands of trees and refiguring the value as of date of purchase);
- the cost basis of the trees left standing on the stand from which trees are being harvested.

When I bought the farm, real-estate agents prized arable acres more than woods. Of course, we know better now, but what criteria should I use at this point in time in determining the cost of a particular stand of trees? A host of assumptions and calculations need to be undertaken to arrive at the cost basis of the trees I had harvested. The task reminds me of an algebraic puzzle with more unknowns than equations, and there are a variety of consistent solutions. Of course, I could make all kinds of assumptions to arrive at a cost evaluation anywhere between $100 to $5,000, and it would probably stand up. My advice is to make reasonable assumptions on your own. Unless your assumptions are totally out of whack, they should be acceptable. In my own case, I concluded a bit arbitrarily (never mind that this is a dirty word in accounting) that the timber I am selling has a cost basis of $2,000. This is very unlikely to be challenged. Nationwide, the IRS has twelve timber experts qualified to determine timber cost basis. They are busy assessing billions in timber sales by Weyerhaeuser and other timber giants. They have no time for our few trees.

Even a professionally obtained appraisal is likely to be as unreliable as your own, although it would be even less likely to be challenged. An IRS agent who also happens to be a forester recently made a presentation at a woodland owners conference. He had never, in the decades of his professional tenure, heard of a case where a small-woodland owner's cost basis evaluation was challenged by the IRS. If this is really true, I could have evaluated the cost of my timber at $20,000 and declared a capital loss. That's a joke, of course, but you can fudge a bit in your favor without taking an unreasonable chance.

Filling Out a Tax Return

As an example on how to complete a Schedule C for a woodland operation, let us assume the following hypothetical transactions (in appendix C, I show the necessary entries for this example):

Cash Receipts

The first thing to do is add up your cash receipts.

A. Sale of timber ($18,750), with a cost basis of $2,000. Enter the figures on Schedule D, part 2, line 8 (page 210).

B. Payments from the government of $1,950 of cost-sharing for planting 3,000 trees. The $1,950 will be deducted from the total cost of planting to establish the cost basis. Please see section H below for necessary entries.

C. CRP payments from the federal government. As related in chapter 23, the government makes payments to farmers for not producing crops on erodible land. It is here assumed that you receive $3,250 from the USDA. It is taxable income. Enter on Schedule C, part 1, line 1.

D. Revenues of $200 from leasing your woodland to hunters. This amount should be entered on Schedule C, part 1, line 1.

E. You received $500 from the DNR for timbers and improvement in your woodland. This is income to be reported on Schedule C, part 1, line 1. (The three sums to be entered on Line 1 total $3,950. See page 208). Any expenses you incurred for the TSI work should be reported in Part 5 of Schedule C.

Expenses

Any money you spend improving any stand of trees constitutes an expense. As long as the expenses you claim appear to be reasonable, an IRS agent is unlikely to give you trouble. If you should ever be audited, it helps to have adequate records (such as invoices and canceled checks) and to employ generally accepted accounting procedures. Common sense should suffice. Below are some examples of typical expenses:

F. You paid $1,200 in real-estate taxes.

If you view your woodland as an vacation home, you should enter the real-estate taxes on Schedule A. I assume here that in a spirit of fairness you allocate $500 of the taxes on your vacation home (enter on Schedule A , line 8, page 207) and $700 on your woodland operation (enter on Schedule C, part 2, line 23, page 208).

G. You paid $300 in interest on a mortgage. Mortgage payments are treated the same as real-estate taxes. In our example we allocate $125 of in-

---

* The book value of the $1,050 cost for planting seedlings is diminishing over seven years and should technically be added to the book value of your property. Because the trees will not be harvested until after the cost of planting has been amortized, there is no reason to include it in your cost basis.

terest to the vacation home and $175 for the woodland operation. Enter the $175 on Schedule C, part 2, line 16a (page 208). The $125 should be entered on Schedule A, line 10 (page 207).

H. You planted 3,000 trees at a total cost of $3,000 (actually, your cost is $1,050 after deducting 65 percent cost-share).*

Planting is an investment that can be amortized. (Amortization is an accounting term meaning the incremental reduction in value of an asset that is not a piece of equipment.) You are also entitled to an investment credit equal to 10 percent of your cost (The investment credit is limited to $5,000 per taxpayer per year, and a balance can be carried forward). Your cost of the planting is $1,050, so your investment credit is 10 percent thereof, or $105 (see page 212). The investment credit can be deducted from your income tax due on page two of Form 1040.

The balance of your planting cost (your outlay less cost-share and tax credit), $997.50, constitutes the book value of the asset and can be amortized over seven years. The amount to be amortized should be entered on line 40 of Form 4562, part 6 (page 214). The annual amortization is $142.50, but only $71.25 can be amortized on the first year.

I. You incur $100 depreciation expense on your barn used for storing equipment and supplies. If the determined cost basis of the barn is $2,000, then the annual depreciation is $100 per year given a twenty-year life. This amount is entered on line 17, part 3 of Form 4562 (page 213).

The purchase of an asset, such as a chain saw or a barn, will have to be depreciated over time. Most tools are to be depreciated over seven years. The IRS publishes a depreciation guide listing the accounting life of any asset you can depreciate. Form 4562 is used to record depreciable assets. For each equipment item you have to state the following: date of purchase, percentage used in business, cost, recovery period, depreciation method, and annual depreciation amount. Most equipment should be depreciated over seven years, but buildings over a longer period.

J. You bought a used bush hog for $350.

The bush hog should be depreciated over seven years. The annual depreciation is figured on Form 4562 (part 2, line 15c, page 213) from which the annual depreciated amount is forwarded to Schedule C.

There is a provision known as section 179 that allows you to convert the purchase of an asset into an expense up to a certain limit, depending on your income. Of course, this is very much to your advantage because as expenses go up your reported taxable income and your income taxes go down. I won't use section 179 in this example for simplicity's sake, but keep in mind that it is to your advantage to use the provisions in section 179. Ask your accountant about it. Section 179 does not apply to reforestation expense.

K. You hired your Amish neighbor to do some pruning and help planting trees at a cost of $825. Enter on Schedule C, part 5 (page 209).

L. You bought $300 worth of gas and oil. Enter on Schedule C, part 5.

I deduct all of it, even if I use some of it for rides in my Gator, which are at least as much for pleasure as they are for business. But nobody can deny that looking at my trees is an important management activity for my woodlands.

M. You bought a lopper pruning shear for $80. I treat all hand tools worth less than $200 as an expense. Enter on Schedule C, part 5.

N. You spent $1,532 traveling to and from your woodland. Enter on Schedule C, part 2, line 10 (page 208).

I made twenty trips to my woodland from Chicago, a distance of 222 miles. Some trips are for pleasure, some very necessary to take care of my trees, as when I prune and confer with the county forester. I treat 50 percent of my mileage as an expense. So I treat ten trips at 444 miles each as an expense. The deduction is 4,440 miles at $.345 per mile, which adds up to $1,532. (The allowable mileage is periodically adjusted by the IRS. The 34.5 cents per mile is for 2001).

O. You hired a consultant to handle a sale of timber. You paid $1,875 for his services (10 percent of sales). You also paid $325 for having some TSI work done. The total of $2,200 is entered on the second page of Schedule C, part 5 (page 209).

P. You paid $2,000 for phone and utilities on your house in your woodland.

Whatever portion of your phone and other utility bills is directly related to woodland management can be treated as an expense. I deduct about 20 percent, which would mean that $400 can be deducted as an expense on Schedule C, line 25 (page 208).

When preparing Schedule C, you have to make decisions in many gray areas. What is pleasure and what can reasonably be charged against your woodland operation? What about the use of the barn, the house, travel, and the cost of purchasing this book? If you bought this book strictly for fun, you may not deduct its purchase, but if the information you derive is useful in tending your forest, it is a deductible expense. I trust that the information contained in this chapter alone would make it eligible to be listed as an expense. It is a judgment call, and even experts (such as your CPA, who most likely will never have encountered the Schedule C of a woodland operation) would end up with different incomes based on the same data. My advice is to try to be fair and reasonable and, in the unlikely event of an IRS audit, be prepared to defend your calculations and assumptions.

As a practical matter, many woodland returns are only a minor part of the typical owner's income tax return, and an IRS auditor will most likely ignore it. There is more to gain (from the auditor's point of view) by scrutinizing other parts of your tax return. So be reasonable, but if you do err, do so in your favor. I used to be afraid that an IRS agent might get angry if I showed a sizable loss for my tree farm, or worse, that an IRS agent could outrageously term my woodland a "hobby" farm. I have since concluded that such guilt feelings are irrelevant. So don't be afraid that even a sizable loss may appear unreasonable. Remember, as a responsible steward of your woodland you are playing an important role in the preservation of our ecosystem. The U.S. government should be grateful to you.

twenty-three

GOVERNMENT SUBSIDIES

Any sensible government should be eager to assure the health of its forests. In many European countries, this is in fact the case. Sadly, in the United States it is not. The U.S. Forest Service, the agency responsible for maintaining our forests, has facilitated the destruction of almost all of U.S. old-growth forests. Moreover, a look at federal agricultural subsidies underscores our government's misplaced priorities with respect to forests. The U.S. Department of Agriculture, the parent organization of the Forest Service, has a budget of $90 billion, of which practically nothing is devoted to private woodlands. I also own some crop land in Minnesota, and I constantly receive such largesse as flexibility payments, loan-deficiency payments, and Conservation Reserve Program (CRP) benefits. But I receive nothing for managing my woodlands in accordance with environmentally friendly principles. So, I have decided to make the following op-ed appeal for a more enlightened forest policy at the USDA.

THE CASE FOR A FEDERAL WOODLAND SUBSIDY

Two years ago, our presidential candidates delighted in proposing a variety of ways to spend our budget surplus. Overlooked is an elementary component of the electorate's life-support system: our forests. Forests serve vital economic and ecological purposes: They are a source of timber and pulp, but more importantly they provide us with water, absorb CO_2, generate oxygen, maintain equilibrium in our climate, and preserve biodiversity. Biodiversity is our genetic heritage. Our government seems to think that ecological health is a free good, gratuitously maintained by nature, no matter how much our forests are abused. This is a mistake.

Timber harvests often involve clear-cutting, which disrupts the ecological viability of forests and, in extreme situations, can destroy a forest for many generations. Moreover, the burning of the rain forests makes it unlikely that they will ever regenerate themselves to their original biodiverse splendor. There is, however, no reason that forests need to be impaired in order to harvest timber. All that is necessary, as environmentalists have argued for years, is sustainable forest management. Sustainability means that no more timber is harvested than what nature regrows. Typically, a stand of trees adds 2 to 3 percent of its volume every year. If timber is harvested periodically at that rate (maybe 10 to 15 percent of the stand every five years), the forest will remain relatively unchanged, with all of its ecological functions intact. The ecological value (biodiversity, carbon sequestration, pure-water generation) of a forest remains at its maximum as long as a forest climate is preserved and trees are allowed to reach maturity.

There is one major problem with sustainable forestry: It is not financially prudent. Conservatively, a sustainable forests allows an average annual harvest of about 2 percent of all standing timber. For example, if an acre of standing oaks has a value of $10,000, 2 percent can be harvested annually, yielding $400 a year. However, if the owner of the woodland decides to cut down all the trees and buy a 6 percent government bond with the proceeds, he would have an income of $600 per year per acre and could still own, utilize, and enjoy the land, or even sell the land after cutting down the trees. Given this disparity of outcomes, it is unreasonable to expect woodland owners to delay harvesting—excepting for the odd rare cases of altruism—simply for the sake of the environment. I suggest that the government should subsidize small woodland owners at a rate of about 1 to 2 percent of inventory per year.

It should not be surprising, then, that sustainable forestry is not the norm in the United States. True, the U.S. Forest Service has begun to shift away from its traditional policy of subsidized give-aways of old-growth timber, so publicly owned forests are in less peril than they once were.* But commercial timber growers, constrained by the dictates of profit maximization, grow timber in short rotations of about twenty-five years. Tree stands are clear-cut and reforested in a manner not very friendly to the environment. Attempts to make them curb their environmentally destructive management practices have been largely fruitless, and our politicians don't seem to care.

More than half of all U.S. forest land, however, is owned neither by the federal government nor the large timber companies but by small-woodland owners. These people are typically interested in recreation, wildlife, and aesthetics—all objectives compatible with sustainable forestry. Certainly, small-woodland owners are interested in making money in their forests, and they too understand that sustainable forestry is an ideal that costs them. Yet many, given an incentive by the government, would be willing to adopt environmentally friendly forestry procedures. They could still sell wood on a sustainable basis, but they would have to agree to abide by a management plans suggested by their state's department of natural resources.

If our society chooses to maintain a healthy environment—and it would irresponsible not to do so—our government needs to pay woodland owners to manage their forests in an environmentally friendly manner. The payoff to our society would justify the cost.

Better management of the globe's environmental health should also be an aim of U.S. policy. Dealing with rain forests in Brazil or Indonesia is an awesome task, involving international cooperation, and it is unfortunate that the U.S. government does not assume a leading role in working out an international agreement. In the meantime, it is unreasonable for the industrial nations that consume most of the world's fossil fuels to expect developing countries to spare their forests without some sort of a subsidy, especially as long as we continue to abuse our own forests. Neither is it reasonable to expect either Brazilian or domestic woodland owners to preserve our environment without some sort of a cost-share arrangement.

A subsidy encouraging domestic woodland owners to operate sustainably would send a message to the world that the United States is seriously addressing the quality of our environment. The benefits to society would be huge, while the cost would be relatively small, roughly $10 to $15 billion a year—something like $100 per acre per year. The benefits of the woodland subsidy would be purer and more plentiful water, less erosion, more carbon sequestration, less severe floods, more

---

* Sadly, however, President George Bush is using the 2002 forest fires as an excuse to schedule massive logging activity. The stated objective is to reduce combustible forests; the reality is that large trees most resistant to burning are harvested.

wildlife, and more biodiversity. In addition to supporting individual small-woodland owners, there might be a need to subsidize the few commercial timber companies who maintain sustainable forests. One way to accomplish this would be to reward them with a right to cut timber in public forests. While timber companies often extol their sustainable management, real sustainable forests are rarely maintained by commercial enterprises.

As a practical matter, an effective subsidy would require standards both of biodiversity and sustainable harvesting practices for eligibility, ensuring that the program did not simply become yet another instance of welfare. In most states, a department of natural resources maintains forestry management plans for some woodlands,* and these plans could be expanded to administer the subsidy without excessive burden. It also bears mentioning that many farmers own some woodlands and would benefit from such a subsidy as well. The USDA has a program in place, known as the Conservation Reserve Program, which pays agricultural landowners for taking land out of production. A similar program, geared to induce woodland owners to harvest sustainably, would have huge environmental benefits for our country.

THE REALITY OF CURRENT POLITICS

It is unfortunate, but not surprising, that no major newspaper was interested in publishing this op-ed piece. It is a reflection of our national priorities, a reflection that Congress is bowing to the well-organized farming lobby, and a reflection of a failure by our society to recognize the utter importance of maintaining the health of our forests.

Our federal government does nothing for small-woodland owners. The few pennies trickling down to the woodland owners do not even pay the overhead of administering the program; they serve little purpose. For example, the allocation for the Stewardship Incentive Program (SIP) for the state of Wisconsin amounted to $60,000 in 1998. This is less than $0.25 for each woodland owner.

States do support woodland owners. Programs offered vary from state to state. The state of Wisconsin budgets $16 million for the Managed Forest Law, which pays all real-estate taxes in excess of $1.74 per acre per year (or $0.74 per acre if you allow public hunting). In return, the woodland owner

* A Wisconsin DNR official I know estimates that fewer than 20 percent of Wisconsin woodland owners have management plans. Even fewer use them as an effective tool. It is certain, however, that management plans would be followed if woodland owners were given a subsidy incentive.

has to abide by a management plan (written by a consulting or a DNR forester), desist from developing the land for twenty-five years, and agree to pay 5 percent of timber harvest revenues to the state. It's a good deal, since the management plan generally specifies sensible procedures (although I am not crazy about the specification of clear-cuts in some cases) and makes some allowances to the owner's wishes.

In addition, a Wisconsin Forest Land Owners Grant Program budgets $2 million for woodland owners, generally for TSI (timber stand improvement), tree planting, erosion control, the writing and enforcement of management plans, the survival of endangered species, and wildlife habitat. Generally, the program pays 65 percent of total costs. If you do your own work, you can pay yourself $15 an hour, which means that you make money participating in the plan. So it is a good idea to talk to your DNR forester and sign up for any program you can. Of course, $2 million for the whole state of Wisconsin is not much, amounting to something around $4 per woodland owner. Surprisingly, the program has not always been oversubscribed, and two years ago I obtained around $7,000 for my woodland, a relatively large amount. This year the program has been oversubscribed, which is a new phenomenon reflecting the interest of woodland owners to do some forestry. So if you are persistent, and if the DNR forester believes that you do good things to your forest, you can get subsidies. You should take advantage of this opportunity. DNR foresters like to work with concerned woodland owners and will channel cost-share money to you. Sign-up (in Wisconsin) is in September on a first-come-first-served basis. I urge you to be aggressive in asking your DNR foresters what programs are available. It is his or her job to facilitate your participation.

THE NEED FOR LOBBYING

Historically, farmers have constituted a vital part of the electorate that no national candidate could ignore. While the percentage of citizens engaged in farming has shrunk to around 2 percent, their political power persists. And it shows! Currently nearly half of farm income is paid by the federal government. Our society totally overlooks the fact that vibrant woodland is more critical to the welfare of the country than an excess of farmers.

Woodland owners do not have a lobby. I belong to three organizations: the Wisconsin Woodland Owners Association, the Walnut Council, and the Tree Farm System. Only the Tree Farm System has a lobby, but its agenda is very conservative, dealing with landowners' rights vis-à-vis the Environmental Protection Agency (EPA) and lobbying against the federal estate tax. I do not consider them environmentally friendly, an impression reinforced by the disgusting "wildlife-enhancing" herbicide ads featured in its magazine.* I am in the unfortunate position that, as with clear-cutting, my feelings are very much in the minority.

The most effective lobbies for environmental causes are organizations such as the Sierra Club and The Nature Conservancy. I am particularly fond of the Forest Service Employees for Environmental Ethics (FSEEE), a group that courageously attempts to steer public policy in the right direction. Some potentially powerful woodland-owners organizations, on the other hand, are woefully ignorant about politics.**

If I were heading a lobbying group for woodland owners, I would make these modest proposals to the federal government:

Provide an incentive for woodland owners to practice sustainable forestry (as outlined in the beginning of this chapter).

Limit clear-cutting. The government could mandate that trees can only be clear-cut by special permit and only when this practice is not ecologically harmful.

Recognize the importance of CO_2 sequestration. People seem to have finally recognized that the enormous amount of fossil fuels burnt around the world probably has caused the global temperature to rise, seriously affecting the health of the planet. CO_2 accumulation in the atmosphere causes the sun's heat rays to be reflected in the atmosphere and thereby increases ambient temperature. The phenomenon is known as the greenhouse effect. The more CO_2 absorbed by plants, the less is the danger of the climate change. As plants bind carbon, oxygen is released into the atmosphere. The absorption of carbon by the plants is known as carbon sequestration. The more vegetable matter a plant comprises, the greater the level of sequestration. There is relatively little carbon sequestration in a wheat field; woods absorb thousands of times more. A point can be made that woodland owners should be compensated for causing carbon to be sequestered. There has been some discussion for a mechanism to buy and sell permits to generate and absorb CO_2. For about two decades, the right to emit pollution into the air (generally by utilities burning fossil fuels) has been a traded commodity. The scheme is an efficient solution for rationing the right to pollute. Some forward-looking thinkers are suggesting a similar arrangement for the use

* The Tree Farm System has 62,000 members. It has a very strong presence in the Midwest, and its principal purpose seems to be awarding tokens of recognition to tree farmers. I once called its office in Washington, D.C., and asked to talk to a forester. I was told there was none on the payroll. For certification of "tree farmers" it utilizes foresters who often are connected to timber buyers.

** If you are concerned about the U.S. Forest Service's mismanagement of our forests, you may want to join FSEEE, a group of courageous folks who value the interests of our nation's forests even at the expense of their own professional careers. Contact FSEEE at P.O. Box 11615, Eugene, OR 97440; or at www.fseee.org.

and absorption of CO_2.[*] Any agreement would have to be international and would require determination of who is responsible for how much use of fossil fuel and what forest owners in which countries should be entitled to payments for sequestering carbon. Conceptually, the benefits could be huge.

Reward the preservation of habitat for endangered species. Some large forest owners are being penalized for having endangered animals on their land. They can not harvest their forest, lest the endangered animals are hurt. Rather than reducing the value of forests inhabited by endangered critters, the government should offer a subsidy and an award for maintaining a biodiverse mature forest. Many a landowner would be very proud to be recognized for harboring endangered animals and plants, and thrilled to receive a small subsidy for doing so. (Maybe even a sign prominently acknowledging the presence of endangered species would be good beginning. I would proudly display mine, and I believe countless others would as well.) This practice would also help to track remaining populations of endangered species.

Do a more imaginative job of administrating the CRP program. As I mentioned earlier in this book, the government's CRP program pays landowners to take erodible land out of production. The landowner receives something like $60 per year for doing nothing, and the land lies idle.

Here is a wonderful opportunity to start forests on these millions of acres with very little expense. If the government would spend a few dollars per acre to rough up the land (a disc, anchor chain, or chisel plough would do the job), all kinds of new vegetation would arise and eventually succeed into a forest. The government does provide some incentive to plant trees on CRP land. Unfortunately, direct seeding is not a sanctioned technique in most states. Meanwhile, though, it allows CRP recipients to plant as few as 250 walnut or aspen trees per acre. Planting so few trees is silly, because they may not be able to compete with grasses and because planting that few trees on a wide spacing will assure that they will never have timber value. Sometimes it seems our forestry policy makers would never pass an elementary forestry class in junior college.

I am confident that sooner or later federal legislators and agency people will recognize the contributions small-woodland owners can make to humanity. I may not be in the current administration, but I am hopeful that it will happen. Our lives may depend on it.

---

* See Robert Hahn and Robert Stavins, *Trading Greenhouse Permits: A Critical Examination of Design and Implementation Issues* (Washington, D.C., Island Press). There is an intelligent discussion of the possibility of trading carbon sequestering coupons in a chapter entitled "Shaping National Responses to Climate Change."

I find it disturbing that with the pervasive waste of the U.S. Government granting subsidies everywhere, woodland owners are ignored. I believe we should lobby as best we can, but more importantly we should remain equally firm in our commitment to pursue environment-friendly forestry practices. Perhaps somewhere along the line our value as the protectors of the environment will be recognized. With luck, that will happen before much more serious deterioration occurs in our environment.

Is it too much to hope that some U.S. congressman will read this chapter—and the next one, a disquisition on the historical importance of wood—and incorporate some of the obvious lessons into our national policy?

twenty-four

AN HISTORICAL PERSPECTIVE

In this chapter I relate the importance of wood in human history. As you will learn, the availability of wood has usually been important in the flourishing and decline of most civilizations. While in our time petroleum has become a most important commodity, historically wood has been a most important ingredient in determining the success of human civilizations.

ANCIENT HISTORY

Four thousand seven hundred years ago, city-states flourished in Mesopotamia. Wood trestles can be backdated to that period.* As local wood supplies were used up, wood was floated down the rivers from the north. The inevitable depletion of the forest was followed by droughts. Later, Sumerian civilizations in the same area imported still more wood from Turkey and Syria to fuel smelters for the production of bronze. Neighboring kingdoms were overthrown to obtain access to forests. The Sumerian civilizations collapsed primarily because deforestation caused excessive amounts of silt, which clogged its waterways and irrigation channels. Worse, continual irrigation caused the sali-

* Adalbert Ebner, *German Forests* (New York: German Library Information, 1940), page 55.

nation of agricultural fields, which proved irreversible and led to drastic reduction in barley yields. By 2000 B.C. Sumerian states ceased to exist, and regional power shifted north to Babylonia. Similarly, later civilizations (such as Knossos on Crete) declined relative to other states on the Greek mainland where timber was in greater supply. Here, also, deforestation brought deadly consequences. Hillsides denuded of ground cover were bombarded by rain drops with greater force, washing away the remaining soil and causing floods downstream. Lack of nitrogen in the soil made it impossible for agriculture to feed the surrounding population. After the soil became infertile, the exposed limestone bedrock and red subsoil came to dominate the Mediterranean landscape. What appeared to be the consequence of a climate change in the area was actually caused by the absence of trees. The population in Greece declined by 75 percent in the 13th and 12th centuries B.C.*

The availability of wood was a central factor in the rise to power of Venice at the dawn of the Renaissance period. The Venetian fleet suffered defeat by the Turks in 1470, but once Venice secured sufficient wood from the southern Alpine slopes, it flourished—until the wood was depleted. Thereafter, shipbuilding shifted to northern Europe, where supplies of wood were more ample.

THE ENGLISH EXPERIENCE

England in the time of Henry VIII was a rather primitive country, but it was covered with vast forests. While England imported most manufactured goods, including glass, iron, weapons, and salt, its principal export was timber. The best Henry's father could do was to increase the English fleet to ten ships at a time when Spanish and Portuguese navies made a fortune in trade and in the exploitation of America. Charles V, the Holy Roman Emperor, regarded Henry VIII as a potential rival and refused to sell arms to England. Rightfully alarmed, Henry undertook to establish a domestic arms industry and close the "cannon gap." This required the conversion of much of England's wood into charcoal. The iron mills in Sussex used large quantities of wood, raising the price of the commodity sharply and as a consequence causing rebellions among the people. Bills were introduced in Parliament to preserve woods, among them one stipulating that "hedgerows under two acres not to be put to coals."

The use of wood for navigation, housing, furniture, casks, carts, wagons, coaches, mining, and the production of iron, lead, glass, brick, and tile quickly depleted English woodland. The government was compelled to reduce the amount of wood used in iron smelting, but to little effect. Landowners virtually never reforested the depleted forests, because they found it more profitable to use the land for pasture. Woodland near population cen-

---

* John Perlin, *A Forest Journey: The Role of Wood in the Development of Civilization* (Cambridge: Harvard University Press, 1989).

ters became depleted. A contemporary commentator observed that "those who live longest would be condemned to fetch their wood farthest." In the seventeenth century, James I forbade the use of timber for firewood and limited the amount of wood available for housing. People were forced to burn straw and manure for heat, which in turn hurt agriculture. While the use of coal in the manufacture of glass reduced the demand for wood somewhat, it was still necessary to use charcoal for the manufacture of iron. Meanwhile, the kings of England financed their high living and military adventures by selling their forests with abandon.

The scarcity of timber caused English planners to look for timber elsewhere. Irish forests had already been depleted. More successful was the importation of timber from Baltic nations. In another scheme to increase the supply of timber, the government built wagonways to bring wood from forests in more remote corners of the kingdom to cities. Later, canals allowed easier transportation of timber and coal. While accessible forests became more and more depleted, English society became wealthy through trade and industry. A big boost to the economy was the development of the technology to use coal for iron production late in the 18th century, an important event in the industrial revolution. The subsequent availability of American timber helped to satisfy the need for wood in Europe.

THE GERMAN EXPERIENCE

Before we return to your forest, I want to relate a history of German woods.* When the Romans tried to conquer Germania, they were repelled by hoards of fierce natives who took refuge in huge forests. The savages established settlements and pastured all kinds of animals in the forest. Interestingly, the most damaging of these were the horses, who roamed freely, especially after A.D. 732, when Pope Gregory III forbade human consumption of horse meat. Cattle were pastured in the woods, as were sheep and goats. Leaves were harvested (especially elm and ash) to be fed to cattle in the winter. Come spring, famished cows (by then weighing less than four hundred pounds) devoured emerging vegetation. Pigs were driven by the thousands into the forest, and in order to provide sufficient feed, it was forbidden to cut down mast-producing trees such as oaks and beeches (i.e., trees producing nuts, acorns, and other seeds that accumulate on the forest floor and serve as food for pigs and other animals). Equally damaging was the use of the forest for honey and wax. Frequently, whole sections were burned to generate flowering woods, or trees were coppiced to induce flowering. Other forests were depleted for firewood and construction timber. Conifers tapped for the production of resin (the raw material for turpentine) were damaged. The removal of leaves, along with the theft of

* I lavish special attention on Germany both because I grew up in Germany and because the silvicultural history of Germany is relatively unknown and interesting, though it has parallels elsewhere in Europe. Much of the information here comes from Wilhelm Bode, *Waldwende* (Munich: Beck'sche Verlagsbuchhandlung, 1994). Unfortunately, the book is not available in English.

humus (which was punished as late as the twentieth century), depleted the soil and slowed regeneration. Also competing for the resources of the forest were deer and wild boars, which the gentry hunted to show off its manliness. When a prince with his entourage descended on the poor country folk, it was not uncommon for the deer kill to exceed a thousand. Country folks always resented the damage done by huntable wildlife. The guardians of the forest, engaged by the gentry, were more concerned with enforcing hunting laws than cultivating trees. Frederick the Great decreed that foresters had to be officers, with their own prestigious military units, a tradition maintained until 1945. By the early nineteenth century, German forests were in a deplorable state.

With the beginning of the industrial revolution came a huge demand for charcoal and timber for mines and various kinds of manufacture. Many of the remaining larger trees were floated down the rivers to Holland for shipbuilding and construction.

In the late eighteenth century, German foresters made the first attempts at reforestation, consisting of leaving some seed trees after the harvest. For a variety of reasons they began to favor conifers, and growing timber became big business. German foresters brought to their trade the precision, control, and military uniformity that characterized the German civil service. Perhaps row after row of straight and uniform pines appealed to this predilection. In any case, the make-up of German forests began to change dramatically. In the Middle Ages, 80 percent of all German trees were deciduous; today, 65 percent are conifers.

In 1990, when Germany suffered immense hurricane losses, monocultural coniferous forests proved particularly vulnerable to wind damage. Mixed forests incurred less damage and recovered faster. Now, a strong movement has arisen in Germany to reintroduce mixed forests.

THE AMERICAN EXPERIENCE

When European pioneers began to settle in America, they found a plentiful supply of wood. The continent being so large, there were different climatic conditions and growing conditions at different parts of the country. In Wisconsin, there were principally two kinds of terrain: the savannah (prairie) and forested area. The savannahs were frequently burned by Indians, and as a result savannah vegetation adapted. Most of the grasses had huge roots and relatively little growth above the surface. There were but few trees. Certain oaks, particularly bur oak, developed a bark thick enough to survive prairie fires (but not necessarily forest fires which generate higher temperature). Jack pines, whose cones would release their seeds prompted by the heat of a fire, also thrived. Where there was no savannah, there were dense woods with huge trees.

Entering an undisturbed forest, easily accessible for harvest, was a new experience for the European settlers. It is easy to see how they imagined America was a paradise of plenty. The historian William Cronon sums this up nicely: "The United States took from the Indians an ecosystem that when viewed through the lens of the marketplace already held great treasures. The attraction of 'free land' was that people could turn this natural wealth into capital with less labor than elsewhere."* Trees were so plentiful that they had no stump value. Viewed another way, they were an impediment to agriculture. One of the first tasks of many settlers was to remove the trees in order to plant grain. Very often this was accomplished by burning.

A contemporary observer termed the Ohio forest as "the grandest unbroken forest of 41,000 square miles that was ever beheld."** While Ohio's forests were primarily hardwood, pines dominated in Michigan, Wisconsin, and Minnesota. So vast were the forests that a contemporary observed that "Upon the rivers which are tributary to the Mississippi, and also those which empty themselves into Lake Michigan, there are interminable forests of pines, sufficient to supply the wants of the citizens of all time to come."*** By the beginning of the 20th century, most of the trees were gone. The land proved to be infertile for agriculture and many farmers could not pay their taxes.

Harvesting was a lot of work, because the trees were chopped down with axes (and, after they were introduced in the 1880s, with crosscut saws). Transporting the trees to market required a lot of hard work and ingenuity. Commonly logs were cut in the winter and floated down the rivers in spring (with the owner's mark burnt on them). Then they were shipped to lumber markets in Chicago.

Logging was dangerous work. Sometimes tree top slash fueled huge fires, occasionally killing scores of people. The worst fire was in Peshtinago, Wisconsin in 1871, burning 1.3 million acres of forest and killing more than 1,500 people.**** Often there were incredible logjams, which required gutsy experts to unlock, a most dangerous undertaking. Sometimes dynamite was used. One logjam on the Menominee River in Wisconsin was so massive that half a billion board feet of timber got stuck.***** Even if accounts of this event were exaggerated, the mass of wood was unimaginably large.

Lumbering was risky as a business, too. In dry winters there was not enough snow and water to transport the logs to the lake harbors. In Great Lakes storms, ships were prone to sink or get stranded. When lumber did not come to market, the operators could not pay the bills, causing unrest among the hired woodcutters who worked 80-hour weeks for about $100 per season.

The abundance of lumber spurred the development of farmland in the prairie states, which were relatively devoid of wood. Railroads transported the lumber to the homesteader and returned with grain for the city population. The settlement of the prairie states happened in a relative short period of time, supported by an "in-

---

* William Cronon, *Nature's Metropolis* (New York: W.W. Norton and Co., 1991), p. 150.

** Francis Baily, writing in 1856, cited by Gerald Jonas, *North American Trees* (Pleasantville, New York: The Reader's Digest Association, 1993), page 127. By 1850, 40 percent of the forests were cut.

*** Jonas, ibid., page 139.

**** Ibid, page 140.

***** Robert Fries, *Empire in Pine* (Madison: University of Wisconsin, 1951), page 45.

SUNKEN TREASURE

It is noteworthy that most logs from northern Wisconsin were white pines, which had a significant advantage in that they have a low specific gravity, low enough so that they would float.* This reminds me of one of my unsuccessful schemes. When I built a dam on my farm, I though it would be nice to have a small float on the lake for sunbathing and for fishing. All I had to do is to drag a few logs into the valley and wait for the water to buoy a raft to the surface. But nothing happened, and the two logs are still securely resting on the bottom on my lake. If I had chosen white pines instead of oaks, I would now have a nice floating raft on which to sunbathe and fish in the summer. Loggers had similar problems floating the timber to the market, as evidenced by thousands of logs still lodged at the bottom of bodies of water. Entrepreneurs are making money salvaging them.

---

exhaustible supply of natural wealth." The wood was a free good from nature. In 1855 Increase Lapham observed: "Few persons . . . realize . . . the amount we owe to the native forests of our country for the capital and wealth our people are now enjoying. Yet without the fuel, the buildings, the fences, the furniture, and [a] thousand utensils, and machines of every kind, the principal materials for which are taken directly from the forests, we should be reduced to a condition of destitution."

After the Civil War, the forests of the Midwest had been largely harvested, and Chicago and its hinterland lost much of their lumber business to the Western states. The ecological damage done was not much noticed, with a few exceptions. An observer in 1867 compared the American rapine of its forest to "the experience of other countries, ancient and modern, whose forests have been improvidently destroyed." He lamented "the effects of clearing land of forest trees, upon springs, streams and rainfall," reminding readers "how (forests) temper winds, protect the earth."**

SUMMARY

It is clear that throughout history humans have abused and depleted forests to advance their short-term aims. They have cut timber mercilessly, destroying biosystems, making countless animal species extinct, causing floods, eroding agricultural land, endangering

---

* To make the southern cypresses more buoyant, loggers girdled the trees to dry them out. Jonas, *North American Trees*, page 142.

** Increase Lapham, *Report on the Disastrous Effects of the Destruction of Forest Trees Now Going On so Rapidly in the State of Wisconsin*, cited in Perlin, *A Forest Journey*, pages 354-55.

water supplies, salinating agricultural fields, poisoning and depleting fisheries, elevating levels of carbon dioxide in the atmosphere and thereby probably altering our climate. The cutting continues, accelerated by chain saws and machines that cause even more deadly havoc in the environment. The rate at which our forests disappear is frightening, especially in South America and Malaysia. No society on earth has ever seriously concerned itself with long-term sustainability of its forests. Efforts to reestablish forests always take a back seat to supplying ever-increasing demand.* Yet the easy availability of vast, virgin forests is a thing of the past. Who knows if we can muster the political will to adopt more sensible forest policy.

* The United States is the only exception to the global trend of diminishing forests, since U.S. consumption approximately equals regeneration. The quaity of our forests, however, has diminished substantially.

twenty-five

CONCLUSION

In my two woodland farms in Wisconsin, I own more than five hundred acres, which is more land than I (or any individual) can manage effectively. I have given a great deal of thought to a better way to use all this land. I have toyed with the following scheme: I'd like to provide building sites for about a dozen houses and sell them to people interested in living in the country and enhancing nature. Each building site owner would have a couple acres of his very own and co-own the remaining five hundred acres with the others and together manage it as an association. I would try to attract folks with a genuine interest in nature. To help assure some philosophical continuity, new members would be accepted by the vote of current residents. With luck, all residents would actively contribute to improving the land.

What appeals to me about such an idea is that more people would be able to enjoy the land, and joint ownership would make it more likely that the woodland would be managed responsibly in perpetuity. The common area could be protected by a conservation easement. There would be opportunities for swimming, hunting, fishing, cross-country skiing, riding, walking, watching, and many other activities. Neighbors would become friends, and common ownership of such a vast area would enable folks to enjoy more than they could on a forty-acre parcel they owned individually. It would be easy to find a local Amish farmer to maintain the property, keep horses, and provide other services for a fee. Real-estate agents have suggested to me that people would rather own forty-acre lots by themselves, so maybe this scheme would not work. Then again, it might not be realistic to expect real-estate agents to understand the spirit behind such a venture.

All of us will be outlived by our woodlands. In my case, perhaps, I hope my forest lives on as a way to cheat my own mortality. I sincerely hope that in centuries to come, those who inherit or buy the land appreciate my efforts and dreams and act in their turn as good stewards. I hope, too, that as a nation—as a species—we come to understand the joy and health of living in harmony with nature. I hope this book inspires you to do your part to get us there.

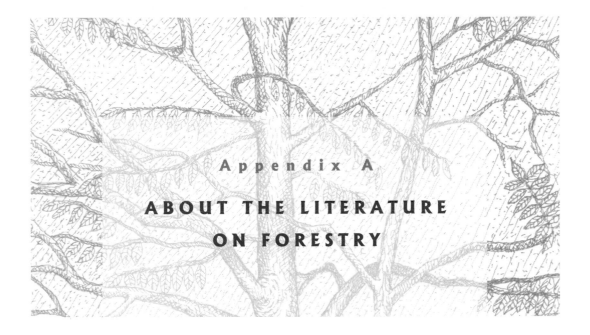

Appendix A
ABOUT THE LITERATURE ON FORESTRY

Like any academic field, forestry has an abundant volume of literature. Many brilliant scientists have spent lifetimes writing about the subject, and countless millions have been spent on research, much of it meticulously documented. When I started cultivating my forest, I expected to learn much from scholarly literature, but I have been disappointed. For the common woodland owner, the vast majority of it is neither easy to understand nor particularly helpful.

Quantitative concepts commonly used in the academic literature, such as the crown competition factor and basal area, are difficult to apply to small woodlots. And university forestry departments have had little to say about issues specific to small-scale tree farming. In general, while some items central to small-woodland management may exist in the academic literature, they are hard to find. Techniques central to small-scale forestry, such as selective cutting (choosing individual stems for harvest), are sometimes mentioned but are more or less dismissed as impractical. Sadly, forestry experts, in my opinion, often betray a lack of moral principle: They discuss techniques such as clear-cutting in great detail but gloss over disastrous consequences of these techniques, such as the diminution of biodiversity and the dangers of global warming. It is difficult to dismiss a suspicion that the power structure of academic forestry is beholden to the lumber industry.

UNIVERSITY EXTENSION PUBLICATIONS

Most states have university extension services that work in conjunction with their state's department of natural resources to publish "best-management practice" sheets geared to the individual woodland owner. Some are very good; others are unreadable, outdated, and counterproductive. Its quality varies from state to state. A "Forest Fact" sheet published by the University of Wisconsin, for example, recommended tall fescue grass as a weed-controlling cover crop for walnut trees. This suggestion borders on malfeasance. One also wonders why a fabulous book like *Woodlands of Wisconsin* by S. A. Wilde is no longer in print, while lesser material is still being published. State extension services should take more care in controlling the quality of the literature they pass out to unsuspecting woodland owners.

I understand that my DNR foresters have used the very textbooks I criticize, and they still have become very good stewards of the environment and are of tremendous help to woodland owners. I believe that much of their knowledge and experience has been acquired by working with individual landowners and by experimentation. The best among them have learned what works and what does not. Some are on the cutting edge of forestry.

I am not familiar with any authoritative book covering the basic principles of forestry suited to small-woodland owners. There are nonetheless some useful books, and I encourage you to acquaint yourself with them and to decide what approaches make the most sense for you. A small list is given below. Please note that I have not undertaken an extensive survey of the literature, but my suggestions may still be useful to you.

RECOMMENDED BOOKS

In the process of writing this book, I have assembled a bookshelf of literature. I cite here only those which I found most helpful to myself and which I view as worthwhile reading for my audience.

Andrew Beattie and Paul Ehrlich, *Wildsolutions* (New Haven: Yale University Press, 2001). You will love this fascinating account of the workings of biodiversity, wonderfully written and brilliantly illustrated.

Mollie Beattie, *Working with Your Woodland: A Landowner's Guide* (Hanover, N.H.: University Press of New England, 1991). This is a very well written and useful guide for woodland owners, although it's geared primarily to the New England ecosystem. It will give you a practical and basic understanding of forestry.

John F. Berger, *Understanding Forests* (San Francisco: Sierra Club Books, 1998). This book is promoted by the Sierra Club as "the best introductory guide to forestry practices and the issues surrounding the preservation of American forests." I concur. It is an easy read, focussed, and well written.

Wilhelm Bode, *Waldwende: Vom Foertserwald zum Naturwald* (Munich: Beck'sche Reihe, 1995). I learned a lot from this German book, which is unfortunately not available in English.

William Cronon, *Nature's Metropolis: Chicago and the Great West* (New York: W. W. Norton and Co., 1981). This book is about the rise of Chicago as a center of commodity exchange. Grain, cattle, and hogs are the most common commodities associated with the mighty Board of Trade, but in the last century lumber markets were also key. Cronon has interesting insights into the lumber trade at its beginnings in the Great Lakes states.

Bernd Heinrich, *The Trees in My Forest* (New York: Cliff Street Books, 1997). A sensitive account of the workings of nature in a Maine woodland.

Paul W. Hirt, *A Conspiracy of Optimism: Management of the National Forests since World War II* (Lincoln: University of Nebraska Press, 1994). An interesting account of how the U.S. Forest Service works, documenting its failure to protect national forests from the worst practices of the timber industry.

Gerald Jonas, *North American Trees* (Pleasantville, New York: The Reader's Digest Association, Inc., 1993). A coffee-table book with spectacular photographs. Interesting, entertaining, and informative.

John Kotar, *Ecologically Based Forest Management on Private Land* (Minneapolis: University of Minnesota Extension, 1997). This small booklet is geared to helping forest professionals apply ecological principles on private woodlands.

John Perlin, *A Forest Journey: The Role of Wood in the Development of Civilization* (Cambridge: Harvard University Press, 1989). I found this book fascinating. Much of chapter 19 of my book is based on Perlin's account.

Ray Raphael, *More People Talk: The People, Politics, and Economics of Timber* (Washington, D.C.: Island Press, 1994). The book is written in a Studs Turkel style, with many personal accounts of people who have worked with timber. It also contains many interesting passages on the politics and economics of timber. I found it interesting and definitely worthwhile reading.

Stephen Spaulding, *So Many Seeds* (Fort Collins, Colorado: Cooperative Extension Resource Center, General Service Center, Colorado State University, 1998). Delightfully written suggestions on how to collect and stratify tree seeds.

Curt Stager, *Field Notes of the Northern Forest* (Syracuse: Syracuse University Press, 1998). An insightful, ground-level account of how organisms survive in a biodiverse environment, written by a host of a NPR program on natural science.

S. A. Wilde, *Woodlands of Wisconsin* (Madison: Cooperative Extension Program, The University of Wisconsin, 1977). This marvelous and insightful small booklet provides an understanding of the workings of forests, regarded from a holistic and philosophical rather than scientific perspective. A great book.

Worldwatch Institute publishes well-researched and informative booklets on key environmental issues, such as *Facing Water Scarcity: How to Shape an Environmentally Sustainable Global Economy*. Intelligently presented position papers. (Worldwatch Publications, 1776 Massachusetts Ave., Washington, DC 20036.)

James A. Young and Cheryl G. Young, *Seeds of Woody Plants in North America* (Portland, Ore.: Dioscorides Press, 1992). A bit on the technical side, this book is nonetheless very helpful to anyone who wants to gather seeds to plant directly. It has many illustrations and a lot of information.

TRADE PUBLICATIONS

Many states have woodland owners' associations, and some of these publish newsletters of interest to woodland owners.

Beware, however, that "trade" literature isn't always what it seems. It is a mixed bag, and you should regard such sources with caution. Some publications may talk a good game about self-sustaining, regenerating, nature-friendly, and biodiverse ecosystems, but their pages are infected with an ever-so-subtle bias toward herbicides, as well as glossy advertisements for the companies that make them.

HOW DOES THIS BOOK FIT INTO THE LITERATURE?

Of course, I hope that this book will become a respected part of the woodland-management library. Its point, however, is less to be authoritative than to be practical. The advice of so-called experts can be wildly misguided—I have many acres of stunted walnut trees to prove it. By the same token, the experience of a humble layman may reveal things that the experts don't know (or worse, don't credit). I return to the mysterious "hedgerow effect" that pines seem to have on walnut trees planted nearby. Some professors who have read this manuscript have actually denied that such a phenomenon can exist. Yet any Doubting Thomas may visit my farm and see for himself what I am talking about.

As I've said before, forestry for the small-woodland owner is more an art than a science. But the science is still important. To succeed in large- or small-scale forestry, you must first assimilate its basic principles and techniques. But for the small-woodland owner especially, more important is the need to understand the myriad anomalies and contingencies that may either shatter or fulfill your silvicultural dreams. The best way to make those contingencies go your way is to study the experiences—the unforeseen failures and the unexpected successes—of those in the trenches of small-scale forestry.

Reading about my own frustrating experiences, I believe, will save you time and disappointment. It will deliver the immense pleasures I have known, and do so with less effort than I expended myself. It should also prepare you to anticipate new problems, to look for new solutions, and perhaps to identify new and better objectives for your woodland. In this sense, I intend the book not to be authoritative, but to be the beginning of a dialogue between stewards, between amateurs in the classical sense of the word. It would please me greatly if it stirred debate at woodland associations, started small-woodland owners talking to each other, and encouraged readers to come forth with their own experiences and know-how, so that I, too, might learn from them. In fact, I encourage readers to visit my web site, www.woodland-management.com, to keep in touch.

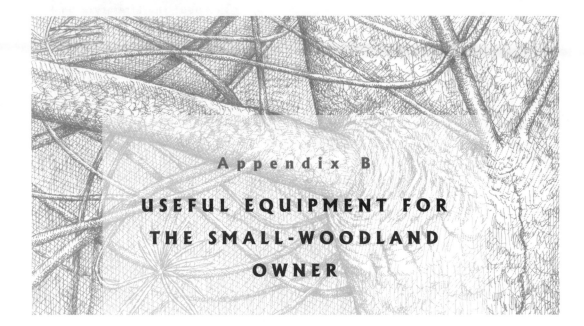

Appendix B

USEFUL EQUIPMENT FOR THE SMALL-WOODLAND OWNER

Below is a list of the equipment I like. Of course, for each tool I list there are many competing products. In most cases I have not gone out of my way to test different makes, so by all means you should weigh the alternatives when you buy equipment. I buy much of my equipment from forestry supply catalogs, but there are many stores where you can buy comparable goods.

The Ben Meadows Co. is particularly good. For a catalog, call 800-628-2068 or visit their web site at www.benmeadows.com. I also recommend Forestry Suppliers, Inc. They can be reached at 800-647-5368 or www.forestry-suppliers.com.

A note on maintenance: While farmers are accustomed to working with machinery and tools, you may not be all that handy. It helps to have a knowledgeable neighbor who can help. It is not uncommon to spend more time messing with your tools and machinery than using it. It pays to be very organized, maintain operation and parts manuals, and have good tools. There is nothing more frustrating if one of your spray nozzles breaks off and you do not have a replacement—especially if the store is not open on Sunday and you are distressed because it is getting late in the season to spray and you had no plans to return to your land for a couple of weeks.

PLANTING TOOLS

Tree planting bar. Also known as a dibble or a spud, it is the standard tool for planting seedlings (Ben Meadows). See the illustration on page 218.

PRUNING EQUIPMENT

Small hand pruner. I like the Snap-Cut Model 19T Pruner (Ben Meadows). It is small enough to fit into your pocket and works consistently.

Large pruning shears. I use the Corona Super-Duty WL6490 Lopper (Ben Meadows), which is capable of cutting three-inch diameter branches.

Motorized pole pruners. I like Echo power pole pruners. They have a long reach (depending on the model, up to nearly thirteen feet). The manufacturer also sells extensions that can extend your reach by another five feet. There are two types of blades: reciprocal action and chain saw. I prefer the reciprocal-action blade. It cuts branches like a sabre saw, which means that it cuts with minimum injury to the tree. You should be careful not to drop or knock your pole pruner when you transport it, because it is easily bent out of shape, which will make it unusable. I have done this to my extension, and it costs about $100 to fix. Another thing to keep in mind is that the reciprocal-action sawblades last for only about two hours of continuous pruning and cost about $3 apiece. They take a little work to replace, but it's all worth it. The Echo pruner makes a difficult job much easier.

Manual pole pruner. You may also want to have a manual pole pruner. My Gilmour pruner has worked reliably. You should get two six-foot extensions (Ben Meadows).

WOOD-CUTTING EQUIPMENT

Chain saw. You should always be aware that a chain saw can be a lethal piece of equipment and should be used with caution and care. Always wear chaps, gloves, and a helmet. If you use the saw above your head (which is a bad idea, but sometimes difficult to avoid), you should wear a safety vest as well. I do not recommend felling large trees unless you are experienced. A small saw (twenty-inch bar) will do fine. Most saws on the market appear reliable. Stihl is my brand of choice.

Small hand pruner.

Large pruning shears

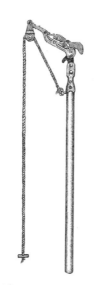

Manual pole pruner.

MOWING EQUIPMENT

I'm not big into mowing regularly around my trees, but it is useful for such things as site preparation and maintaining paths for my Gator. A wide variety of mowing equipment is available from any lawn-care or farm-implement dealer.

Bush hog. The bush hog is a square mower attached to a farm tractor and driven by the tractor's power take-off (or PTO). It has rotating blades that chop up everything to four inches in diameter. It is very useful for cutting paths, mowing between rows of trees, and clearing brush. It is a standard piece of equipment available at places selling farm implements. (See illustration on page 4.)

Bush trimmers. If you want something smaller than a bush hog attached to a tractor, bush trimmers are the thing. They're souped-up lawn mowers, some with a chain saw on a rotating disc capable of cutting five-inch trees. These typically have bicycle-type wheels on either side and are easy to walk behind. Check the following web site: www.drtrimmers.com.

SPRAYING EQUIPMENT

Blueing compound. People mix this compound in with whatever they're spraying. For a while I did, too. It's supposed to help you see what area you've sprayed by turning it slightly blue. But the stuff is hard to see and expensive as well. I have discontinued using bluing compound and am now using the Hansel and Gretel approach: I drop small pieces of plastic tape to show where I have sprayed. The pieces of tape are not offensive and disappear after a short period of time. Still, if you prefer using bluing compound, look for it at any farmer's co-op.

Hand pump sprayer. To dispense herbicides, you need a hand sprayer with a manual pump. There are many makes and models, and I have no particular preference. You can buy them through catalogs or from agricultural implement dealers. (See the illustration on page 51.)

Motorized sprayer. If you have a larger area, it pays to have a motorized sprayer. Basically there are two types:

• *A pump attached to a tractor's power take-off.* I used to use such a contraption, but it did not work terribly well (as related in chapter 5). The hoses tended to get tangled up, and as the trees became taller it proved difficult to maneuver the tractor between the rows without being continually whacked by branches.

• *A motorized sprayer that fits on a vehicle of some sort.* I have been very happy using a Fimco sprayer, which has a gas engine of its own and fits on my Gator. It has an eight-foot spraying band (five feet if you fold back the side extension). It has a fifty-gallon tank and is reliable and easy to use. It takes two people to load the sprayer on the Gator, but only one to do the spraying. You can buy the Fimco sprayer from any agricultural implements dealer. (See the illustration on page 49.)

TRANSPORT

The Gator. The Gator, made by John Deere, is a sort of cross between a go-cart and a tank. There are four-wheel and six-wheel models. I own a six-wheel Gator. It has a driver's seat and a passenger's seat in front and a dumpable cargo bed in back. I built a wood platform that fits in the bed and accommodates two more passengers comfortably. It safely negotiates incredibly steep hills, and though I have come close, I have never tipped it over. It takes an amazing amount of abuse. Its fat tires make for great traction and minimal compaction—which is key for driving through your woodlands. It is small and flexible, making it easy to negotiate tight spots. It has become indispensable for hauling and getting about. It is no exaggeration to say that since I bought my Gator I enjoy my land much more. In fact, one drawback of the vehicle is that it's so convenient and handy that you'll probably walk your land less. Its one significant operational drawback is that it does not function very well in snow (the snow packs underneath and you just can't move). Overall, you and your guests will love it. The Gator costs roughly $9,000 and can be bought from any John Deere dealer. (See the illustration on page 6.)

MISCELLANEOUS SUPPLIES

Tree shelters. These are plastic tubes many woodland owners use to shield seedlings from animals and to act as a sort of greenhouse to accelerate growth. The tubes sound better in theory than they work in practice, however. Often the plant a tube is supposed to shield dies, at other times the tube gets blown over. Tubes are also unkind to birds, which often mistake them for nesting sites, fly into them, and can't get out (the manufacturer furnishes netting to minimize this problem). Bucks also love the tubes for testing their antlers, which reduces the tubes to shreds. I do not recommend the

Paint spray gun.

tubes, except perhaps to mark the spot where you planted a seedling. Tubex makes the leading model.

Colored tape. To flag or mark trees, colored tape made of elastic plastic is very handy. You just tear off the desired length and tie it around a tree. I use it primarily to mark keepers. It lasts for several years, although the color fades over time. It is available in several colors and comes in three-hundred-foot rolls (Ben Meadows).

Flags. Flags can be very useful to pinpoint locations where you have planted seeds or seedlings. You may think that you can remember where you've planted, but chances are you won't. Little flags come in a variety of sizes and colors (Ben Meadows).

Tree-marking paint. If you're subcontracting somebody to log or release some trees, it helps to mark trees to be cut. I even mark trees I plan to cut myself. Walking through a stand with a chain saw in hand, it's easier to cut when the trees have been marked on a previous occasion. I prefer to buy my paint in quart-size containers onto which you can screw the sprayer (Ben Meadows).

Paint Spray Gun. With a range of ten feet, a spray gun can make it much easier to mark trees. I have used the IDICO gun (Ben Meadows), which screws onto a quart can. I suggest cleaning the spray gun with paint thinner after each use because the nozzle can get gummed up.

MISCELLANEOUS HAND TOOLS

Come-along. This tool is a godsend on those occasions when you need to move a heavy object, such as a car in a ditch, a stuck tractor, or Gator. If you find an anchor (something like a tree will do) you wrap the cable part of the come-along around it and crank a ratchet. In forestry, this is especially useful for pulling down a felled tree whose branches are stuck on surrounding trees, preventing it from falling properly. Used correctly, a come-along pulls some pretty heavy things. I use a More Power Puller (Ben Meadows).

Fencing tool. It is an indispensable tool if you ever work with your fences. It cuts, pulls, removes staples, and hammers. It should be available in any country hardware store.

Yuppie tools. I used to buy out of yuppie catalogues. It's fun, but not productive. Most gadget tools are more picturesque than useful.

CHEMICALS

Deer repellent. An effective spray-on deer repellent is Durapel. The active ingredient is Birex, the same substance used to keep kids from biting their fingernails. It's easy to spray on and persists for months. Contact the Treessentials Company (www.treessentials.com).

Herbicides. Those in vogue change annually. The most commonly used poison is Roundup, but new formulations with different capabilities appear on the market continually. The best place to buy herbicides is from the farmers co-op in the nearest town. You can also buy it more expensively from catalogues.

Appendix C

INCOME TAX FORMS

1040

Department of the Treasury - Internal Revenue Service

U.S. Individual Income Tax Return 2001 (99)

IRS Use Only - Do not write or staple in this space.

Label (See instructions on page 19.)

For the year Jan. 1-Dec. 31, 2001, or other tax year beginning _____, 2001, ending _____

OMB No. 1545-0074

Your first name and initial **TIMBER**	Last name **TAXPAYER**

Your social security number **999-99-9999**

Spouse's social security number

Use the IRS label. Otherwise, please print or type.

Home address (number and street). If you have a P.O. box, see page 19. **1000 FOREST DRIVE** — Apt. no.

City, town or post office, state, and ZIP code. If you have a foreign address, see page 19. **WOODALE, WI 88888**

▲ **Important!** ▲
You **must** enter your SSN(s) above.

You   Spouse

Presidential Election Campaign (See page 19.)

Note. Checking "Yes" will not change your tax or reduce your refund.

Do you, or your spouse if filing a joint return, want $3 to go to this fund? . . . . ▶ Yes No Yes No

Filing Status

Check only one box.

1. [X] Single
2. [ ] Married filing joint return (even if only one had income)
3. [ ] Married filing separate return. Enter spouse's social security no. above and full name here. ▶
4. [ ] Head of household (with qualifying person). (See page 19.) If the qualifying person is a child but not your dependent, enter this child's name here. ▶
5. [ ] Qualifying widow(er) with dependent child (year spouse died ▶ _____). (See page 19.)

Exemptions

6a	[X] **Yourself.** If your parent (or someone else) can claim you as a dependent on his or her tax return, do not check box 6a	
b	**Spouse**	

No. of boxes checked on 6a and 6b **1**

c Dependents:

(1) First name Last name	(2) Dependent's social security number	(3) Dependent's relationship to you	(4) ✓ if qualifying child for child tax credit (see page 20)

If more than six dependents, see page 20

No. of your children on 6c who:
- lived with you
- did not live with you due to divorce or separation (see page 20)

Dependents on 6c not entered above

Add numbers entered on lines above ▶ **1**

d Total number of exemptions claimed . . . .

Income

Attach Forms W-2 and W-2G here. Also attach Form(s) 1099-R if tax was withheld.

If you did not get a W-2, see page 21.

Enclose, but do not attach, any payment. Also, please use Form 1040-V.

7	Wages, salaries, tips, etc. Attach Form(s) W-2	7	
8a	Taxable interest. Attach Schedule B if required	8a	
b	Tax-exempt interest. Do not include on line 8a	8b	
9	Ordinary dividends. Attach Schedule B if required	9	
10	Taxable refunds, credits, or offsets of state and local income taxes (see page 22)	10	
11	Alimony received	11	
12	Business income or (loss). Attach Schedule C or C-EZ	12	-2,458.25
13	Capital gain or (loss). Attach Schedule D if required. If not required, check here . . . ▶ [ ]	13	16,750.00
14	Other gains or (losses). Attach Form 4797	14	
15a	Total IRA distributions	15a		b Taxable amount (see page 23)	15b	
16a	Total pensions and annuities	16a		b Taxable amount (see page 23)	16b	
17	Rental real estate, royalties, partnerships, S corporations, trusts, etc. Attach Schedule E	17	
18	Farm income or (loss). Attach Schedule F	18	
19	Unemployment compensation	19	
20a	Social security benefits	20a		b Taxable amount (see page 25)	20b	
21	Other income. List type and amount (see page 27) _____	21	
22	Add the amounts in the far right column for lines 7 through 21. This is your total income . . ▶	22	14,291.75

Adjusted Gross Income

23	IRA deduction (see page 27)	23		
24	Student loan interest deduction (see page 28)	24		
25	Archer MSA deduction. Attach Form 8853	25		
26	Moving expenses. Attach Form 3903	26		
27	One-half of self-employment tax. Attach Schedule SE	27		
28	Self-employed health insurance deduction (see page 30)	28		
29	Self-employed SEP, SIMPLE, and qualified plans	29		
30	Penalty on early withdrawal of savings	30		
31a	Alimony paid b Recipient's SSN ▶ _____	31a		
32	Add lines 23 through 31a	32		
33	Subtract line 32 from line 22. This is your adjusted gross income . . . . ▶	33	14,291.75	

For Disclosure, Privacy Act, and Paperwork Reduction Act Notice, see page 72.

Form **1040** (2001)

Form 1040 (2001)   Page **2**

Tax and Credits	34	Amount from line 33 (adjusted gross income)	**34** 14,291.75
Standard Deduction for -	35a	Check if: ☐ You were 65 or older, ☐ Blind; ☐ Spouse was 65 or older, ☐ Blind. Add the number of boxes checked above and enter the total here . . . . ► **35a** ☐	
● People who checked any box on line 35a or 35b or who can be claimed as a dependent, see page 31.	b	If you are married filing separately and your spouse itemizes deductions, or you were a dual-status alien, see page 31 and check here . . . . ► **35b** ☐	
	36	Itemized deductions (from Schedule A) or your **standard deduction** (see left margin)	**36**
	37	Subtract line 36 from line 34	**37** 14,291.75
● All others:	38	If line 34 is $99,725 or less, multiply $2,900 by the total number of exemptions claimed on line 6d. If line 34 is over $99,725, see the worksheet on page 32	**38** 2,900.00
Single, $4,550	39	Taxable income. Subtract line 38 from line 37. If line 38 is more than line 37, enter -0-	**39** 11,391.75
Head of household, $6,650	40	**Tax** (see page 33). Check if any tax is from **a** ☐ Form(s) 8814 **b** ☐ Form 4972	**40**
	41	Alternative minimum tax (see page 34). Attach Form 6251	**41**
Married filing jointly or Qualifying widow(er), $7,600	42	Add lines 40 and 41 . . . . ►	**42**
	43	Foreign tax credit. Attach Form 1116 if required	**43**
Married filing separately, $3,800	44	Credit for child and dependent care expenses. Attach Form 2441	**44**
	45	Credit for the elderly or the disabled. Attach Schedule R	**45**
	46	Education credits. Attach Form 8863	**46**
	47	Rate reduction credit. See the worksheet on page 36	**47**
	48	Child tax credit (see page 37)	**48**
	49	Adoption credit. Attach Form 8839	**49**
	50	Other credits from: **a** ☐ Form 3800 **b** ☐ Form 8396 **c** ☐ Form 8801 **d** ☒ Form (specify) 3468	**50** 105.00
	51	Add lines 43 through 50. These are your **total credits**	**51** 105.00
	52	Subtract line 51 from line 42. If line 51 is more than line 42, enter -0- . . . . ►	**52** .00
Other Taxes	53	Self-employment tax. Attach Schedule SE	**53**
	54	Social security and Medicare tax on tip income not reported to employer. Attach Form 4137	**54**
	55	Tax on qualified plans, including IRAs, and other tax-favored accounts. Attach Form 5329 if required .	**55**
	56	Advance earned income credit payments from Form(s) W-2	**56**
	57	Household employment taxes. Attach Schedule H	**57**
	58	Add lines 52 through 57. This is your **total tax** . . . . ►	**58** .00
Payments	59	Federal income tax withheld from Forms W-2 and 1099	**59**
	60	2001 estimated tax payments and amount applied from 2000 return . .	**60**
If you have a qualifying child, attach Schedule EIC.	61a	**Earned income credit (EIC)**	**61a**
	b	Nontaxable earned income **61b**	
	62	Excess social security and RRTA tax withheld (see page 51)	**62**
	63	Additional child tax credit. Attach Form 8812	**63**
	64	Amount paid with request for extension to file (see page 51)	**64**
	65	Other payments. Check if from **a** ☐ Form 2439 **b** ☐ Form 4136	**65**
	66	Add lines 59, 60, 61a, and 62 through 65. These are your **total payments** . . . . ►	**66**
Refund	67	If line 66 is more than line 58, subtract line 58 from line 66. This is the amount you **overpaid**	**67** .00
Direct deposit? See page 51 and fill in 68b, 68c, and 68d. ►	68a	Amount of line 67 you want **refunded to you** . . . . ►	**68a**
	b	Routing number _____ ► **c** Type: ☐ Checking ☐ Savings	
	d	Account number _____	
	69	Amount of line 67 you want applied to your **2002 estimated tax** ► **69**	
Amount You Owe	70	**Amount you owe.** Subtract line 66 from line 58. For details on how to pay, see page 52 . . . . . ►	**70** .00
	71	Estimated tax penalty. Also include on line 70 . . . . **71**	

Third Party Designee
Do you want to allow another person to discuss this return with the IRS (see page 53)? ☐ **Yes. Complete the following.** ☐ **No**
Designee's name ► _____ Phone no. ► _____ Personal identification number (PIN) ► _____

Sign Here
Joint return? See page 19.
Keep a copy for your records.

Under penalties of perjury, I declare that I have examined this return and accompanying schedules and statements, and to the best of my knowledge and belief, they are true, correct, and complete. Declaration of preparer (other than taxpayer) is based on all information of which preparer has any knowledge.

Your signature ►	Date	Your occupation	Daytime phone number
Spouse's signature. If a joint return, **both** must sign.	Date	Spouse's occupation	

Paid Preparer's Use Only

Preparer's signature ►	Date	Check if self-employed ☐	Preparer's SSN or PTIN
Firm's name (or yours if self-employed), address, and ZIP code ►		EIN	
		Phone no.	

JSA

1A1220 3.000   Form **1040** (2001)

SCHEDULES A&B (Form 1040)	Schedule A - Itemized Deductions	OMB No. 1545-0074

SCHEDULES A&B
(Form 1040)

Department of the Treasury
Internal Revenue Service   (99)

Schedule A - Itemized Deductions
(Schedule B is on back)
▶ **Attach to Form 1040.** ▶ **See Instructions for Schedules A and B (Form 1040).**

OMB No. 1545-0074

2001

Attachment
Sequence No. **07**

Name(s) shown on Form 1040

TIMBER TAXPAYER

Your social security number

999-99-9999

Medical and Dental Expenses

Caution. Do not include expenses reimbursed or paid by others.

1 Medical and dental expenses (see page A-2) . . . . | 1 |
2 Enter amount from Form 1040, line 34 · · · · · · · · | 2 |
3 Multiply line 2 above by 7.5% (.075) . . . . | 3 |
4 Subtract line 3 from line 1. If line 3 is more than line 1, enter -0- . . . . | 4 |

Taxes You Paid

(See page A-2.)

5 State and local income taxes . . . . | 5 |
6 Real estate taxes (see page A-2) . . . . | 6 |
7 Personal property taxes . . . . | 7 |
8 Other taxes. List type and amount ▶ _____
   VACATION HOME | 8 | 500.00 |
9 Add lines 5 through 8 . . . . | 9 | 500.00 |

Interest You Paid

(See page A-3)

Note.
Personal interest is not deductible.

10 Home mortgage interest and points reported to you on Form 1098 | 10 | 125.00 |
11 Home mortgage interest not reported to you on Form 1098. If paid to the person from whom you bought the home, see page A-3 and show that person's name, identifying no., and address ▶
_____
_____ | 11 |
12 Points not reported to you on Form 1098. See page A-3 for special rules . . . . | 12 |
13 Investment interest. Attach Form 4952 if required. (See page A-3.) . . . . | 13 |
14 Add lines 10 through 13 . . . . | 14 | 125.00 |

Gifts to Charity

If you made a gift and got a benefit for it, see page A-4.

15 Gifts by cash or check. If you made any gift of $250 or more, see page A-4 . . . . | 15 |
16 Other than by cash or check. If any gift of $250 or more, see page A-4. You must attach Form 8283 if over $500 . . | 16 |
17 Carryover from prior year . . . . | 17 |
18 Add lines 15 through 17 . . . . | 18 |

Casualty and Theft Losses

19 Casualty or theft loss(es) Attach Form 4684. (See page A-5.) . . . . | 19 |

Job Expenses and Most Other Miscellaneous Deductions

(See page A-5 for expenses to deduct here.)

20 Unreimbursed employee expenses - job travel, union dues, job education, etc. You must attach Form 2106 or 2106-EZ if required. (See page A-5.) ▶ _____
_____ | 20 |
21 Tax preparation fees . . . . | 21 |
22 Other expenses- investment, safe deposit box, etc. List type and amount ▶ _____
_____ | 22 |
23 Add lines 20 through 22 . . . . | 23 |
24 Enter amount from Form 1040, line 34 · · · · · | 24 |
25 Multiply line 24 above by 2% (.02) . . . . | 25 |
26 Subtract line 25 from line 23. If line 25 is more than line 23, enter -0- . . . . | 26 |

Other Miscellaneous Deductions

27 Other- from list on page A-6. List type and amount ▶ _____
_____ | 27 |

Total Itemized Deductions

28 Is Form 1040, line 34, over $132,950 (over $66,475 if married filing separately)?
   ☐ No. Your deduction is not limited. Add the amounts in the far right column for lines 4 through 27. Also, enter this amount on Form 1040, line 36. } . . . ▶ | 28 | 625.00 |
   ☐ Yes. Your deduction may be limited. See page A-6 for the amount to enter.

For Paperwork Reduction Act Notice, see Form 1040 instructions.

Schedule A (Form 1040) 2001

JSA
1A1400 2.000

SCHEDULE C (Form 1040)	**Profit or Loss From Business**	OMB No. 1545-0074
Department of the Treasury Internal Revenue Service (99)	(Sole Proprietorship) ▶Partnerships, joint ventures, etc., must file Form 1065 or Form 1065-B. ▶Attach to Form 1040 or Form 1041. ▶See Instructions for Schedule C (Form 1040).	**2001** Attachment Sequence No. **09**

Name of proprietor	Social security number (SSN)
TIMBER TAXPAYER	999-99-9999

A Principal business or profession, including product or service (see page C-1 of the instructions)
TREE FARM

B Enter code from pages C-7 & 8 ▶ 113000

C Business name. If no separate business name, leave blank.

D Employer ID number (EIN), if any

E Business address (including suite or room no.) ▶ 1000 FOREST DRIVE
City, town or post office, state, and ZIP code   WOODALE, WI 88888

F Accounting method: (1) [X] Cash (2) [ ] Accrual (3) [ ] Other (specify) ▶ _____

G Did you "materially participate" in the operation of this business during 2001? If "No," see page C-2 for limit on losses . . . . [X] Yes [ ] No

H If you started or acquired this business during 2001, check here . . . . ▶ [ ]

Income

1	Gross receipts or sales. Caution. If this income was reported to you on Form W-2 and the "Statutory employee" box on that form was checked, see page C-2 and check here . . . . ▶ [ ]	1	3,950.00
2	Returns and allowances	2	
3	Subtract line 2 from line 1	3	3,950.00
4	Cost of goods sold (from line 42 on page 2)	4	
5	Gross profit. Subtract line 4 from line 3	5	3,950.00
6	Other income, including Federal and state gasoline or fuel tax credit or refund (see page C-3)	6	
7	Gross income. Add lines 5 and 6 . . . . ▶	7	3,950.00

Expenses. Enter expenses for business use of your home **only** on line 30.

8	Advertising	8		19	Pension and profit-sharing plans	19	
9	Bad debts from sales or services (see page C-3)	9		20	Rent or lease (see page C-4):		
				a	Vehicles, machinery, and equipment . . .	20a	
10	Car and truck expenses (see page C-3)	10	1,532.00	b	Other business property	20b	
				21	Repairs and maintenance	21	
11	Commissions and fees	11		22	Supplies (not included in Part III)	22	
12	Depletion	12		23	Taxes and licenses	23	700.00
13	Depreciation and section 179 expense deduction (not included in Part III) (see page C-3)	13	125.00	24	Travel, meals, and entertainment:		
				a	Travel	24a	
14	Employee benefit programs (other than on line 19)	14		b	Meals and entertainment . .		
15	Insurance (other than health)	15		c	Enter nondeductible amount included on line 24b (see page C-5) . .		
16	Interest:						
a	Mortgage (paid to banks, etc.) . . .	16a	175.00	d	Subtract line 24c from line 24b	24d	
b	Other	16b		25	Utilities	25	400.00
17	Legal and professional services	17		26	Wages (less employment credits)	26	
18	Office expense	18		27	Other expenses (from line 48 on page 2)	27	3,476.25

28	Total expenses before expenses for business use of home. Add lines 8 through 27 in columns . . . . ▶	28	6,408.25
29	Tentative profit (loss). Subtract line 28 from line 7	29	-2,458.25
30	Expenses for business use of your home. Attach Form 8829	30	
31	Net profit or (loss). Subtract line 30 from line 29. • If a profit, enter on Form 1040, line 12, and also on Schedule SE, line 2 (statutory employees, see page C-5). Estates and trusts, enter on Form 1041, line 3. • If a loss, you must go to line 32.	31	-2,458.25
32	If you have a loss, check the box that describes your investment in this activity (see page C-6). • If you checked 32a, enter the loss on Form 1040, line 12, and also on Schedule SE, line 2 (statutory employees, see page C-5). Estates and trusts, enter on Form 1041, line 3. • If you checked 32b, you must attach Form 6198.	32a [X] All investment is at risk. 32b [ ] Some investment is not at risk.	

For Paperwork Reduction Act Notice, see Form 1040 instructions.   Schedule C (Form 1040) 2001

JSA

Schedule C (Form 1040) 2001

Page **2**

Cost of Goods Sold (see page C-6)

33 Method(s) used to value closing inventory: **a** ☐ Cost **b** ☐ Lower of cost or market **c** ☐ Other (attach explanation)

34 Was there any change in determining quantities, costs, or valuations between opening and closing inventory? If "Yes," attach explanation . . . . ☐ Yes ☐ No

35 Inventory at beginning of year. If different from last year's closing inventory, attach explanation	**35**	
36 Purchases less cost of items withdrawn for personal use	**36**	
37 Cost of labor. Do not include any amounts paid to yourself	**37**	
38 Materials and supplies	**38**	
39 Other costs	**39**	
40 Add lines 35 through 39	**40**	
41 Inventory at end of year	**41**	
42 Cost of goods sold. Subtract line 41 from line 40. Enter the result here and on page 1, line 4	**42**	

Information on Your Vehicle. Complete this part **only** if you are claiming car or truck expenses on line 10 and are not required to file Form 4562 for this business. See the instructions for line 13 on page C-3 to find out if you must file.

43 When did you place your vehicle in service for business purposes? (month, day, year) ▶ 04/10/1996 .

44 Of the total number of miles you drove your vehicle during 2001, enter the number of miles you used your vehicle for:

a Business 4,440 **b** Commuting 0 **c** Other 6,700

45 Do you (or your spouse) have another vehicle available for personal use? . . . . ☒ Yes ☐ No

46 Was your vehicle available for personal use during off duty hours? . . . . ☒ Yes ☐ No

47 a Do you have evidence to support your deduction? . . . . ☒ Yes ☐ No

b If "Yes," is the evidence written? . . . . ☒ Yes ☐ No

Other Expenses. List below business expenses not included on lines 8-26 or line 30.

AMORTIZATION	71.25
GAS & OIL	300.00
SMALL TOOLS	80.00
CONSULTING SERVICES	2,200.00
DAY LABOR-TREE MAINTENANCE	825.00
48 Total other expenses. Enter here and on page 1, line 27 . . . . **48**	3,476.25

Schedule C (Form 1040) 2001

JSA
1X0120 2.000

SCHEDULE D (Form 1040) Department of the Treasury Internal Revenue Service (99)	Capital Gains and Losses ▶ Attach to Form 1040. ▶ See Instructions for Schedule D (Form 1040). ▶ Use Schedule D-1 to list additional transactions for lines 1 and 8.	OMB No. 1545-0074 2001 Attachment Sequence No. 12

Name(s) shown on Form 1040

TIMBER TAXPAYER

Your social security number

999-99-9999

Short-Term Capital Gains and Losses - Assets Held One Year or Less

(a) Description of property (Example: 100 sh. XYZ Co.)	(b) Date acquired (Mo., day, yr.)	(c) Date sold (Mo., day, yr.)	(d) Sales price (see page D-5 of the instructions)	(e) Cost or other basis (see page D-5 of the instructions)	(f) Gain or (loss) Subtract (e) from (d)	
1						

2 Enter your short-term totals, if any, from Schedule D-1, line 2 . . . . **2**

3 **Total short-term sales price amounts.** Add lines 1 and 2 in column (d) **3**

4 Short-term gain from Form 6252 and short-term gain or (loss) from Forms 4684, 6781, and 8824 . . . . **4**

5 Net short-term gain or (loss) from partnerships, S corporations, estates, and trusts from Schedule(s) K-1 . . . . **5**

6 Short-term capital loss carryover. Enter the amount, if any, from line 8 of your 2000 Capital Loss Carryover Worksheet . . . . **6** ( )

7 **Net short-term capital gain or (loss).** Combine lines 1 through 6 in column (f). **7**

Long-Term Capital Gains and Losses - Assets Held More Than One Year

(a) Description of property (Example: 100 sh. XYZ Co.)	(b) Date acquired (Mo., day, yr.)	(c) Date sold (Mo., day, yr.)	(d) Sales price (see page D-5 of the instructions)	(e) Cost or other basis (see page D-5 of the instructions)	(f) Gain or (loss) Subtract (e) from (d)	(g) 28% rate gain or (loss) * (see instr. below)
8 SALE OF TIMBER	06/10/1974	10/30/2001	18,750.00	2,000.00	16,750.00	

9 Enter your long-term totals, if any, from Schedule D-1, line 9 . . . . **9**

10 **Total long-term sales price amounts.** Add lines 8 and 9 in column (d) **10** 18,750.00

11 Gain from Form 4797, Part I; long-term gain from Forms 2439 and 6252; and long-term gain or (loss) from Forms 4684, 6781, and 8824 . . . . **11**

12 Net long-term gain or (loss) from partnerships, S corporations, estates, and trusts from Schedule(s) K-1 . . . . **12**

13 Capital gain distributions. See page D-1 of the instructions **13**

14 Long-term capital loss carryover. Enter in both columns (f) and (g) the amount, if any, from line 13 of your 2000 Capital Loss Carryover Worksheet . . . . **14** ( )( )

15 Combine lines 8 through 14 in column (g) **15**

16 **Net long-term capital gain or (loss).** Combine lines 8 through 14 in column (f) **16** 16,750.00

Next: Go to Part III on the back.

* **28% rate gain or loss** includes all "collectibles gains and losses" (as defined on page D-6 of the instructions) and up to 50% of the eligible gain on qualified small business stock (see page D-4 of the instructions).

For Paperwork Reduction Act Notice, see Form 1040 instructions.

Schedule D (Form 1040) 2001

JSA
1A2011 2.000

Schedule D (Form 1040) 2001   Page **2**

	Taxable Gain or Deductible Loss		

17 Combine lines 7 and 16 and enter the result. If a loss, go to line 18. If a gain, enter the gain on
Form 1040, line 13, and complete Form 1040 through line 39 . . . . | **17** | 16,750

> **Next:** • If both lines 16 and 17 are gains **and** Form 1040, line 39, is more than zero, complete
> Part IV below.
> • Otherwise, skip the rest of Schedule D and complete Form 1040.

18 If line 17 is a loss, enter here and on Form 1040, line 13, the **smaller** of **(a)** that loss or
(b) ($3,000) (or, if married filing separately, ($1,500)). Then complete Form 1040 through line 37 . . . | **18** (|)

> **Next:** • If the loss on line 17 is more than the loss on line 18 **or** if Form 1040, line 37, is less
> than zero, skip **Part IV** below and complete the **Capital Loss Carryover Worksheet**
> on page D-6 of the instructions before completing the rest of Form 1040.
> • Otherwise, skip **Part IV** below and complete the rest of Form 1040.

	Tax Computation Using Maximum Capital Gains Rates		

19 Enter your unrecaptured section 1250 gain,
if any, from line 17 of the worksheet on
page D-7 of the instructions . . . . | **19** |

**If line 15 or line 19 is more than zero, complete the worksheet on
page D-9 of the instructions to figure the amount to enter on lines
22, 29, and 40 below, and skip all other lines below. Otherwise,
go to line 20.**

20 Enter your taxable income from Form 1040, line 39 . . . . | **20** |

21 Enter the **smaller** of line 16 or line 17 of
Schedule D . . . . | **21** | 16,750

22 If you are deducting investment interest
expense on Form 4952, enter the amount
from Form 4952, line 4e. Otherwise, enter -0- . | **22** |

23 Subtract line 22 from line 21. If zero or less, enter -0- . . . . | **23** | 16,750

24 Subtract line 23 from line 20. If zero or less, enter -0- . . . . | **24** |

25 Figure the tax on the amount on line 24. Use the Tax Table or Tax Rate Schedules, whichever applies | **25** |

26 Enter the **smaller** of:
• The amount on line 20 **or**
• $45,200 if married filing jointly or qualifying widow(er);
$27,050 if single;
$36,250 if head of household; or
$22,600 if married filing separately   } . . . . | **26** | 16,750

**If line 26 is greater than line 24, go to line 27. Otherwise, skip lines
27 through 33 and go to line 34.**

27 Enter the amount from line 24 . . . . | **27** | 16,750

28 Subtract line 27 from line 26. If zero or less, enter -0- and go to line 34 . . | **28** |

29 Enter your qualified 5-year gain, if any, from
line 7 of the worksheet on page D-8 . . . . . . | **29** |

30 Enter the **smaller** of line 28 or line 29. . . . . | **30** |

31 Multiply line 30 by 8% (.08) . . . . | **31** |

32 Subtract line 30 from line 28 . . . . | **32** |

33 Multiply line 32 by 10% (.10) . . . . | **33** |

If the amounts on lines 23 and 28 are the same, skip lines 34 through 37 and go to line 38.

34 Enter the **smaller** of line 20 or line 23 . . . . | **34** |

35 Enter the amount from line 28 (if line 28 is blank, enter -0-) . . . . | **35** |

36 Subtract line 35 from line 34 . . . . | **36** |

37 Multiply line 36 by 20% (.20) . . . . | **37** |

38 Add lines 25, 31, 33, and 37 . . . . | **38** |

39 Figure the tax on the amount on line 20. Use the Tax Table or Tax Rate Schedules, whichever applies . | **39** |

40 **Tax on all taxable income (including capital gains). Enter the smaller of line 38 or line 39 here
and on Form 1040, line 40** . . . . | **40** |

                                                                                            Schedule D (Form 1040) 2001

Form **3468**	**Investment Credit**	OMB No. 1545-0155
Department of the Treasury Internal Revenue Service (99)	▶ Attach to your return. ▶ See separate instructions.	**20**01 Attachment Sequence No. **52**

Name(s) shown on return
TIMBER TAXPAYER

Identifying number
999-99-9999

Current Year Credit

1 Rehabilitation credit (see instructions for requirements that must be met):

a Check this box if you are electing under section 47(d)(5) to take your qualified rehabilitation expenditures into account for the tax year in which paid (or, for self-rehabilitated property, when capitalized). See instructions. **Note:** *This election applies to the current tax year and to all later tax years. You may not revoke this election without IRS consent* . . . . ▶ ☐

Enter the amount of qualified rehabilitation expenditures and multiply by the percentage shown:

b Pre-1936 buildings . . . . _____ x 10% (.10) | **1b** |
c Certified historic structures . . . . _____ x 20% (.20) | **1c** |

    (1) Enter the assigned NPS project number or the pass-through entity's employer identification number (see instructions) _____

    (2) Enter the date that the NPS approved the Request for Certification of Completed Work (see instructions) . . . . _____

d (1) Enter the date on which the 24- or 60-month measuring period begins _____ and ends _____

    (2) Enter the adjusted basis of the building as of the beginning date above (or the first day of your holding period, if later) . . . . _____

    (3) Enter the amount of the qualified rehabilitation expenditures incurred, or treated as incurred, during the period on line 1d(1) above . . .

e Rehabilitation credit from an electing large partnership (Schedule K-1 (Form 1065-B), box 9) . . . | **1e** |

2 Energy credit. Enter the basis of energy property placed in service during the tax year (see instructions) . . . . . . _____ x 10% (.10) | **2** |

3 Reforestation credit. Enter the amortizable basis of qualified timber property acquired during the tax year (see instructions) ___1,050.00___ x 10% (.10) | **3** | 105.00

4 Credit from cooperatives. Enter the unused investment credit from cooperatives . . . . | **4** |

5 **Total current year investment credit. Add lines 1b through 4** . . . . | **5** | 105.00

Tax Liability Limit (See Who Must File Form 3800 to find out if you complete Part II or file Form 3800.)

6 Regular tax before credits (see instructions) . . . . | **6** | 1,000.00
7 Alternative minimum tax (see instructions) . . . . | **7** |
8 Add lines 6 and 7 . . . . | **8** | 1,000.00

9a Foreign tax credit . . . . | **9a** |
b Credit for child and dependent care expenses (Form 2441, line 9) . . . . | **9b** |
c Credit for the elderly or the disabled (Schedule R (Form 1040), line 20) . | **9c** |
d Education credits (Form 8863, line 18) . . . . | **9d** |
e Rate reduction credit (Form 1040, line 47) . . . . | **9e** |
f Child tax credit (Form 1040, line 48) . . . . | **9f** |
g Mortgage interest credit (Form 8396, line 11) . . . . | **9g** |
h Adoption credit (Form 8839, line 14) . . . . | **9h** |
i District of Columbia first-time homebuyer credit (Form 8859, line 11) . . . | **9i** |
j Possessions tax credit (Form 5735, line 17 or 27) . . . . . | **9j** |
k Credit for fuel from a nonconventional source . . . . . . | **9k** |
l Qualified electric vehicle credit (Form 8834, line 20) . . . . . | **9l** |
m Add lines 9a through 9l . . . . | **9m** |

10 Net income tax. Subtract line 9m from line 8. If zero, skip lines 11 through 14 and enter -0- on line 15. . . . . | **10** | 1,000.00
11 Tentative minimum tax (see instructions) . . . . | **11** |
12 Net regular tax. Subtract line 9m from line 6. If zero or less, enter -0- . . . | **12** |
13 Enter 25% (.25) of the excess, if any, of line 12 over $25,000 (see instructions) . . . . | **13** |
14 Enter the greater of line 11 or line 13 . . . . | **14** |
15 Subtract line 14 from line 10. If zero or less, enter -0- . . . . | **15** | 1,000.00
16 **Investment credit allowed for the current year.** Enter the **smaller** of line 5 or line 15 here and on Form 1040, line 50; Form 1120, Schedule J, line 6d; Form 1120-A, Part I, line 4a; Form 1041, Schedule G, line 2c; or the applicable line of your return . . . . | **16** | 105.00

For Paperwork Reduction Act Notice, see separate instructions.

Form **3468** (2001)

JSA
1X1710 4.000

Form **4562**	**Depreciation and Amortization** (Including Information on Listed Property)	OMB No. 1545-0172
Department of the Treasury Internal Revenue Service (99)	▶ See separate instructions. ▶ Attach this form to your return.	**20**01 Attachment Sequence No. **67**

Name(s) shown on return	Business or activity to which this form relates	Identifying number
TIMBER TAXPAYER	TREE FARM	999-99-9999

Election To Expense Certain Tangible Property Under Section 179
Note: *If you have any "listed property," complete Part V before you complete Part I.*

1	Maximum dollar limitation. If an enterprise zone business, see page 2 of the instructions	**1**	$24,000
2	Total cost of section 179 property placed in service (see page 2 of the instructions).	**2**	
3	Threshold cost of section 179 property before reduction in limitation	**3**	$200,000
4	Reduction in limitation. Subtract line 3 from line 2. If zero or less, enter -0-	**4**	
5	Dollar limitation for tax year. Subtract line 4 from line 1. If zero or less, enter -0-. If married filing separately, see page 2 of the instructions	**5**	

(a) Description of property	(b) Cost (business use only)	(c) Elected cost	
6			

7	Listed property. Enter amount from line 27	**7**	
8	Total elected cost of section 179 property. Add amounts in column (c), lines 6 and 7	**8**	
9	Tentative deduction. Enter the smaller of line 5 or line 8	**9**	
10	Carryover of disallowed deduction from 2000 (see page 3 of the instructions).	**10**	
11	Business income limitation. Enter the smaller of business income (not less than zero) or line 5 (see instructions) . . .	**11**	
12	Section 179 expense deduction. Add lines 9 and 10, but do not enter more than line 11	**12**	
13	Carryover of disallowed deduction to 2002. Add lines 9 and 10, less line 12 . . . . . ▶	**13**	

Note: *Do not use Part II or Part III below for listed property (automobiles, certain other vehicles, cellular telephones, certain computers, or property used for entertainment, recreation, or amusement). Instead, use Part V for listed property.*

MACRS Depreciation for Assets Placed in Service Only During Your 2001 Tax Year (Do not include listed property.)

Section A - General Asset Account Election

14 If you are making the election under section 168(i)(4) to group any assets placed in service during the tax year into one
or more general asset accounts, check this box. See page 3 of the instructions . . . . ▶ ☐

Section B - General Depreciation System (GDS) (See page 3 of the instructions.)

(a) Classification of property	(b) Month and year placed in service	(c) Basis for depreciation (business/investment use only - see instructions)	(d) Recovery period	(e) Convention	(f) Method	(g) Depreciation deduction
15a 3-year property						
b 5-year property						
c 7-year property		350.00	7 YRS	MACRS	S/L	25.00
d 10-year property						
e 15-year property						
f 20-year property						
g 25-year property			25 yrs.		S/L	
h Residential rental property			27.5 yrs.	M M	S/L	
			27.5 yrs.	M M	S/L	
i Nonresidential real property			39 yrs.	M M	S/L	
				M M	S/L	

Section C - Alternative Depreciation System (ADS) (See page 5 of the instructions.)

16a Class life					S/L	
b 12-year			12 yrs.		S/L	
c 40-year			40 yrs.	M M	S/L	

Other Depreciation (Do not include listed property.) (See instructions beginning on page 5.)

17	GDS and ADS deductions for assets placed in service in tax years beginning before 2001	**17**	100.00
18	Property subject to section 168(f)(1) election	**18**	
19	ACRS and other depreciation	**19**	

Summary (See page 6 of the instructions.)

20	Listed property. Enter amount from line 26	**20**	
21	Total. Add deductions from line 12, lines 15 and 16 in column (g), and lines 17 through 20. Enter here and on the appropriate lines of your return. Partnerships and S corporations - see instructions	**21**	125.00
22	For assets shown above and placed in service during the current year, enter the portion of the basis attributable to section 263A costs	**22**	

For Paperwork Reduction Act Notice, see page 9 of the instructions.   Form **4562** (2001)

JSA

Form 4562 (2001)   Page **2**

Listed Property (Include automobiles, certain other vehicles, cellular telephones, certain computers, and property used for entertainment, recreation, or amusement.)

Note: *For any vehicle for which you are using the standard mileage rate or deducting lease expense, complete only 23a, 23b, columns (a) through (c) of Section A, all of Section B, and Section C if applicable.*

Section A - Depreciation and Other Information (Caution: *See page 7 of the instructions for limits for passenger automobiles.)*

23a Do you have evidence to support the business/investment use claimed?	Yes	No	23b If "Yes," is the evidence written?	Yes	No

(a) Type of property (list vehicles first)	(b) Date placed in service	(c) Business/ investment use percentage	(d) Cost or other basis	(e) Basis for depreciation (business/investment use only)	(f) Recovery period	(g) Method/ Convention	(h) Depreciation deduction	(i) Elected section 179 cost
24 Property used more than 50% in a qualified business use (see page 6 of the instructions):								
		%						
		%						
		%						
25 Property used 50% or less in a qualified business use (see page 6 of the instructions):								
		%				S/L -		
		%				S/L -		
		%				S/L -		

26 Add amounts in column (h). Enter the total here and on line 20, page 1 . . . . | **26** |

27 Add amounts in column (i). Enter the total here and on line 7, page 1 . . . . | **27** |

Section B - Information on Use of Vehicles

Complete this section for vehicles used by a sole proprietor, partner, or other "more than 5% owner," or related person.

If you provided vehicles to your employees, first answer the questions in Section C to see if you meet an exception to completing this section for those vehicles.

	(a) Vehicle 1		(b) Vehicle 2		(c) Vehicle 3		(d) Vehicle 4		(e) Vehicle 5		(f) Vehicle 6	
28 Total business/investment miles driven during the year (do not include commuting miles - see page 2 of the instructions)												
29 Total commuting miles driven during the year												
30 Total other personal (noncommuting) miles driven												
31 Total miles driven during the year. Add lines 28 through 30												
	Yes	No	Yes	No	Yes	No	Yes	No	Yes	No	Yes	No
32 Was the vehicle available for personal use during off-duty hours?												
33 Was the vehicle used primarily by a more than 5% owner or related person?												
34 Is another vehicle available for personal use?												

Section C - Questions for Employers Who Provide Vehicles for Use by Their Employees

Answer these questions to determine if you meet an exception to completing Section B for vehicles used by employees who **are not** more than 5% owners or related persons (see page 8 of the instructions).

	Yes	No
35 Do you maintain a written policy statement that prohibits all personal use of vehicles, including commuting, by your employees?		
36 Do you maintain a written policy statement that prohibits personal use of vehicles, except commuting, by your employees? See page 8 of the instructions for vehicles used by corporate officers, directors, or 1% or more owners		
37 Do you treat all use of vehicles by employees as personal use?		
38 Do you provide more than five vehicles to your employees, obtain information from your employees about the use of the vehicles, and retain the information received?		
39 Do you meet the requirements concerning qualified automobile demonstration use? (See page 8 of the instructions.)		

Note: *If your answer to 35, 36, 37, 38, or 39 is "Yes," do not complete Section B for the covered vehicles.*

Amortization

(a) Description of costs	(b) Date amortization begins	(c) Amortizable amount	(d) Code section	(e) Amortization period or percentage	(f) Amortization for this year
40 Amortization of costs that begins during your 2001 tax year (see instructions beginning on page 8):					
TREE PLANTING	05/01/2001	997.50		7 YRS	71.25
41 Amortization of costs that began before your 2001 tax year				**41**	
42 Total. Add amounts in column (f). See page 9 of the instructions for where to report				**42**	71.25

Glossary

Note: This glossary contains some terms and information that I think readers will find useful. Some of these terms are not covered elsewhere in the book.

acre. 43,560 square feet.

agroforestry. The use of forest as an economic resource for products other than wood. Such products might be mushrooms, a row crop growing between rows of seedlings, ginseng, or silvopasture (for the grazing of livestock). In my opinion, using forest as pasture is a bad idea because cattle kill seedlings and compact the soil.

alluvium. Soil matter deposited by flowing water. Winds have deposited alluvial soil in much of southwestern Wisconsin from deposits left by glaciers in the Mississippi valley.

allelopathy. The harmful effect of chemicals produced by a plant on nearby competitive plants.

annual growth increment. The growth of a tree in any one year, as shown by the width of a tree ring.

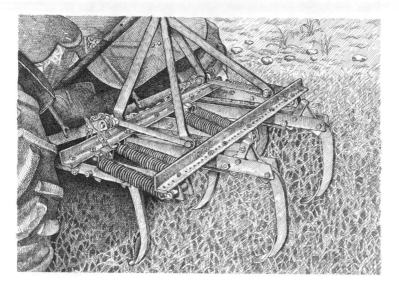

Chisel plow.

anthropogenic. Caused by human activity.

aspect. The orientation of a slope relative to a compass. If you are standing on the top of a hill looking down, and you are facing north, the plot of land in question is said to have northern aspect. North-facing slopes are cooler than south-facing slopes.

board foot. 144 cubic inches of wood, most often thought of as a piece of board 1 foot x 1 foot x 1 inch. Larger volumes are measured in units of MBFT, which is to say a thousand board feet. One MBFT of hardwood weighs between five thousand and nine thousand pounds. One MBFT of softwood weighs between four thousand and six thousand pounds.

bolt. One hundred inch-long logs, usually eight to twelve inches in diameter.

Btu. British thermal unit, a measure of heat produced. Some trees burn better and longer than others, and this difference is measured in Btus.

bush hog. A powerful mower mounted behind a tractor. It consists of a box about five-feet square, in which a rotating blade chops off weeds, grass, or seedlings.

butt log. The first log above the stump.

cambium. The layer of cell tissue between the inner bark of a tree and the wood. Cambium cells are fast growing. Cells added by new growth thicken the stem while pushing the bark to the outside.

chisel plow. A farm implement attached to a tractor that has bent arms to scratch channels in the earth at a depth set by the operator, up to about a foot.

clear-cutting. A method of harvesting in which all trees in an area are cut at the same time. Many environmentalists believe that clear-cutting is harmful to the forest ecology.

climax forest. A forest that has reached a point in its succession where its community of plants will reproduce themselves ad infinitum, that is until a disturbance changes the living conditions. A maple forest is often thought of as a climax forest because maples are shade-tolerant and will reproduce themselves.

commercial thinning. Partial harvesting of commercial trees with the aim of accelerating the growth of remaining tress.

conifers. Trees producing their seeds in cones. Examples are pines, redwoods, firs, spruces, cypresses, and yews.

Conservation Reserve Program (CRP). A program whereby the federal government pays landowners to establish a permanent vegetative cover, instead of growing crops, on land prone to erosion. Trees are not considered a crop. The terms of the contract are changing. Typically the contract is ten years (fifteen years if you plant trees). To be eligible you have to grow crops of some sort in at least three out of five years before enrolling in the program. The amount of money you get depends on the fertility of the land (you actually "bid" for it), presently around $65 per acre per year in Wisconsin.

coppice. A cut made right through the trunk of a tree with the aim of regenerating new shoots from the stump. This may be done low or high on the trunk, for the purpose of producing a new, straighter bole, for inducing flowering to attract bees, or for providing forage for animals. Coppicing is the usual way of regenerating oak and aspen clear-cuts.

cord. A quantity of wood logs, eight-feet long, where the ends fit into a four-foot square. A cord is 128 cubic feet of wood (including bark and air space).

crop tree. A tree destined to become a harvestable money tree, selected because of its vigor, form, and position in the canopy.

crown. The upper part of the tree (above the bole or stem) that contains most of the branches and leaves and is exposed to the sun. In a forest, crown positions are classified as dominant, co-dominant, intermediate, or sup-

Dibble.

pressed. A tree with a dominant crown has direct access to sunlight and does not touch neighboring trees. A tree with a co-dominant crown has direct access to sunlight but touches other crowns. A tree with an intermediate crown is struggling for access to direct sunlight. A tree with a suppressed crown is totally shaded by neighboring trees.

cull tree. A tree with no commercial wood value because of decay and/or undesirable shape.

cutover. Land that has been previously logged.

DBH. Diameter at breast height, four and a half feet aboveground (on the uphill side of the tree).

deciduous trees. Trees that drop their leaves at the end of a growing season.

dibble. A spade-like tool used for planting trees.

disturbance. An environmental change affecting tree growth, such as windthrow or fire.

driftless area. The portion of southwest Wisconsin, northeastern Iowa, and southeastern Minnesota that escaped the last ice age, characterized by hilly terrain and the absence of glacial drift.

ecology. The study of living organisms and their environment.

epicormic sprout. A small shoot, smaller than a branch, caused by sunlight directly hitting the trunk. Often caused by releasing a tree from competing neighbors, epicormic sprouting can cause imperfections in the tree's wood. For this reason, shade-tolerant trees are often cultivated around veneer trees to shade their trunks.

frass. Insect feces, as well as the debris produced by plant-chewing insects.

Gator. A four- or six-wheeled vehicle, part go-cart and part tank, that is great for riding around on your land and transporting supplies. This well-designed machine is extremely difficult to tip over and provides countless hours of fun. Kids love it. (See the illustration on page 4.)

girdle. A deep, closed cut that rings the circumference of a tree trunk and that will gradually kill it. Cutting a girdle is a relatively effortless way to cull a tree.

high-grading. The frowned-upon practice of removing valuable trees from a stand and leaving inferior trees. Timber cutters who do this make more money and leave the landowner with inferior woods.

intolerant trees. Trees that need direct sunlight to flourish.

kerf. Width of a cut made by a saw blade or chain.

leader. The central growing shoot or sprout of a tree. It will become the main log.

Lyme disease. An unpleasant nervous system disorder affecting humans bitten by certain deer ticks that burrow into the skin. If you scratch a scab and notice some movement, it may be a deer tick. Under a magnifying glass, it looks like a crab. If a colored circle forms around the bite, it was a Lyme tick. Get antibiotics as soon as possible, and you should be okay.

management plan. A document outlining management goals, objectives, and practices for a forest. Management plans are usually drawn up for woodland owners by DNR foresters, but they may be prepared by a consulting forester as well.

mast. Fruits and seeds of shrubs and trees eaten by animals. Mast trees in a forest encourage wildlife.

MBFT. One thousand board feet of one-inch-thick wood. The most common measure of a quantity of wood to be used for lumber or veneer.

microclimate. A meteorological condition specific to a small tract of land (such as a hedgerow) where moisture, shading, and temperature combine to generate growing conditions different from those found in the general area.

monoculture. The cultivation of a single species of plant to the exclusion of other species.

mycorrhizae. (myco is Greek for fungus and rhizo means root). These fungi form a symbiotic relationship with roots of plants. Part of the fungus lives among the root cells while their filaments remain outside. The fungus takes up water and nutrients essential for plant growth. Without mycorrhizae most plants would grow poorly or die.

natural regeneration. The reproduction of trees from seed, stump sprouts, or root suckers, without the help of humans.

nurse tree. A tree that provides support (such as shade, wind protection, or nutrients) to a cultivated tree.

old-growth forest. Mature forest not disturbed by human activity.

perpetual mixed forest (PMF). A forest that is ageless (i.e., containing young, adolescent, mature, dying, and dead trees) and made up of many species.

plantation. An area planted or seeded by humans.

pole-sized trees. Trees between five and eleven inches in diameter.

rhizome. An underground part of a root (a runner) from which a new stem sprouts.

rotation. The elapsed time required for trees to reach economic maturity (that is, between a timber harvest and the succeeding harvest).

rototiller. An implement (either self-propelled or attached to a tractor) that digs up earth similarly to a disc or a chisel plow. It consists of a shaft rotating at a right angle to the direction of travel, on which arms dig up the earth. It is typically used to prepare a garden plot for cultivation.

sapling. Young tree two to four inches in diameter.

scarification. Scratching the soil surface to allow seeds to establish themselves. Traditionally, an anchor chain is used for this purpose. Some prefer a chisel plow. Scarification also refers to the technique of hastening germination by cracking or scratching seeds. Sandpaper is useful here.

shelterwood. A harvesting scheme whereby most trees are cut with the exception of a few seed trees which may be cut after a new stand of seedlings has been established.

silviculture. The art and science of tending a forest.

site index. The projected height of a given species of trees at age fifty on a given site. This is a measure of site fertility.

site preparation. Procedures used to help a new plantation to be successful, such as mowing, scarification, herbiciding, or tilling.

skidder. A self-propelled machine designed to drag logs behind it.

snag. A standing dead tree.

stumpage. The value of standing trees in a plot before they are cut.

succession. The sequence of plant communities over time in the absence of disturbances.

sustained yield. The amount of timber that can be continuously extracted in perpetuity without affecting the quality and inventory of a forest.

thinning. The removal of trees to encourage growth of selected residual trees.

timber stand improvement (TSI). Management procedures, such as thinning or pruning, that improve the long-term value of a stand of trees.

totholz. Dead wood that attracts insects and mosses important to biodiversity and wildlife. German forestry practices suggest leaving between 5 and 10 percent of your trees to decay in your woodland.

transpiration. The absorption of water by plants and subsequent release of water vapor into the atmosphere.

understory. Vegetation under the canopy.

veneer. High quality wood cut into thin sheets for use in overlay. Only the best quality logs are destined to be veneer.

water bar. A little berm on a slope designed to duct water in order to minimize erosion.

watershed. An expanse of land from which water flows into a body of water.

wick applicator. A tool that releases herbicide through a sponge. The operator wipes it on the plant. You may also use a stain applicator to do the same job.

windthrow. The uprooting of trees by a storm.

yarding. The moving of logs from the stump to a loading area.

yuppie tools. Many catalogues offer for sale items of fanciful utility that usually have clever names and concepts behind them and that tend to be expensive. My advice: Don't even look at the catalogues. The pleasure resides solely in perusing the catalogs. You will be disappointed as soon as you try to use a yuppie tool. Buy your stuff from a professional catalog.

Index

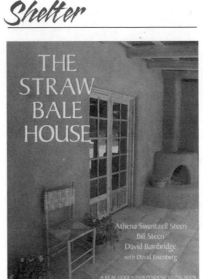